CLEAR
HOLD
BUILD

CLEAR
HOLD
BUILD

How the Free State won the Irish Civil War

GARETH PRENDERGAST

EASTWOOD

First published 2025 by Eastwood Books
Dublin, Ireland

www.eastwoodbooks.com
www.wordwellbooks.com

3

Eastwood Books is an imprint of the Wordwell Group

Eastwood Books
The Wordwell Group
Suite 5
Hub17
Corrig Road
Sandyford Business Park
Dublin, Ireland

The Wordwell Group is a member of Publishing Ireland, the Irish Book Publishers' Association.

© Gareth Prendergast, 2025

ISBN: 978-1-916742-56-7 (Paperback)
ISBN: 978-1-916742-87-1 (ePub)

The right of Gareth Prendergast to be identified as the Author of this work has been asserted in accordance with the Copyright, Designs and Patents Act 1988.

All rights reserved. No part of this book may be reprinted or reproduced or utilised in any form or by any electronic, mechanical or other means, now known or hereafter invented, including photocopying and recording, or in any information storage or retrieval system, without the permission in writing from the Publishers.

British Library Cataloguing in Publication Data.
A catalogue record for this book is available from the National Library of Ireland and the British Library.

Copyediting by Conor Reidy
Layout and design by Wordwell
Printed in Ireland by Sprint Books

For Sarah

CONTENTS

Foreword	ix
Acknowledgements	xii
Preface	xiv
Introduction	xvii
1. Counterinsurgency	1
Generate	5
2. Generation of the National Army	7
3. Training and Equipping the National Army	19
Clear	39
4. Shaping Operations: The Conventional Phase of Warfare in Munster	41
Map 1	59
5. The Cork Landings: The Decisive Operation	60

Hold 85

6. Establish Civil Security 87

7. A Learning Organisation 112

8. Establish Civil Control 130

   Map 2 145

9. Information Operations 146

Build 159

10. The Restoration of Essential Services 161

11. Supporting Governance 180

12. Supporting the Economy 192

Conclusion 210

Bibliography 229

Notes 241

FOREWORD

While a great deal has been written about counterinsurgency over the past two decades – much of it by me – to date the Irish Civil war has not been examined in depth by a scholar of counterinsurgency. Gareth Prendergast has now remedied that gap in our understanding of an interesting but understudied effort to defeat an insurgency that has important lessons for both academics and practitioners.

The reason counterinsurgency research has, um, exploded over the past two decades is the American counterinsurgency effort in Iraq. While it may not be intuitive that the world's greatest power could have much to learn from the Irish Free State Army's efforts to defeat the Irish Republican Army in a war that didn't last a year, this veteran of the American war in Iraq would strenuously take the opposite tack. As Prendergast argues in his very first chapter:

> To the neutral observer, it seems obvious that the National Army won the civil war because of superior numbers and equipment. But those advantages could easily have been squandered by neglecting the support of the population. Throughout history, heavy-handed tactics, disregard for public opinion, clumsy operations resulting in excessive civilian damage, illegitimate governance, an absence of local security and lack of essential services, errors of judgement, and a failure of common sense have proven devastating to military campaigns. When military leaders and their armies fail to capitalise on initial support from the local

population, they waste their original advantage. The forces of liberation can become an army of occupation because of poor planning and lack of cultural awareness. This was the problem faced by the leaders of the National Army during the civil war.

Let me be very clear: this was also the problem faced by the leadership of the American Army during the Iraq War. In fact, I cannot write a better description of the mistakes the American Army made in the initial phases of its occupation of Iraq in 2003, proving (not for the first time) that if history doesn't repeat itself, it certainly rhymes. Had this book existed in 2003 – and, more importantly, had the American national security team read and understood its lessons – history might have turned out very differently indeed.

The path that the Free State's Army followed to defeat the Irish Republican Army (IRA) is also a road map that could have been used to make the American war in Iraq shorter and less costly for both the Americans and their allies and the people of Iraq. Prendergast's very title covers the most important realisation that America stumbled onto years into its bloody war in Iraq: that sweep and clear operations are useless unless the counterinsurgent government leaves forces behind to hold the area that has been cleared of insurgents, and then builds a better government and future for the people of the afflicted region. There is enormous wisdom in the three words "Clear, Hold, and Build", and the fact that those techniques worked in Dublin and Cork in much the same way they did a century later in Baghdad and Ramadi indicates that counterinsurgency doctrine may be on to something that transcends culture, race, language, and religion – that creating regional security and then building a government that meets the needs of the people is a strategy for all armies to ponder, in as many cases as they can muster.

Prendergast's work is impressive, but so is the commitment of his Army to giving him the time and resources required to become a serving officer with a doctorate. The demands of defeating irregular wars demand soldiers with a working understanding of politics, economics, and cul-

FOREWORD

ture as well as artillery and infantry tactics. The work Prendergast has done in writing *Clear-Hold-Build* is a gift to the worldwide community of soldiers and scholars who study insurgency and counterinsurgency; the example he sets of a soldier who craves learning at the highest level, has implications for the Irish Army for generations to come. Officers in his army, and in mine, would benefit greatly from reading this important work and applying the counterinsurgency principles he so adeptly describes to the future irregular wars that will inevitably challenge us all.

John A. Nagl, D.Phil.
Lieutenant Colonel, US Army (Retired)

ACKNOWLEDGEMENTS

I would like to acknowledge a vast array of people who have supported me over the six years and more that it has taken to bring this project to fruition. First, thanks go to my excellent supervisors, Dr David Fitzgerald and Dr John Borgonovo from University College Cork, who, with great dedication and professionalism, took me on board and helped me build the research that underpinned the doctoral thesis on which this book is built. Next, I must thank my family, my wife Claire, and my children Eva, James, and Shane, who gave me the time and backing I needed. And without my father, Jim, I could not have finished this work.

To everyone at UCC who helped me, most particularly Danielle, Richard, and Sara in the Graduate Studies Office and Kathy, Yasmine, and Éadaoin in the UCC Skills Centre, I offer heartfelt thanks. I am also grateful to Dr Tim Hoyt, Dr Andy Bielenberg, Dr Donal O'Driscoll and Dr Andrew McCarthy for all their help and academic support. I would also like to thank Mr Tim McKane and Dr John Kuehn from the US Command and General Staff College for their assistance and advice in starting me off on this journey.

Special thanks are due to Brendan O'Shea for his wonderful encouragement and help when times were difficult. I would also like to thank Dr David Murphy and Professor Marian Lyons in Maynooth University for allowing me to start this journey. To all my proof-readers along the way – Stephen, Terry, Tony, and the Terrace gang of Francesco, Paul, Matthias, and NJ … and particularly Gary Walsh and Pat Burke, who

ACKNOWLEDGEMENTS

stuck with me until the bitter end – thanks everyone. I thank Lar Joye for his support and Sean Boyne, who shared his research notes with me on the civil war during the COVID-19 lockdown, when all the archives were closed. Thanks also to Damien Brett, Kilkenny County Council Library Services, for sourcing some particularly important books. To Brian McCarthy, thank you for answering my questions on the foundation of the Civic Guards. Special thanks must go to Camilla Blakeley for comprehensive editorial support and to Gary Blakeley for his design expertise. To Sarah Carey and my uncle Patsy in Enfield thank you for discussing the importance of family involvement and significance of the local narrative.

Finally, I thank Mick Roche and Paul Shorte for their IT skills, and Tom Reddy and Paul for helping me to produce the initial maps. To all the Staff in the Defence Forces Directorate of Training, thank you for all your support. To Sue Ramsbottom and her excellent staff in the Defence Forces Library, and to all those in the Irish Military Archives, especially Stephen and Daniel, thanks so much for your continued assistance.

PREFACE

In the summer of 1919 my grandfather, Patrick Prendergast, enlisted in the IRA. The force had been formed just six years earlier as the Irish Volunteers to battle for independence from British rule.

Prendergast joined his local Kerry unit: A Company (Ballyhar) of the 4th (Killarney) IRA Battalion. He remembered being approached by two men dressed in trench coats while undergoing his initial tactical training in the Kerry foothills. One of them was his unit commander. They asked young Patrick about his freedom of movement as the son of a prominent cattle dealer.[1] When he announced that he could travel all over Ireland without suspicion under the guise of selling cattle, Prendergast was taken off the basic infantry line and converted into an intelligence operative for the IRA.

After Ireland had endured first a war of independence and then a civil war, Patrick married Rose Murphy in 1926, and they settled in Enfield, County Meath. Rose was also from Kerry but had attended the Holy Faith Boarding School in Glasnevin, County Dublin. She would often tell her children how, as an eighteen-year-old student, she had watched out the windows of Holy Faith as British artillery shelled the centre of Dublin City during Easter Week, 1916. She recalled the flames that lit up the night sky during this brief but fierce rebellion. But Rose also told a softer story from her school days. Just before the summer holidays in 1916, a young officer in British Army uniform walked into her classroom, marched up to the girl who sat beside her, and kissed her goodbye. That officer was Emmet Dalton, and he was heading off to the Western Front. By September, he had won the Military Cross for gallant actions in the Battle of Ginchy.

In the aftermath of the First World War, Dalton left the British Army and, like many other veterans, enlisted in the IRA to fight in the Irish War of Independence. In the civil war that followed he sided with Michael Collins and the pro-Treaty forces, becoming a Major General in the National, or Free State, Army at the ripe old age of twenty-four. In August 1922, along with his deputy commanding officer, Major General Tom Ennis, Dalton launched a very successful amphibious operation to seize Cork from the anti-Treaty IRA. Still based in Cork that November, Dalton found time to marry Alice Shannon, the girl he had kissed goodbye six and a half years before.

Tom Ennis was a very able and experienced second-in-command to Dalton. He is often remembered for triumphantly travelling through the city streets of Cork in an armoured car known as 'the Manager.' It was said he could be seen standing upright in the vehicle, 'like a ship's captain on the bridge.'[2]

Ennis was a veteran of the 1916 Easter Rising, and he was undoubtedly sheltering in those burning Dublin buildings watched by Rose and her school friends. He was actively involved in most of the major IRA operations in Dublin throughout the War of Independence, including the attack on the Customs House and the assassination of British intelligence agents at Mount Street on the morning of 21 November 1920. That afternoon – on what came to be known as Bloody Sunday – Tom Ennis and other IRA men who were involved in the shootings played for Dublin against Tipperary in a football match at Croke Park when a mixed force of police and military stormed the field and began shooting in reprisal. Less than two years later, on 28 June 1922, Ennis was prominent in the battle of the Four Courts in Dublin, which started the Irish Civil War. This time he was standing with the pro-Treaty forces bombarding the Republicans who were barricaded within. While fighting first with the IRA during the War of Independence and then with the

Free State, Ennis was shot twice, once in the hip and once in the pelvis, thus cutting short his football career.

Born in Enfield, County Meath, in 1892, Ennis was the same age as his first cousin John Ryan, who many years later became my other grandfather. The pair were classmates and neighbours as well as relatives. Ryan's father, who died four months before John was born, was a Royal Irish Constabulary police officer, and John followed in his father's footsteps. That put the cousins on opposite sides during the War of Independence, as so many other cousins and siblings and parents and children were. Yet John Ryan and Tom Ennis remained good friends after surviving that blighted period. Tom attended the wedding when John married Agnes Duffy in 1932, presenting the newlyweds with a beautiful silver tea set. Agnes was a schoolteacher in Dublin, but she was originally from Scotstown, County Monaghan, in Ulster.

The familial and the political constantly intersect and circle one another through the complex pattern of modern Irish history. As a young officer in the Irish Defence Forces during the Troubles, I was based in Monaghan, on the border with Northern Ireland. It was during this time, on a beautiful summer's day in 1990 while I was on my first foot patrol near my grandmother's hometown of Scotstown, that I was called a "Free State bastard" for the very first time.

INTRODUCTION

> War with the foreigner brings to the fore all that is best and noblest in a nation—civil war all that is mean and base.
>
> Frank Aiken, quoting an old priest, 3 August 1922

The Irish Free State was forged in the flames of a bitter civil war fought between 28 June 1922 and 24 May 1923. It eventually brought to an end a decade of insurrection and conflict that opened with the Home Rule Crisis of 1913–14, endured the War of Independence from 1919 to 1921, and closed with the end of the civil war.

Over that turbulent period, Ireland was transformed from an important part of the British Empire into a divided island: one portion within the United Kingdom, the rest a nascent state. The civil war was one of the most divisive and violent aspects of these troubled times, as the young and idealistic leadership that had spearheaded the fight for independence decimated itself in the final year of internecine violence, leaving a vacuum at the top that the newly established Irish Free State would find very hard to fill. What caused such a deeply felt and deeply wounding conflict?

In 1921, the British government needed to end the Anglo-Irish War, which was unpopular both domestically and internationally. A Labour Party commission investigating conditions in Ireland during the war concluded that 'things are being done in the name of Britain which make our name stink in the nostrils of the whole world.'¹ When a truce came into effect on 11 July 1921, suspending the War of Independence, many IRA fighters believed that it would last for only two or three weeks, and worked to make the most of the breathing space to prepare to continue the fight for the much sought-after republic.² An IRA Quarter Master General (QMG) Logistics Report indicates that by December 1921, the Republicans had sufficient arms and ammunition to fight with greater intensity than at any time during the previous two and a half years of conflict. The IRA leadership knew this, nullifying any argument that the Anglo-Irish Treaty signed on 6 December 1921 was a military necessity due to want of armaments.³

Under the Treaty, Ireland would become a dominion, styled the Irish Free State, rather than a republic. The Free State would enjoy sovereignty subject to inclusion within the British Commonwealth of Nations and to other imperial trappings. The anti-Treaty – or Republican – elements of the IRA strongly objected to continued citizenship within the British Empire enshrined in an oath of allegiance to the Crown. Their distaste was magnified by the partitioning of the island of Ireland, as six counties were to form Northern Ireland and remain in the United Kingdom.⁴

Arthur Griffith, the founder of Sinn Féin and one of the leading Irish negotiators, said he had signed the Treaty in the belief that the end of the conflict of centuries was at hand.⁵ Others were less optimistic and more philosophical. Michael Collins remarked that he had signed his own death warrant.⁶ As part of the Irish delegation in London, Collins and Griffith did not report back to Dublin before signing the final document, infuriating the President of Dáil Éireann (Irish Parliament) Éamon de Valera when the news emerged.⁷ Some in the IRA believed the delegation members should have been arrested for exceeding their authority by signing without first referring the matter to Cabinet.⁸ In public, de Valera vehemently denounced the fact that the negotiating team had not achieved the status of a republic for Ireland; in private he was more realistic. Prominent pro-Treaty parliamentarian, Liam de Róiste, noted in his diary that nationalist activist Eoin MacNeill, one of the founders of Óglaigh na hÉireann, 'From conversations with dev [de Valera] in 1919–20, the latter certainly considered then that "The Republic" could not be achieved; that it was a good fighting position: That another arrangement would sometime become inevitable.'[9]

A week after the Treaty delegates returned to Ireland, debates over ratification began in Dáil Éireann, the parliament of the newly-minted state. For and against, the speakers were passionate and uncompromising. Collins argued that after a lapse of 750 years, the country would be left with a parliament to make laws for the peace, order, and good government and with it an executive responsibility to that parliament.[10] Ernie O'Malley, a prominent IRA divisional commander in Munster, reminded his peers of the opposite point of view: 'How often had we vowed, as we sat around the turf fires, or as we tramped with squelching feet … that we in our generation would finish the fight.'[11]

For the most part, those who opposed the Treaty 'could see no good in it, looking down from the height of the Republic, seeing it as degradation and sheer loss.'[12] Mary MacSwiney, a Teachta Dála (TD, or deputy), supported the common Republican sentiment: 'Without the machinations of the Irish Republican Brotherhood (IRB) led by Collins, the Treaty would not have been supported by 5 percent of the TDs.' O'Malley, MacSwiney, and a large minority of IRA volunteers condemned the agreement as failing to achieve the national aspiration.

Debates continued both in and out of the Dáil. As Christmas approached, churches overflowed with congregants who listened to sermons by a largely pro-Treaty clergy calling for peace, while the country started to fracture along ideological and political lines. The press tended to approve. County councils expressed agreement or disagreement. In Cork, the Chamber of Commerce laid out signature books for business leaders to record their support.[13] Constitutionalist bodies such as the South of Ireland Cattle-Traders and the Cork Legion of Ex-Servicemen similarly endorsed the agreement.[14] After the Christmas recess, when politicians had had a chance to reflect, a vote was called.[15] With 64 in favour, 57 against, the Dáil voted in early January 1922 for acceptance of the Treaty. Most of the pro-Treaty TDs did so on pragmatic grounds, to avoid further war, rather than out of any enthusiasm for the document.[16] Two days after the vote, de Valera resigned as president of Dáil Éireann, and Arthur Griffith was elected in his place.

Up until June 1922, those on both sides of the debate made constant, strenuous efforts to produce an acceptable political compromise, but at the same time both Republicans and the transitional pro-Treaty Provisional Government prepared for hostilities.[17] What troubled Michael Collins most during this period of uncertainty was the effect on his beloved IRA, now divided into anti-Treaty Republican forces and the National Army.[18] Collins tried to satisfy his former comrades to prevent the split. He would rather have had any one of anti-Treaty advocates such as Liam Lynch, Liam Deasy, Tom Hales, Rory O'Connor, or Tom Barry on his side than a dozen like de Valera.[19] The rupture affected the vast majority of IRA members, who became, as Ernie O'Malley put it, 'two parties now, Republican and Free State, those who believed in an absolutely independent Ireland and those who wished to become a Dominion of the British Empire.'[20]

A general election called for 16 June 1922 and supported by the British government allowed Irish voters a voice on Treaty ratification. Secretary of State for the Colonies Winston Churchill was anxious for a victory by Treaty supporters to legitimise the agreement in the eyes of the Irish population.[21] The results validated this strategy, returning the pro-Treaty faction of Sinn Féin with 58 seats, the anti-Treaty faction with 36, Labour with 17, the Farmers' Party with 7, Unionists (Trinity College) 4, and Independents 6.[22]

The Free State Provisional Government saw the outcome as a mandate to proceed with full implementation of the Treaty. The pro-Treaty side believed there could be no doubt that the overwhelming majority wished for the crisis to be settled peaceably. The shadows of conflict continually hung over the burgeoning state, however, as it struggled to formulate itself into a functioning entity. The Free State faced its greatest challenge within a few months of its establishment, as the country slid into civil war.

INTRODUCTION

The IRA repudiated Dáil Éireann control and established its own executive, setting up a new headquarters in the judicial centre of Dublin, the Four Courts. Initially the British were satisfied with the Provisional Government response. On 19 April 1922, Churchill wrote to Prime Minister David Lloyd George that he thought the British government was 'wise to put up with the occupation of the Four Courts until public opinion is exasperated against the raiders. I feel a good deal less anxious than I did a fortnight ago.'[23] Churchill's upbeat attitude would have been reinforced by a letter he received from Alfred Cope, the assistant under-secretary for Ireland during this period. Cope remarked, 'The mutineers [IRA] are commandeering food etc. from the local shopkeepers and thus making themselves very unpopular. It would not pay the P.G. [Provisional Government] to take drastic action at the moment.'[24]

The British General Officer Commanding Ireland, General Nevil Macready, who commanded the British troops operating in Ireland, also urged the importance of avoiding a wider conflict, 'because it is probable that Rory O'Connor, [the leader of the Republican armed men in the Four Courts] hopes to embroil British Troops in order to bring about unity in the Irish Republican Army against a common enemy.'[25] The British were fully aware of the anti-Treaty strategy of trying to drag them back into a fight in order to re-unify the IRA against them and the Treaty. As such they held firm and put their trust in the newly-formed Irish Free State government (or National Government). As Macready put it, for obvious political reasons, if Irish rather than British government representatives put their 'foot down and assert[ed] their authority strongly ... they would have the country behind them, except a few hundred, or possibly thousand, extremists, like Rory O'Connor and Co., who will resist *any* form of settled Government.'

While internal and external debates went on in Britain and Ireland, events took a dramatic turn across the Irish Sea. On 22 June 1922, IRA members in London apparently decided unilaterally to assassinate British Army Field Marshal Sir Henry Wilson on his own doorstep.[26] This sent shockwaves through Westminster and Whitehall, even though Wilson's extremism probably posed more of a threat to British mainstream politics than it did to Irish Republicanism.[27] John Borgonovo asserts that the British government wrongly blamed the assassination on Republican militants from the Four Courts, and demanded that the National Government move against them.[28] In contrast, Ernie O'Malley and his fellow anti-Treaty IRA (hereby called the IRA) volunteers believed that Wilson had been shot on the instructions of the IRB, meaning Michael Collins, Patrick O'Hegarty, and Richard Mulcahy.[29]

The threat of action by the British government was real and reinforced by British troops still to be evacuated from Ireland. In a handwritten letter to Collins, Prime Minister Lloyd George wrote that 'documents have been found upon the murderers of Field-Marshal Sir Henry Wilson which clearly connect the assassins with the Irish Republican Army, and which further reveal the existence of a definite conspiracy against the peace and order of this country.'[30]

The British Cabinet instructed Macready to prepare a full-scale assault on the Four Courts using tanks, aircraft, and field artillery. On 24 June, London decided that the attack should go ahead the following day. Macready took a dim view of this project. In his view, the assassination had thrown the British Cabinet into panic. Churchill was even talking of air action (a habit the Colonial Office had got into overseas) and how to disguise British aircraft in Free State colours.[31] Historian Keith Jeffrey suggests that Macready deliberately delayed acting on his orders from London to avoid precipitating Anglo–Irish relations into crisis.[32]

On the same day, the Four Courts IRA garrison added another layer of defiance by kidnapping General J.J. O'Connell, Deputy Chief of Staff of the pro-Treaty forces.[33] On 27 June, Churchill stood up in the House of Commons to declare that if the Four Courts siege did not 'come to an end, and a speedy end, then it is my duty, on behalf of his Majesty's Government, to say that the Treaty has been formally violated'. Facing pressure from all directions, the National Government issued an ultimatum to the Four Courts garrison on 28 June to evacuate. The IRA did not comply.

INTRODUCTION

On the night of 27–28 June, National Army troops commanded by General Tom Ennis began shelling the Four Courts.[34] Artillery and ammunition had been given to the National Army by the British and moved into firing positions. The IRA claimed that the 'British were observing the results of artillery fire and they would report to their new allies [the National Army].'[35] Whether the British were observing or not is unconfirmed, but the artillery pieces were definitely handed over to Free State soldiers by members of the 17th Battery Royal Field Artillery Regiment from a British Army depot in the Phoenix Park on the night in question. With British assistance, two guns were hitched to the backs of Lancia armoured trucks and straw placed on the truckbeds to protect the artillery shells. British Army unit commander Major Colin McVean Gubbins recorded in the Division war diary that two eighteen-pounders had been handed over to the Provisional Government on 27 June 1922.[36]

The shelling of the Four Courts by National Army troops was effective, and for the next few days fighting shifted to Sackville Street, in the centre of Dublin. As had happened in the Easter Rising of 1916, Republican forces briefly occupied prominent buildings, but by 5 July the fighting came to a close – and with it the first volley of the Irish Civil War.[37]

To the neutral observer, it seems obvious that the National Army won the civil war because of superior numbers and equipment. But those advantages could easily have been squandered by neglecting the support of the population. Throughout history, heavy-handed tactics, disregard for public opinion, clumsy operations resulting in excessive civilian damage, illegitimate governance, an absence of local security and lack of essential services, errors of judgement, and a failure of common sense have proven devastating to military campaigns. When military leaders and their armies fail to capitalise on initial support from the local population, they waste their original advantage. The forces of liberation can become an army of occupation because of poor planning and lack of cultural awareness. This was the problem faced by the leaders of the

National Army during the civil war, and an analysis of the solutions they found forms the core of this book. In other words, how did the Free State convert local victories and initial tactical successes into overall victory?

Most studies of the war have focused on geography, chronology, personality, or military history. By contrast, I use counterinsurgency doctrine as a framework, focusing on the actions of the National Army in the southern province of Munster, and in particular on Cork city and county. Various excellent studies have already covered war activities in the counties that constitute Munster.[38] As Pat McCarthy does in *The Irish Revolution, 1912–23: Waterford*, I want to bring fresh scholarship to an analysis that makes local revolutionary experiences available to a wider audience. In the military realm, tactics teach the use of armed forces in engagements, while strategy teaches the use of engagements to achieve the goals of the war. McCarthy gives his readers a better understanding of how strategic actions influence tactical events by demonstrating the connection between political policies and local activities. Similarly, Joe Power in *Clare and the Civil War* expertly demonstrates how the course of the conflict in Clare was dictated to a large extent by military events beyond the county's borders, and in particular with respect to control of the strategic city of Limerick.[39] The current study demonstrates that tactical successes in Cork and Munster were directly related to the overall strategic success of the Free State. In my opinion, the conflict in Cork and Munster was the decisive operation for the Free State in the entire civil war and for that reason, analysing the National Army actions in this theatre of war is an important methodology in explaining how the Free State won the Irish Civil War. However, unlike McCarthy and Power, I interweave the counterinsurgency doctrine of Clear–Hold–Build throughout my investigation in order to describe how National Army victories in Cork and Munster achieved strategic and national significance.

The so-called Munster Republic was an attempt by the IRA to establish an independent entity during the early months of the civil war. It is hard to define territorially but contained the counties south of the anti-

Treaty defensive line that stretched from Limerick City to Waterford. South of this line were the counties of Cork, Kerry, Waterford, and substantial parts of Limerick and Tipperary. In 1922, the Munster Republic became a direct and substantial threat to the newly-established sovereignty and viability of the Free State. As a result, General Macready wrote to Churchill to warn that the Republic (meaning those who refused to accept the partition of Ireland) held sway in Cork and the surrounding country and that there was no sign of Provisional Government authority.[40] In other words, the Free State was nowhere to be seen. This was a dangerous precedent because, as the *Irish Times* helpfully pointed out, 'two opposing Governments cannot exist in the same country.'

Historian Peter Hart describes the Munster Republic as a simulacrum of statehood that possessed a police force, tax collectors, censors, and even postage stamps but commanded little loyalty and less legitimacy.[41] Cork became its de facto capital and, therefore, a focal point for IRA resistance to the Free State. Over 10 per cent of the National Army was deployed in the county during the conflict and soldiers there received nearly 15 per cent of its overall fatalities.[42] General Richard Mulcahy stated that after initial summer clearance operations of 1922, the most significant military problem facing the National Army was in the area of Cork and also Waterford, Kerry, and Limerick.[43]

Munster was thus the focus of the main effort for the National Army and Cork the site of its decisive operation. T. Ryle Dwyer describes fighting in Munster as the most intense in the country during the entire civil war, and he focuses on the fighting in Kerry, describing it as particularly severe and robust. He speculates that Free State troops in Kerry operated in a way similar to that of an occupying force because most of them could not be recruited locally.[44] As a direct result, efforts in Kerry became focused more on what is known in military circles as 'compellence – coercion through force or threat of force – than on winning hearts and minds or emphasising good governance. In comparison, Michael Hopkinson contends, after initially intense conventional fighting, the occupation of Cork was not as severe or robustly conducted because most of the

National Army soldiers had been recruited locally.[45] Thus the Free State strategy in Cork and other Munster regions was a better combination of compellence and good governance than activity in Kerry, and is hence more suitable for a doctrinal examination of how the civil war was won.

The leadership of the National Army of course did not have the luxury of referring to counterinsurgency doctrine during its struggle for survival, but its methods closely resembled the counterinsurgency tactics, doctrine, and strategy that are taught and practised by modern Western militaries.

An insurgency can take on the characteristics of a civil war, yet there is a difference in form.[46] In Ireland's case, the country was divided over the terms of a peace treaty on an ideological, rather than a religious or socio-political, basis. The campaign that was conducted by the National Army had all the hallmarks of a well-prosecuted counterinsurgency campaign using an identifiable doctrine and strategy. Doctrine helps to simplify complexity, and this was most evident with respect to utilising local forces, providing a legitimate government at national and local levels, establishing civil control, using information operations successfully, and protecting and restoring essential services, the economy, and governance.

It is a difficult proposition to generate and train a professional army for counterinsurgency operations. Drawing on my own experience, particularly with a European Union Training Mission in Mali, I believe that such undertakings require several key elements, among them a doctrine, a training cadre, suitable recruits and logistical support. *An t-Óglách*, the journal for the Irish Volunteers, then Irish Republican Army, and later the National Army, declared in its 16 December 1921 issue, 'The army is the servant of the nation and will obey the national will expressed by the chosen representatives of the people and interpreted through the proper military channels.' Thus, even before ratification of the Anglo-Irish Treaty, the foundations of a disciplined and regimented army had been laid.

No evidence has emerged that any of the Free State military leadership had studied counterinsurgency or small wars theorists such as Colonel C.E. Callwell, whose classic *Small Wars: Their Principle and Practice* was published first in 1896 and was available in updated editions during this period. But the fact that in most correspondence and reports the Free State leadership referred to the anti-Treaty IRA as 'irregulars' ties in with Callwell's definition of small wars as 'operations of regular armies against irregular, or comparatively speaking irregular forces.'[47]

An t-Óglách carried various articles on military history throughout the civil war. Basic tactical lessons such as how to defend a village and how to conduct ambushes are numerous. Although there is no immediate evidence of counterinsurgency or small wars theory in its pages, the importance of winning the support of the population is emphasised, as are other indirect lessons on counterinsurgency. An editorial entitled 'Fight Fair' in the 27 January 1923 issue, outlines in detail the Hague Convention of 1907, underscoring the necessity to conduct operations 'in accordance with laws and customs of war.' The 10 June 1922 edition actually asks 'What is the problem?' in an article on the principles of war. Students in defence academies and universities throughout the Western world are very familiar with this question and with the importance of understanding the problem before formulating the solution, as recent US Army doctrine on design methodology makes clear.

Strong advocacy for a connection between the National Army and the population is also prevalent in *An t-Óglách* through this period, as the 31 March 1922 edition makes clear in an editorial entitled 'The IRA and the People':

> It would be a criminal act to break this sacred alliance between the [National] Army and the people, and no good volunteer would be guilty of such an act. During the war [1919–21] the people stood by the army, and it is now the army's turn to show that it will stand by them and respect their rights.
>
> (*An t-Óglách*, 31 March 1922)

Although *An t-Óglách* did not quote particular small wars theorists, its articles certainly promulgated what they preached. National Army practice in the field against the IRA points to the fact that its leadership tried to be a learning organisation at all levels and had a basic understanding of counterinsurgency tactics and strategy.

A WORD ABOUT RESEARCH

> Ireland is big enough for great things and great movements, but it is too small for Civil War. Civil War means death and destruction. It means the material ruin of the nation and the moral degradation of its people.
> (*Kilkenny People*, 15 April 1922)

Many of the National Army's civil war files held in Irish Military Archives were destroyed for political reasons after a change of government in 1932. Accurate report writing was, in any case, not fully utilised until a reorganisation of the National Army in January 1923 brought new professionalism. For that reason, I have had to rely heavily on the private papers and correspondence of the leadership on both sides of the conflict, on newspaper articles, and on war correspondence reports from the period.[48] For events after January 1923, the National Army reports in the National Archives of Ireland were invaluable. Additionally, archival material in Britain helped to fill the vacuum, uncovering files and information that might otherwise have been destroyed by the Irish in 1932.

Researching a civil war is always fraught, re-opening old wounds and evoking ideological, family, and historical biases that can lead to heated debates. Historian Anne Dolan explains that a civil war can bring shame and silence, noting that 'the memory of the Irish Civil War has been assumed, distorted, misunderstood. It has been manipulated, underestimated, but most of all ignored.'[49] Writing a popular textbook 50 years after the end of hostilities, F.S.L. Lyons refers to the war as 'burned so deep into the heart and mind of Ireland that it is not yet possible for the historian to approach it with the detailed knowledge or the objectivity which it deserves.'⁵⁰

The political systems and security forces of Ireland were born from the ashes of this violent conflict, however, and a hundred years later they deserve to be fully understood. Similarly, the counterinsurgency strategy of the National Army during this bitter campaign and the strategic successes it produced need to be comprehended so that we can learn from them. I am mindful that local histories are still alive with stories of alleged atrocities committed by both sides, and that one of the most tragic consequences of the civil war was the death of many IRA leaders who had fought the British Army to a standstill during the War of Independence. Because of these underlying tensions, my investigation concentrates on policies and doctrine used at the strategic and operational levels, rather than on skirmishes in the towns and villages of Ireland. I have no wish to become mired in local controversies and casualty figures or to dwell on the names of combatants; my aim is to connect tactical actions to strategy and to analyse the operational planning and execution of the campaigns conducted by the National Army.

The Irish Civil War was a watershed. It marked the end of an era in which gunmen had controlled Irish politics and revolutionary thinking. As a direct consequence, governmental authority and civilian control were fully asserted over the new National Army. Constitutional opposition came to separate itself from the IRA, permitting a new political system to emerge free from the shadows of collusion and civil government to be rightfully re-established.⁵¹

1

COUNTERINSURGENCY

> Counterinsurgency is not just thinking man's warfare—it is the graduate level of war.
>
> US Special Forces officer, Iraq, 2005

French military theorist David Galula once remarked that 20% of counterinsurgency is military and 80% is everything else. A successful counterinsurgency campaign is dominated not by military action but by actions that improve security and quality of life for the local population. Effective counterinsurgency operations combine military force with a policy that diminishes support for the insurgents by undermining their cause and building a more attractive alternative. The population doesn't have to approve of the counterinsurgent force, but actions should be taken that allow it to accept and respect that force. Counterinsurgency operations therefore need to encompass all aspects of national power: the diplomatic, information, military, and economic elements sometimes referred to as DIME.

One of the principal tenets of modern military counterinsurgency doctrine is known as Clear–Hold–Build. This construct forms the framework of the current analysis, which considers how the work of various theorists informs contemporary doctrine associated with counterinsurgency. It is hoped that this fresh analytical lens will open up and contribute to debate on the Irish Civil War.

CLEAR–HOLD–BUILD DOCTRINE

> The key variable in determining whether organizations adapt or die is not at the lower levels but at the top; key leaders have to determine that real change is required. If they make that decision, it is comparatively easy to transmit instructions on how to respond to changes in the environment; in the military, such instructions are called "doctrine".
>
> John A. Nagl, Knife Fights, 37

Doctrine is a trailing indicator of inherited practices and a receptive intellectual environment. It brings together tactical and operational routines developed by units to meet current contingencies.[2] The concept of Clear–Hold–Build is a by-product of US Counterinsurgency and Stability doctrines, as expressed in Field Manuals (FM) 3-24 and 3-07.[3] These doctrines combine operations in offence (finding and eliminating the insurgent), defence (protecting the local populace), and stability (rebuilding infrastructure, increasing the legitimacy of the local government, and bringing the rule of law to the area).[4] A Clear–Hold–Build doctrinal operation is executed in a specific area, with the following objectives:

- Clear: Create a secure physical and psychological environment.
- Hold: Establish firm government control of the populace and area.
- Build/Rebuild: Gain the populace's support.[5]

Successful counterinsurgency rests on a well-informed plan and the efficient use of resources that are not primarily military, although in a combat zone military forces might be the only ones able to complete certain elements of the plan.[6] For that reason, they need to be adaptable and flexible in stability operations and kinetic warfare. Thus, the Clear–Hold–Build doctrinal concept takes into account the necessity for hard military actions to underpin and function in tandem with the philosophy of winning hearts and minds.

Counterinsurgent forces must provide security as well as restore essential services, encourage good governance, and support economic development. These goals are wrapped up in a comprehensive information operations campaign. Consequently, my interpretation and understanding of FM 3-24 describes, prosecuting a counterinsurgency campaign that requires the promotion of the following fundamental provisions inherent in the Clear–Hold–Build framework:

- Generate: establishment/generation of a host nation army
- Clear: clearance operations against insurgent forces
- Hold: provision of civil security and civil control; targeted use of information operations
- Build: restoration of essential services; good governance and support of the economy and a safe and secure society.[7]

A discussion of these provisions forms the basis of the ensuing chapters.

FM 3-24 was heavily influenced by classical counterinsurgency theorists, perhaps none of whom was more important than David Galula. To American military intellects, his ideas were a revelation: defending the population, conducting information operations, dealing with the root causes of insurgency, and a civil–military fusion in which the military assumed many governance and police functions.[8] Roger Trinquier, another French classical counterinsurgency leading light, also influenced FM 3-24 in terms of his belief that military operations must be backed up by a comprehensive civil-military campaign.[9]

American theorist Edward Luttwark took a different view, contending that FM 3-24 offers only a compendium of practices, procedures, and tactics that discount the fact that insurgencies are political phenomena. As such, he declared, 'its prescriptions are in the end of little or no use and amount to a kind of malpractice.'[10] Gian Gentile supports Luttwark's view: 'The simple truth is that we have bought into a doctrine for counterinsurgencies that did not work in the past, as proven by history, and whose efficacy and utility remain problematic today.'[11]

However problematic the practices and procedures advocated by FM 3-24 may at times have been, I contend that when properly adopted they can and have turned tactical victories into strategic success. The Clear–Hold–Build counterinsurgency operations conducted by the National Army are a case in point, bringing overall success for the pro-Treaty side.

This is my starting point.

GENERATE

The three pillars of force generation are manning, training, and equipping. These three elements feed directly into the readiness of a state to secure its territorial integrity, and also engage in proficient combat operations.

> US Army, STAND-TO! *Army Readiness Guidance*, 2016

2

GENERATION OF THE NATIONAL ARMY

> A standing army is necessary for Ireland, the absence of it has been the cause of all her misfortunes for 700 years. There is no safety for any country unable to defend itself.
>
> Colonel Maurice Moore to IRA Chief of Staff Richard Mulcahy,
> 12 January 1922

Article 8 of the Anglo-Irish Treaty, 6 December 1921, permitted the new Irish Free State to raise a standing army. For the first time in over seven hundred years, Ireland had the right to raise its own defence forces and defend its territorial integrity:

> Article 8. With a view to securing the observance of the principal and international limitations of armaments, if the government of the Irish Free State establishes and maintains a military defence force, the establishment thereof shall not exceed in size such proportion of the military establishments maintained in Great Britain as that which the population of Ireland bears to the population of Great Britain.

Compared to what had been conceded in either the 1914 Home Rule Act or the 1920 Government of Ireland Act, this was momentous. To fully grasp the opportunity and secure the country, the Free State had to build an effective defence force quickly, taking the initial step by recruiting a nucleus of 4,000 men. Normally the complex process of raising, training, and equipping a military force takes a substantial amount of time and money, but impending war required the Free State leaders to act without delay to create a robust army that could defend the Treaty and take control of the territory of the fledging state.[1]

The three pillars of force generation are manning, training, and equipping. They feed directly into the readiness of a state to secure its territorial integrity and engage in proficient combat operations.[2] The British government, realising the importance of a functioning defence force in the Irish Free State, acted as a guarantor. The existence of the new standing army was assured by British direct support in the form of weapons and equipment and indirect support in the form of available trained manpower. These veterans formed the cadre force of the National Army, providing the leadership, weapons expertise, and training mainstay.

BRITISH SUPPORT FOR THE IRISH NATIONAL ARMY

> Do not try to do too much with your own hands. Better the Arabs do it tolerably than do it perfectly. It is their war, and you are to help them, not to win it for them.
>
> T.E. Lawrence, *Twenty-Seven Articles,* 20 August 1917

Exorbitant financial implications and war weariness reduced the chances of British military re-intervention in Irish affairs without strong political support in Britain. Ireland had been offered dominion status because elite British public opinion determined that the government's controversial counterinsurgency tactics in Ireland had not been successful and undermined its good name abroad, especially in the United States.[3]

Towards the end of the Anglo-Irish War, public opinion in Britain had been soured by the activities of the British security services, as newspapers filled with stories of the Black and Tans and Auxiliary paramilitary forces excesses deepened the feeling that London had lost control of its forces in Ireland. Public opinion across the dominions and in the United States condemned British actions and caused Prime Minister David Lloyd George to fear the unravelling of the empire.[4] General Sir Nevil Macready, who was to be the last British military commander in Ireland, was also horrified at the excesses of the Royal Irish Constabulary (RIC), especially its Auxiliary Division, and so reduced contact with them to a minimum.[5]

Compared to the turmoil consuming Ireland, the Treaty was an outstanding success for the British government, enjoying such overwhelming acceptance in Britain that the Irish question could now be regarded as closed.[6] Yet, the British government feared that IRA volunteers who opposed the Treaty remained a significant threat to the new Irish Free State, the Anglo-Irish Protestant community still living in Ireland, and the new state of Northern Ireland. Lloyd George expressed his concern to Michael Collins in a letter dated 23 June 1922:

> Other information has reached His Majesty's Government showing that active preparations are on foot among the irregular elements of the IRA to resume attacks upon the lives and property of British subjects both in England and Ulster. The ambiguous position of the Irish Republican Army can no longer be ignored by the British Government.[7]

Along with Winston Churchill, his secretary of state for the colonies, Lloyd George adopted a pragmatic approach by actively but quietly equipping and indirectly manning and training the Irish National Army.[8] In other words, the British establishment employed a hybrid strategy – similar to that applied by T.E. Lawrence during the Arab Revolt of the First World War – in which it was considered better that the Irish perform the task of defeating the anti-Treaty IRA tolerably, albeit with

British support, than have the British re-enter the conflict and re-unifying the Irish in opposition. That approach had a further advantage in that Churchill did not want the Irish Provisional Government ordering weapons and ammunition from elsewhere.[9]

Not only did Churchill wish to prevent the Irish from fostering security arrangements with other countries but he also wanted to avoid a security vacuum following the complete withdrawal of British forces from Free State territory. The British understood the need for a coherent Irish National Army to support their exit strategy, and as theorist John Nagl explains, the best exit strategy in a counterinsurgency campaign is to strengthen and support the capabilities of the host nation security forces left behind.[10] Churchill evidently agreed, writing to Under-Secretary for Ireland Sir Alfred Cope, 'We shall certainly not be able to withdraw our troops from their present positions until we know that the Irish people are going to stand by the Treaty, neither shall we be able to refrain from stating the consequences which would follow the setting up of a republic.'[11]

The British government believed that the existence of British-backed Irish troops was the most acceptable solution to the conflict facing the fledgling state. Beyond the political benefits, Irish soldiers had other advantages over young British Army soldiers who 'might as well have been in Nepal' in terms of their cultural and linguistic understanding of the strategic environment.[12] The situational awareness of local Irish soldiers would be a significant force multiplier during the Free State counterinsurgency campaign, especially in intelligence, information engagement, negotiations, and targeting. They understood the operational environment far better than foreign troops and could provide excellent human intelligence.[13]

Churchill also understood that the moral costs of continuing a British counterinsurgency campaign in Ireland were too high, asking 'What was the alternative? It was to plunge one small corner of the empire into an iron repression, which could not be carried out without a mixture of murder and counter-murder.'[14] Supporting the National Army was the best way for the British to negotiate the political conundrum that was Ireland.

THE ORGANISATION OF THE NATIONAL ARMY

From its inception, the Irish National Army was modelled on the British Army, initially with good reason and almost by default.[15] Because it was busy fighting for survival, the army urgently needed regimentation and the ability to organise itself easily. Whether explicitly following British example or simply drawing on general experience, it was determined that the General Headquarters (GHQ) of the National Army would comprise the departments of the Commander-in-Chief, Chief of Staff, Adjutant-General, Quartermaster-General, and Director of Intelligence. The first headquarters was established at Beggar's Bush Barracks, Dublin, on 31 January 1922. Detailed, hand-drawn organisational charts show the National Army command structure from Commander-in-Chief down to General Officers Commanding District Commands and Officer Commanding Battalions. Senior staff officers included the Adjutant General (AG), Quarter Master General (QMG), Assistant Adjutant General, Directors of Intelligence; Communications; Personnel; Discipline; Operations and Training, and Judge Advocate General.[16] Michael Collins was appointed the first Commander-in-Chief, leaving the running of the government to W.T. Cosgrave, who became President of the Executive Council. Richard Mulcahy was appointed as both Chief of Staff of the army and Minister for Defence. The conduct of the civil war was vested in a war council consisting of Collins, Mulcahy, and General Eoin O'Duffy, who was a deputy Chief of Staff in the initial National Army.[17]

A significant boost to the pro-Treaty side came with the IRA split of early 1922, when the staff of the Quartermaster-General's department, based primarily in Dublin and under the command of General Seán Mac Mahon, transferred en masse to the National Army in the second week of

February.¹⁸ These very capable and respected officers brought their expertise from the IRA into the National Army, and most of them remained prominent in its formative years.¹⁹ Although British Army veterans filled many key positions within the National Army because of their experience and knowledge, the GHQ predominantly comprised IRA volunteers.²⁰ From the start, the National Army GHQ continued to call itself the IRA in spite of raised eyebrows in the British House of Commons.²¹

While Collins was Commander-in-Chief, he also quietly moonlighted as president of the Supreme Council of the IRB, an association that suggests an underlying IRB influence on the leadership of both the Free State government and the army.²² The IRB was a secret, oath-bound society established in 1858 as the Fenian Brotherhood; it maintained a small, powerful nucleus within the Irish Volunteers and later the IRA.²³ Ernie O'Malley, a prominent IRA commander, contended that during the War of Independence the leadership of the IRA, especially those members based in Dublin, was dominated by the IRB. Like Collins, Mulcahy belonged to both the IRB and the IRA and helped to recruit key IRA figures into the National Army, especially from eastern Ireland.

The actual influence of the IRB on the National Army is nonetheless difficult to gauge. Its membership never exceeded 5 per cent of the total strength of the IRA, but it controlled positions of authority. Many officers who were IRB men and on the Supreme Council were also on the staff of GHQ.²⁴ Some IRA members (not in the Brotherhood) claimed that the IRB controlled 'most of the administrative machinery of the Army and could direct the manner of its operations.'²⁵

The Free State War Council was set up in order to exert governance and control over, and provide support to, the fledgling army. It should be noted as a progressive step into a modern democracy that the War Council had a civilian majority and was given considerable powers to limit the army's autonomy. It possessed the authority to enquire into the administration of any military department, and it could recommend the removal of any officer, including generals.²⁶ However, according to Mulcahy, the council never functioned as a definite body.²⁷

The Free State had various governance advantages over the IRA, as historian Eunan O'Halpin describes. The first was British backing, giving access to financial support and military equipment. The second was the guidance provided by Collins, who in the words of one army officer was, in pre-truce days, not only the Commander-in-Chief but also 'the man'. The third and most important advantage was that Mulcahy, the Chief of Staff, had a clear and strategic vision of what he wanted to achieve, namely a permanent and centrally controlled defence force that would take its orders from the elected government.[28] This would feed directly into the organisational structures of the National Army.

THE FREE STATE RECRUITING CAMPAIGN

To form an effective counterinsurgent force, the National Army had to expand rapidly. A recruiting campaign in early-1922 was initially successful, but by the outbreak of the civil war in June, anti-Treaty elements of the IRA still outnumbered the National Army and retained an advantage in battle experience. Unlike the Republicans, however, its recourse to First World War veterans meant that the Free State government had the resources to quickly expand its army.[29] It is difficult to calculate how many former British Army soldiers of Irish origin were serving in the National Army during the civil war. The army census of November 1922 details every member of the organisation but does not list previous military employment. Perhaps one of the best assessments can be found in a speech given in Dáil Éireann in 1926 that put the figure at about half of the almost 60,000 men in the National Army of the period.[30]

Returning First World War veterans were spread throughout Ireland. The 1926 national census identifies 150,000 ex-servicemen still resident in the Free State, a figure that does not include those who were living in the newly-created Northern Ireland or who had since died or emigrated. Certain urban areas in the provinces of Leinster and Munster contained a disproportionate share. In 1924, the total population of Dublin was

304,802, some 30,000 of whom – nearly 10 per cent – were British Army veterans. The population of Cork City in the same year was 76,673, of whom 16,000 were British Army or Navy veterans, a whopping 21 per cent.[31] Assuming these figures reflect something similar to the civil war period, this was a very sizeable pool of experienced soldiers for the National Army to exploit, especially after it had seized and occupied Cork and other Munster cities.

In fact, all the cities of Munster proved to be a ripe recruitment ground for the National Army. Limerick and Waterford also contained very sizeable percentages of ex-servicemen, at 9.9 per cent and 13.5 per cent, respectively. Remarkably, although the Kerry town of Tralee and its surrounds formed one of the most violent anti-Treaty battle zones of the civil war, the area was also a former recruiting centre and depot for the Munster Fusiliers of the British Army, with 2,116 veterans of that force living within its environs.[32] Clearing, seizing, and holding these Munster towns and cities would prove vital to the Free State recruitment campaign. To open up their populations to the recruitment mechanism, Free State bases were established in most urban locations throughout the province and elsewhere. In total the National Army occupied 367 bases across Ireland, some 17.4 per cent of them in Cork. The bases would provide the much-needed security infrastructure within which to recruit successfully and securely from the local population and to pay Free State soldiers. The prospect of payment enticed many to join, especially in areas of economic decline. Free State soldiers received the then generous wage of 25 shillings per week and their keep, making a staggering impact on needy labourers and ex-British soldiers.[33] IRA volunteers, by contrast, were not only unpaid but were in danger of losing precious employment while on active service, although many joined up at prospect of food and shelter.[34]

Unemployment was very high in the new Irish Free State; some 46 per cent of all Irish ex-servicemen from World War I were drawing so-called out-of-work donations in November 1921.[35] As a result of financial enticements, the National Army, therefore, grew substantially and Irish veterans of the Great War were perfectly happy to apply their skills in return for employment and a regular salary. Feelings of isolation may also have contributed to the active enlistment of veterans. In the immediate aftermath of the First World War, veterans faced a somewhat unwelcoming country in turmoil, and the National Army offered a ready-made refuge and repository for their talents.[36] The fighting acumen, skills, and discipline of these soldiers would be better utilised on home soil and for a cause that was not inconsistent with their ideology.

DESIRED STRENGTH AND DISPOSITION

> The defence of national territory is the raison d'être of an army; it should always be capable of accomplishing this objective.
>
> Roger Trinquier, *Modern Warfare*, 3

As noted, Article 8 of the Anglo-Irish Agreement permitted the Irish Free State to maintain a military force for territorial security – but also stipulated that it could not exceed the size of military establishments maintained in Great Britain in terms of the respective populations.[37] This pragmatic approach was immediately undermined when the IRA started to fracture into pro and anti-Treaty factions. As the split grew, the British authorities' intention was not to restrict the size of the National Army but to strengthen it, believing that unless this was done correctly, the IRA could defeat the Free State forces in an armed confrontation.[38] This would have been a strategic and political disaster for Britain and signalled a significant reversal of their newly-established and evolving policy for Ireland.

The IRA leadership took advantage of the Truce with the British in the second half of 1921 to enrol new recruits, in case hostilities began again. O'Halpin points out that this resulted in entire 'Trucer' companies in some divisions, doubling the IRA's total paper strength from roughly 30,000 to an estimated 70,000.[39] John Borgonovo suggests the figure could actually be higher, based on a Department of Defence Military Service Pensions membership roll that shows a nominal strength of 115,550 IRA volunteers, almost all of whom were part-time activists.[40]

How many of the Truce IRA were active fighters from the War of Independence and how many supported the Treaty or were neutral, is an open question. Michael Hopkinson believes the anti-Treaty side had the advantage at the start of the civil war, with around 13,000 active fighters, while just 9,700 IRA members joined the National Army following the split.[41] In a statement to the Army Inquiry Committee in 1924, Free State general Seán Mac Mahon reported that the National Army numbered roughly 8,000 men at the start of the conflict – a quarter the size of its enemy. He also noted that only around 6,000 members of the early National Army had been armed, and just 5,000 fully uniformed and equipped.[42] A large portion of initial Free State recruits, according to Mac Mahon, had never handled a rifle. He recalled men being taught the mechanism of their weapon, 'very often on the way to a fight.'[43]

Taking into account various elements and combat ratios to ensure victory, Free State soldiers would have to substantially outnumber and be better equipped than those the IRA could assemble on the conventional or non-conventional battlefield. In fact, the Free State would have to recruit a number of soldiers comparable to the withdrawing British Army troops. The average strength in station for British Army troops in Ireland during the peak of the War of Independence, in October 1920 was 55,800 all ranks, with 20,000 of these deployed in the British Army 6th Division Area of Responsibility, Munster.[44] Even by October 1921, British Army strength in Ireland still stood at an estimated 57,000.[45]

The National Army would have to recruit similar numbers, but there was a difference. Most would possess the significant advantage of local knowledge. Another advantage was that the veteran recruits who enlisted in the Irish National Army possessed combat experience from the First World War, whereas British Army soldiers serving in Ireland had on the whole been relatively new recruits.

RECRUITMENT SUCCESS AND ARMY SIZE

On 6 July 1922, the Provisional Government issued a nationwide call to arms, placing newspaper advertisements to attract new recruits for the National Army, ideally 'trained men ... of good character ... able to handle firearms.'[46] The response was remarkable, as up to 1,000 men presented themselves at recruiting centres each day.[47] On 7 July, the authorised strength of the National Army was increased to 35,000 (15,000 regulars and 20,000 reservists), and 5,000 new recruits joined the National Army in the weeks after the Four Courts attack.[48] As forces loyal to Collins and the Treaty advanced south and west into Munster and Connaught, potential recruits who wanted to support the National Army but had been living quietly in IRA-controlled areas were able to make their allegiances known. Among them were Irish veterans of the First World War, 'who had been careful to conceal their opinions during the "Tan Fight"', as the War of Independence was known.[49] Once free from IRA influence they started to populate the ranks of the National Army and had the opportunity to demonstrate their proven skills for their new employers.

In July 1922, General Mulcahy signed General Order No. 1, organising the army into the Eastern District Command, the Western District Command, and the Southern District Command.[50] The district command names demonstrated the ambition of Free State government not only to expand the army but also to enhance and enable governance at all levels as the civil war progressed. The districts were then further divided into the 1st Northern, Eastern, Curragh, Western, South Western, and 2nd Southern commands. Additional organisational changes were made as the strength of the army increased and by the end of August 1922, eight territorial commands were introduced.[51] Charles Townsend asserts that the creation of these district or regional commands in the National Army made it possible – at least in principle – for the Free State to develop a strategic plan of action that created a vital advantage over their IRA adversaries.[52] Active recruitment continued throughout the war and by August 1923, a total 60,000 men were on the National Army payroll.[53]

THE COST OF A STANDING ARMY

For a nascent country, an expensively assembled army may be an indulgence, but for the Irish Free State – in the throes of a violent insurgency – it became a necessity. By late-1922, the initial force of 1,246 officers, 25,970 men, and 2,000 Railway Corps cost an estimated £7,245,000 per annum to maintain, or approximately £241 per head.[54] This was an enormous expense for a newly independent state to sustain. Other security entities, such as the Civic Guard and the Railroad Protection and Maintenance Corps, cost well over £1 million each in 1922–23. There was also a considerable expense involved in housing prisoners captured during the civil war.[55] By 1923–24, with total expenditure of £7,500,000 on the National Army and £1,250,000 on compensation, some 30 per cent of all national expenditure was devoted to defence.[56] Interestingly, however, shifting priorities meant that when peace was won the security budget was slashed, tumbling from £11 million in 1924 to just over £1 million in 1932.[57]

The financial burden fostered resentment, and certain factions of the government wanted the money to be spent elsewhere. In particular, Kevin O'Higgins, who served as economic affairs and later justice/home affairs minister, resented the budgetary primacy of the National Army during this period, alleging that the army top brass ran their campaign without oversight from other members of the government.[58] When Richard Mulcahy sat as the minister for defence in the Dáil in order to give an account of the National Army, O'Higgins maintained he was a soldier rather than a minister. At a time when his civilian colleagues were housed together in ministerial blocks for safety, Minister for Defence Mulcahy lived and worked in Portobello Barracks and was actively engaged in National Army activities, a division that exacerbated distrust been civilian and military leaders. Any criticism of the army's performance by Cabinet also made Mulcahy defensive, highlighting his estrangement from government and straining relations between the army and Cabinet.[59]

3

TRAINING AND EQUIPPING THE NATIONAL ARMY

Training is for the known and education is for the unknown.

Anonymous

As civil strife ensued, the Free State leadership was determined to win, and in a remarkable achievement the National Army GHQ (General Headquarters) staff was able to assemble, train, and direct a new conventional force with the combat capabilities to do so, despite being initially outnumbered. In order to accomplish this the National Army needed to instil regimentation, good order, discipline, and professionalism, significantly by tapping the skills of newly recruited Irish veterans. These men joined the National Army in large numbers as readymade soldiers with training in combat and military discipline. They made up for the army's lack of tradition and experience and would form the initial cadres that helped make local recruiting contacts.[1]

During the Truce and prior to the civil war, Lieutenant General J.J. (Ginger) O'Connell, a US Army National Guard (non-combat) veteran, was appointed as assistant Chief of Staff of the National Army with responsibility for training and organising the regular army. Among the other veterans who joined O'Connell in the training environment was ex-British Army officer Emmet Dalton, who was promoted to Major

General and acted as liaison with the British at the start of the Irish Civil War. Demonstrating his willingness to immerse fellow veterans in a standardised training and education regime, Dalton recruited a number of Irishmen who had been British Army officers. With these men on board he was able to organise a training schedule and cadre for the different areas, especially at the Curragh.[2] The professional skills and organisational abilities of these veteran officers and non-commissioned officers made them an extremely valuable asset for the National Army. A large proportion became actively involved in ongoing improvements, in particular the successful reorganisation of the National Army in January 1923.[3]

Chief of Staff Richard Mulcahy also urged the use of sound men who had served in the British Army in order to fill the knowledge and experience vacuum.[4] Lieutenant Colonel Patrick Paul a British Army veteran who had fought with the IRA during the War of Independence, similarly identified the benefits of placing veterans in key training positions: 'Hunting round, I found that there were quite a few other men who had seen service in the British army during the war, like myself, and I arranged to take advantage of their training by having them appointed as instructors.'[5]

Meanwhile, after Dalton arrived in Cork, he recruited numerous British Army veterans as soldiers and instructors, with 5,000 ex-servicemen offering their services. Some of them had been previously operating in order to assist his entry into the city. All officers under Dalton's command were in agreement that these were the most disciplined and effective troops under and … 'I have formed the nucleus of two more companies, making the four companies one battalion called the 1st Cork Reserve.'[6]

Colonel Maurice Moore, a former British Army officer, offered his services in this recruiting effort. In a letter to Mulcahy, he outlined the numbers available and advantages of recruiting ex-British Army veterans:

> All the Irish Regiments in the English [British] Army are about to be disbanded (16 Battalions of Infantry and 3 Regiments of Cavalry); their officers are to be given an option of transfer to English and Scotch units or to receive a bonus on discharge. Those men enlisted in Ireland will, it is presumed, be sent to Ireland and added to the unemployment list. There are already about 80,000 discharged soldiers unemployed in Ireland ... Many of these are anxious to join an Irish army.[7]

Collins acknowledged the contribution that ex-British officers and servicemen of vast experience could provide 'if we could get the right type.'[8] Even with the influx of many First World War veterans, however, it took time to get the force ready for war.[9] Eventually, the integration of these veterans and their specialist skills into the National Army would take on Roger Trinquier's dictum that training should be conducted by specialised volunteer cadres, officers, and NCOs who will ultimately assume charge.[10]

By 1923, an official tally showed that 1,163 officers in the National Army had experience of British Army service, approaching 50 per cent of the overall strength of Free State officers.[11] It is unclear how many of them had been officers in the British military as well, and how many had been enlisted men. Dalton explicitly mentioned recruiting former officers, whereas W.T. Cosgrave noted how difficult it was to find former British Army officers of a certain class.[12] Regardless of their previous service history, the training capabilities and junior leadership of these veterans was important because it provided and strengthened the discipline and fighting acumen of the new National Army.

General Mac Mahon, giving evidence to the Army Inquiry Committee of 1924, estimated that during the civil war, 75 per cent of National Army officers had been in the IRA before the Truce and 25 per cent had joined up after.[13] Among those joining later, many had First World War combat, logistical and administrative experience. Despite their much-needed skills, however, their inclusion was controversial. IRA veterans in the National Army, who had not fought in the Great War, at times believed that the ex-British Army veterans received preferential treatment.[14] These perceptions led Mulcahy to advise that the Free State should 'absorb the best of the disbanded Irish Regiments in a way that will get over any stigma on us for them—and get them in [and] broken up sufficiently to be able to absorb them.'[15] As a result, veterans were used in key leadership roles and as a training staff, comprising a significant proportion of the training cadre. This was a key force multiplier because, as Mulcahy told General Seán Mac Eoin in August 1922, 'We are simply going to break up what we have of an army if we leave it any longer in small posts and do not give it proper military training.'[16]

TRAINING CADRE SKILLS

Serving in a new Irish force must have seemed attractive to unemployed ex- British Army soldiers. M.R. Walker, the chair of the Legion of Irish Ex-Servicemen, seemed eager for members of his organisation to have the opportunity to serve, and perhaps receive preference, in the new army. On 25 July 1922, Walker contacted Collins about making about 500 men available for service, including artillerymen, machine gunners, motor drivers, engineers, and signallers. The National Army leadership realised that these veterans would be a vital factor in the combat effectiveness and training expertise of a growing army, and Dalton sent a list of requirements to Walker, asking for training instructors, weapons experts, military police, armourers, aircraft riggers and fitters, drivers, and medical personnel. Political sensitivities dictated that although first-class instructors would receive an extra £5 per week, they would have no specific military rank.[17]

As the war progressed, weapons training and safety became a priority. Throughout the fighting, the Free State suffered 105 fatalities from accidental shootings and suicides, over 13 per cent of total National Army fatalities during the conflict.[18] On 21 October 1922, the *Irish Times* reported that steps needed to be taken 'to instruct troops in the proper use of weapons', and veteran soldiers were instrumental in improving the training standards for new recruits.

Former officers of the British Army were also necessary to staff the National Army's special services.[19] Their technical expertise and corporate knowledge formed the foundation of the training, tactics, techniques, and procedures adopted by the National Army.

As the National Army continued to grow over the course of the war, so too did the proportion of ex-British servicemen, along with their level of responsibility. Likewise, resentment against them increased, notably after the occupation of the towns in the West and South, where the recruitment pool was particularly well-stocked.[20] Regardless of what former IRA volunteers believed, however, veterans who changed allegiance from Britain to Ireland found no inconsistency in transferring their obedience to new masters and reapplying their military skills.[21] As they consistently demonstrated their specialised skills as fighters or trainers to their new employers, they proved the adage that once a soldier, always a soldier.

FREE STATE TRAINING SCHOOLS

To be effective, training must be linked to policy and an overarching doctrine. It must have seemed natural for the army to model itself on its British equivalent initially, since that was what the rest of the Irish government was doing.[22] Irish military training doctrine at the beginning of the civil war had many similarities to the British doctrine and originally mirrored what the veterans had learned in their previous service.

Nevertheless, the initial training and the doctrine adopted had to be improved, adapted, and regularised to meet Irish needs. First World War veteran, Major General Diarmuid McManus of the National Army, described the military knowledge of average junior officers at the start of the war as 'absurdly nil' and stressed the necessity of employing ex-British soldiers.[23] His fellow generals concurred, and Collins went so far as to adopt delaying tactics to avoid conflict with the IRA until the army was, to some extent, trained and ready to fight.[24]

Even before the end of the War of Independence, the IRA (at that point the precursor to the National Army) understood the need to formalise training. The 1921 IRA GHQ staff wanted to develop a professional officer corps with a dedicated program of training and education. To this end, they ordered all field divisions to set up camps to provide uniform levels of training for officers, as prescribed by a centralised organisation.[25]

The first training manuals issued to all volunteers by GHQ emphasised close-order drill and administration above all other skills.[26] *An t-Óglách,* the journal of the IRA and later of the National Army, was used to update its readership about ongoing combat operations and to impart training and education. Prior to and during the civil war, it published material on doctrine, tactics, strategy, and the principles of war. Editions from 27 May, 3 June, and 10 June 1922 carry articles on these principles, quoting such theorists as Prussian field marshal Helmuth von Moltke, French army chief of staff Ferdinand Foch, Swiss officer Antoine-Henri Jomini, and Eduard von Peucker.[27] The 3 June 1922 edition refers to such edicts as von Moltke's declaration that 'the teaching of military knowledge has before all the object of bringing the student to utilise his intellectual equipment' and von Peucker's comment that 'there is a long distance between an intellectual conception and their priceless faculty which allows a man to make acquired military knowledge the basis for his decisions.' An article entitled 'The Characteristics of Modern Warfare' in the 24 June 1922 issue quotes Prussian military theorist Carl von Clausewitz: 'War is produced by, and receives its form, from the ideas, feelings and relations which obtain at the moment it breaks out.' Its publication was well timed, considering that fighting began on the 28 June.

To guarantee British funding and support, the National Army had to constantly prove its training standards, professionalism, and combat performance. In April 1923, Under-Secretary for Ireland Alfred Cope told Churchill of the improving capabilities of the newly-formed Free State, or Provisional Government, and its army: 'McKeown [Major General Seán Mac Eoin] put up a good show at Sligo over the week-end and the P.G. [Provisional Government] behaved very well in Dublin yesterday'.[28]

To enhance the developing capabilities of its soldiers, the Free State enabled the foundation of professional training schools. The highest priority was given to training schools that instructed soldiers in how to use British-supplied equipment effectively. After the British handed over five MKI and four MKII 18-pounders, for example, the National Army consolidated the equipment and organised an artillery school.[29] The 18-pounder guns had been scattered across the various Free State military barracks. On 23 March 1923, they were grouped together and the artillery school was formed in Clancy Barracks, Islandbridge, County Dublin. On 5 June, Colonel Patrick Mulcahy was then promoted to Officer Commanding (OC) Artillery Corps.[30] Rolls Royce, Peerless, and Lancia armoured cars were similarly consolidated and formally reined in on 14 September 1922 under Captain Joe Hyland as OC Armoured Car Corps, which would constitute the first cavalry corps of the National Army.[31] Throughout the conventional and non-conventional phases of the civil war, specialist training considerably enhanced the effectiveness of combined arms operations.

In January 1923, the National Army undertook an overall re-organisation into 65 independent battle-grouped battalions.[32] These battalions needed to be instructed in tactics and the use of the weapons and equipment at their disposal, courtesy of British logistical supplies. In April, centralised training was launched with courses for company commanders, machine gunners, NCOs, and cooks conducted in the Curragh Camp. A school of instruction was soon established, and so the first seeds of a military college were being sown even before the civil war ended.[33] The combat experience and theoretical knowledge that had been obtained over the previous months of fighting and from various British

Army veterans was used to formulate the doctrine and training syllabi for these schools and their designated courses.

NATIONAL ARMY DISCIPLINE

Alfred Cope referred to an underlying indiscipline within the National Army early in the conflict: 'Forces will have to be pulled up firmly both in leadership and on the part of officers and men.'[34] In Cork, Liam de Róiste mentioned, 'In many cases, apparently, the firing is wanton by men of the National Forces: like the Irregulars [IRA], they have not the discipline or steadiness of old trained forces.'[35] In Limerick, O'Duffy declared the national troops to be 'a disorganised, in-disciplined and a cowardly crowd … When a whole garrison was put in jail owing to insubordination, the garrison sent to replace them often turned out to be worse. One group of 300 reinforcements were absolutely worthless, 200 of them having never handled a rifle before.'[36]

Many of the new recruits were raw and needed to be transformed into disciplined soldiers. Economic Affairs Minister Kevin O'Higgins sent a memo to Free State Executive Council, asking how this army of 'raw lads' with no experience of fighting were to cope with hardened units of the IRA that saw themselves as custodians of the Republican ideal.[37] Emmet Dalton, Diarmuid McManus, Patrick Paul, and other British Army veterans in the National Army recognised that discipline, culture, morale, and fighting spirit are key traits in a professional and regimented army, and they became the driving force behind Richard Mulcahy's long-running efforts to create a military culture that echoed the rules of soldierly behaviour set by regular armies elsewhere. The easy-going familiarity of the revolutionary forces would be out of place in the new Free State order.[38]

In a letter to Mulcahy in September 1922, Dalton remarked that the ex-servicemen were 'conspicuous by their better discipline, deportment and efficiency than my other troops.'[39] This discipline and regimentation needed to be spread throughout the organisation, but the generally positive reception afforded to veteran soldiers by the Free State General Staff was not universal. Within the lower ranks, some of the new Irish recruits were less keen on the discipline being imposed and resented the former British Army NCOs for doing so. Some British intelligence reports went so far as to suggest, 'There is absolutely no discipline in the Free State army and things are getting worse. Men who have been NCOs in the British army are killed if they start enforcing discipline and it is put down to an ambush or accident.'[40]

While there is no clear evidence of anything so drastic occurring, the political and social ramifications of recruiting so many veterans worried both the British and the Free State leadership. 'Upon reviewing the situation' in Cork, said Dalton, 'I foresaw the possible bad political effect of recruiting [too many] ex-servicemen.'[41] But they were needed because, as de Róiste recorded, the National Army soldiers were 'not well disciplined and very badly officered.'[42] Cosgrave assured the Earl of Desart that the army was gradually weeding out ruffians but noted a difficulty: 'The best old soldiers were accustomed to serve under officers who were skilled and of a class they respected and … officers of this class they could not get.'[43]

The leadership of the National Army set about introducing additional corrective measures to counter the threat posed by indiscipline. Collins told the new legal service officer, Cahir Davitt, to draw up a code of discipline for the army, as well as rules of procedure for courts martial. Davitt purchased a copy of the British Army *Manual of Military Law* and got down to work.[44]

A very trying and stressful period followed, but discipline more or less held within the National Army – with notable exceptions – as new officers with British experience sharpened control in the provinces.[45] Discipline was further boosted by continuous training and education, a practice that continued after the civil war ended. A review from 16 November 1923 stated that 'training of troops continues to be brisk with discipline good.'[46] The consensus was that most of the disciplinary problems had stemmed from the transition from a guerrilla force into a professional standing army. As army administration became more systemised and more formalised, conditions improved.[47] At the Army Inquiry Committee of 1924, Professor (and Major-General) James Hogan, the former head of intelligence, noted his belief that the army had undergone extraordinary improvement 'from December 1922 until April 1923, although a slight breakdown in control had occurred with the cessation of hostilities.'[48]

EQUIPPING AND SUSTAINING THE NATIONAL ARMY

> Amateurs talk tactics. Professionals practise logistics.
>
> Anonymous

Logistics is a relatively new word to describe a very old practice: the considerable undertaking of supplying, equipping, moving, and maintaining an armed force. As the initial chief liaison officer with the British, Dalton was fortunate to have the willing support of the British government in providing weapons and supplies.

The greatest need on both sides was for heavier calibre weapons, particularly in the earlier conventional exchanges, and the British made these exclusively available to the National Army. On 22 June 1922, prior to the Battle of the Four Courts, Lloyd George sent a letter to Collins underwriting an explicit British commitment to the security of the Irish Free State: 'Assistance has on various occasions been given to Dominions of the Empire in cases where their authority was challenged by rebellion on their soil; and His Majesty's Government are prepared to place at your disposal the necessary pieces of artillery which may be required or otherwise to assist you as may be arranged.'[49] Artillery is a significant combat multiplier and the supply of these guns gave the National Army a marked advantage over its IRA adversary, particularly when they were crewed by former British Army soldiers.

British support to the National Army proved continuous and reliable, as demonstrated in a telegram from Churchill to Under-Secretary for Ireland Alfred Cope: 'You should do everything in your power to persuade Mr. Collins to draw arms from the British Government, which has a large surplus. I am quite ready to continue the steady issue of arms to trustworthy Free State troops.'[50] In a letter dated 17 April 1922, Cope informs Churchill of his progress to date: 'I have supplied 6,000 rifles which is the limit authorised by you. May I supply a further thousand to-day and another thousand during the week. I am satisfied the P.G. [Provisional Government] is in earnest in dealing with the mutineers [IRA].'[51] Churchill replied positively, agreeing to 'further issue of 1,000 rifles to-day and 1,000 later in the week total 8,000 also the twenty Lewis guns you should obtain concurrence both of Viceroy and Commander-in-Chief in both cases.'[52] Having received this authorisation, Cope reported that he had in fact already supplied 34 Lewis guns and requested authority to supply 20 more than were required.[53] A letter from 'M.E.A.' to Churchill indicates the quantity of equipment, arms, and ammunition issued to the National Army by the British as of 2 September 1922:

Rifles:	27,400
Revolvers:	6,606
Lewis guns:	246
Vickers machine guns:	5
Rifle ammunition:	4,745,848
Revolver ammunition:	435,280
Grenades:	8,495
18-pounder guns (12 authorised):	9
18-pounder ammunition:	2160.[54]

The supply of weapons and ammunition to the National Army had a substantial impact on its combat effectiveness. Correspondence in early 1923, shows that the Free State received 14,744 rifles from the newly-disbanded RIC and 27,052 other rifles from the British, for a total of more than 40,000.⁵⁵ This is noteworthy because it demonstrates, first, that the vast majority of National Army troops received their weapons from Britain, and second, that most RIC rifles went to the National Army on the disbandment of that force rather than going to arm a new Irish civic police force.

While gladly receiving arms and equipment from the British, however, Michael Collins was also covertly liaising with the IRA to supply arms to IRA units in Northern Ireland. In March 1922, with the approval of Collins, Irish Republicans in Germany loaded the schooner *Hannah* with six tons of rifles and ammunition at Breman. It landed in Helvick, Waterford, and dispersed the weapons by road via Dublin primarily to the northern divisions.⁵⁶ In total, the Third Northern Division received 600 rifles and 60,000 rounds of ammunition, divided evenly among its three brigades.⁵⁷ Collins also organised a secret rifle swap in May 1922, as Free State rifles supplied by Britain were swapped with IRA rifles, which were then sent to arm the IRA in Ulster.⁵⁸ These activities suggest that Collins had alternative plans for Northern Ireland as late as May 1922 and was still trying to avoid a civil war in the remainder of the country. The Northern Ireland government discovered this activity, however, and had reliable information that a quantity of munitions supplied by the British government to the Free State government was finding its way to the IRA in the North. It pushed the Free State government to disclaim the IRA in the North and cease giving them assistance.⁵⁹ Eventually these activities did decrease, and Collins' death in August 1992 perhaps, as Bill Kissane contends, removed the last person in the Free State government with a strong protective interest in northern Catholics.⁶⁰

As well as being better armed than their opponents, the National Army was more mobile. By early July 1922, the British government had handed over 355 vehicles to the transport fleet of the National Army.⁶¹ According to a British government report, 79 armoured Lancia trucks and 153 Crossley tenders (15 of them armoured) were supplied.⁶²

Correspondence between Collins and Cosgrave offers somewhat different figures, stating that by August 1922 the Free State had received 13 Rolls-Royce 1920 pattern armoured cars, 7 Peerless armoured cars, and 111 Lancia armoured personnel carriers.[63] In December, the British transferred 20 trucks, 12 touring cars, and 4 mobile search lights.[64] Armour offered protection, mobility, enhanced freedom of movement and also increased firepower, depending on the type of armoured vehicle. This gave an advantage to the Free State during the subsequent fighting with the IRA.

The British also supported the formation of the Irish Air Corps by supplying planes, pilots, and mechanics.[65] The first 13 pilots to fly with the National Army Air Corps were veterans of the Royal Air force and its earlier incarnation, the Royal Flying Corps, notably Charlie Russell and James Fitzmaurice.[66] The first aircraft landed in Baldonnel during the summer of 1922 and soon the Air Corps was equipped with three Bristol Fighters, two Avro Instructional Machines, one Martinsyde Passenger aircraft, and a single-seater S.E.5, operating from both Baldonnel and Fermoy airfields. Over a brief 12 months, the air arm blossomed in size and efficiency.[67] The Free State enjoyed air supremacy for the entirety of the conflict, which substantially increased the intelligence, surveillance, and reconnaissance capabilities of the National Army.

BRITISH CHANGE IN POLICY

The Conservative administration that came to power in Britain in October 1922 was less favourably disposed to the Irish Free State, and started to reduce the support that had been provided by Lloyd George and Churchill. The new British secretary of state for the colonies, the Duke of Devonshire, complained to the Irish governor general, T.M. Healy, 'Supplies which have been furnished to the Provisional [Free State] Government were drawn from surplus stocks which remained over from the late war … The drain on these stocks has been large and continuous.'⁶⁸ Britain wanted financial remuneration for the equipment it had supplied, and in early 1923, Devonshire informed Healy of the change in policy:

> Under no conditions can he hand over any Rolls Royce armoured cars because they cannot be replaced within many months ... A telegram has already been sent to say that six Peerless armoured cars are at the disposal of your Government in Dublin to which the conditions stated in this telegram do not apply and which can be handed over forthwith.⁶⁹

The remainder of the telegram continues in the same vein, as Devonshire goes on to emphasise that munitions will no longer be supplied 'at short notice on the old informal lines.'

As 1923 progressed and the British government became more confident that the Irish National Army would be victorious, it introduced a firmer method of accountancy and accountability for weapons procurement. Financial agreements made between the British and Free State governments in London on 12 February 1923 provided the outline of the new policy. The cost of munitions supplied to the Irish government up to that point would 'constitute a debt to be funded for the purpose of adjustment at the ultimate financial settlement ... on the understanding that the Irish Free State agree to pay cash for future supplies'.⁷⁰

A fortnight later, a letter from the director of equipment and ordnance stores within the British War Office to the high commissioner for the Irish Free State clarified that the Treasury would deal with the financial end of the agreement, in accordance with practice.⁷¹ The British were willing to supply some combat assets by the older methods, but payment was required for the more attractive weapons and equipment requested.

As British public representatives started to enquire into the cost of supporting the Irish National Army, political pressure put an end to covert backing. A report out of the House of Commons notes that 'the arrangement whereby munitions, arms and stores were handed over by the British Government to Free State Government, subject to subsequent valuation … came to an end on 12 February [1923] last.'⁷²

The tightening of financial screws by the new British government had an effect. On the 14 February 1923, the Aireacht Airgid (Irish minister for finance) reported that the Free State stocks were exhausted and that he had 4,000 men without arms. He requested the following list of supplies from the British: '10,000 rifles, 200 Lewis Guns, and 100 Vicar Guns as well as 4,000,000 rounds of .303 ammunition and 2,000,000 rounds of .303 Special Ammunition.'⁷³ There is no record of order fulfilment. In March 1923, James McNeill, an Irish Free State emissary in London, was informed that the Irish quartermaster-general or his representative would be in attendance in London with a view to getting assistance from persons in the British War Office who had experience in dealing with such purchasing. The following month, the Office of the Free State Commander-in-Chief asked McNeill for '40,000 Boots & Leggings, 30,000 Tunics and Caps and 100,000 pairs of breeches.'⁷⁴

The Free State government pragmatically responded to the new British policy by accepting British weapons but neglecting to pay for them on time – or at all. This was a financial necessity since 30 per cent of its entire budget was spent on defence during 1922 and 1923.⁷⁵ On 25 June 1923, the British secretary of state for the colonies was still looking for payment of '£5301.19.10d for two Rolls-Royce armoured cars supplied to the Free State the previous October.⁷⁶ A record that the debt was paid has yet to be discovered.

Yet, notwithstanding the new policy and haggling over payment, the British government could still be relied on to supply the National Army with much-needed ordnance, ammunition, and logistics. This was a major advantage for the National Army and undoubtedly raised its combat effectiveness and fighting acumen relative to the anti-Treaty IRA side, which got very little outside assistance and found it increasingly difficult to supply its forces as the war progressed.

IRA FORCE GENERATION AND LOGISTICAL PROBLEMS

'Despite all the rhetoric and occasional bombast the anti-Treaty Republican side had made no adequate preparation for civil war,' writes historian Michael Hopkinson.[77] In March 1922, the anti-Treaty elements of the IRA (from now on called IRA) organised a convention 're-affirming the IRA's loyalty to the Republic.'[78] An executive was elected, Liam Lynch was appointed chief of staff, and Liam Mellows was made quartermaster-general. Liam Deasy, the former head of the West Cork Brigade, replaced Lynch as O/C 1st Southern Division.[79] Other prominent positions in the IRA command structure were given to Rory O'Connor as director of engineering, Jim O'Donovan as director of chemicals, and Seán Russell as director of munitions. Ernie O'Malley took on the role of director of organisation.[80]

The leadership of the IRA contained various strands, from moderate to extreme. Cathal Brugha, who was killed during early fighting in Dublin, has often been seen as a symbol of violent republicanism, but even he was shouted down for perceived moderation by his more extreme colleagues Rory O'Connor and Liam Mellows.[81] The pre-emptive occupation of the Four Courts by O'Connor and Mellows, before IRA logistical alignment and preparations, did not bode well for the Republican war effort.

O'Malley clearly saw the urgent need for leadership, appropriate staff work, and effective administration: 'The sooner we form an independent headquarters, the better … The men do not know what to do. Time is on the side of the others to wear us down.' Billy Pilkington, another IRA commander, agreed. Noting that the Free State controlled the press, the clergy, and the supply of arms, he declared, 'I vote we here and now form an independent headquarters.' Although O'Malley understood the necessity, he also admitted that it was probably pointless because the 'Free State will be maintained with the arms which the British have sold.'[82]

At the outset of the civil war, at least the numerical advantage appeared to be on the other foot, as anti-Treaty forces dominated the provinces of Ulster, Connacht, and Munster.[83] Only 7 of 16 IRA divisions were loyal to the Free State Ministry of Defence, and the largest divisions – the 1st and 2nd Southern – were anti-Treaty.[84] Nevertheless, 'nationally, the IRA possessed only about 3,000 rifles in 1921, with nearly all of these captured from British forces ... Rifle ammunition remained paltry with an average of forty-three rounds available per weapon.'[85] Such shortages were common even in the comparatively well-armed Cork units. Cork 5th Brigade commander Ted O'Sullivan assessed that each battalion of approximately 500 men had an average of just 8 to 10 rifles.[86]

By the time the conflict was underway the situation had improved somewhat for the IRA. Hopkinson notes that a Free State government source put anti-Treaty IRA numbers at 12,900, with 6,780 rifles.[87] William Kautt contends that it is difficult to know how many IRA volunteers were active but that because most of the IRA arms supply centres in Britain and overseas were against the Treaty, the volunteers at least had the advantage of established networks and experienced smugglers. These networks were also known to Free State personnel, however, meaning that arms and munitions shortages were ongoing. Kautt suggests that smuggling – an enterprise he refers to as 'irregular logistics' – continues to be one of the great requirements for guerrilla forces like the IRA. For that reason, counterinsurgent forces must devote considerable time and resources to counter the threat.[88]

The availability of rifles, equipment, and ammunition to the IRA substantially increased prior to fighting as a result of numerous raids on RIC barracks. One of the most significant was conducted on the Clonmel RIC Barracks by Ernie O'Malley's IRA 2nd Division on 26 February 1922.[89] Some 300 rifles, 200,000 rounds of ammunition, seven machine guns, four armoured cars, and hundreds of grenades were captured.[90]

The Clonmel raid was augmented on 29 March 1922 when the RFA *Upnor* steamed from Haulbowline, in Cork, bound for Devonport, England. By raiding the *Upnor*, the leadership of the IRA hoped to acquire enough guns and ammunition to keep 'Collins and Mulcahy out of Cork.'[91] In an audacious plan, the raiders boarded the vessel, locked the crew below deck, and according to one account unloaded 381 rifles, 727 pistols, 33 Lewis guns, 6 Maxim machine guns, and 25,000 rounds of ammunition in Ballycotton Bay, the most significant capture of weaponry by the IRA during the revolutionary period.[92] An IRA report from 1st (Cork) Brigade of the 1st IRA Division puts the tally from the *Upnor* at '80 tons of machine guns, rifles and ammunition.'[93] John Borgonovo estimates that the raid doubled the 1st Southern Division supply of weapons, including thousands of rounds of precious .303 ammunition, while Tom Mahon makes what he calls a 'conservative estimate' of 1,000 rifles, 2,000 grenades, and up to 200,000 rounds of small arms ammunition, suggesting that this single exploit supplied most of the weaponry and munitions to the IRA in Munster and allowed them to fight a more effective insurgency.[94]

Crucially, the *Upnor* also contained numerous crates of high explosives, giving the IRA the means to mass produce landmines and explosive devices.[95] This would lead to a destructive campaign by IRA engineers on the Free State freedom of movement – and significantly on transport infrastructure in the province of Munster. By 1924, the British government was still looking for £29,972 in compensation for the weapons and ammunition stolen from the *Upnor* by the IRA in 1922.[96]

However successful the IRA was at capturing and seizing weapons, it was difficult to gain substantial support from an international sponsor, although it did have some successes. Desmond FitzGerald, a Free State minister, wrote to Mulcahy in December 1922 that the IRA was getting weapons and munitions in from England 'in fairly large quantities' through shipping companies, while in New York 'the Dockers would help willingly to smuggle the guns out' for the cause.[97] Despite that support, the IRA leadership as a whole failed to seize the opportunity to influence US political opinion and remobilise Irish-Americans.[98] As a last ditch attempt, Liam Lynch despatched Seán Moylan to the United States to purchase arms, telling him in February 1923 of the need for 'even a few [artillery guns], with sufficient shells,' because he believed it 'would finish the business here.'[99] These supplies never materialised.

Though better equipped, especially in Cork, than it had been throughout the War of Independence, the IRA did not have the discipline, training, or regimentation of their pro-Treaty adversaries. O'Malley vented his frustration to Seán Lemass over IRA tardiness and neglect of training, and also wrote to Liam Deasy lamenting that even after raids, 'the men are scattered and the equipment and armament poor.'[100] Ultimately this would have substantial consequences for the insurgency campaign conducted by the IRA against the Free State government.

AN INSTRUMENT OF THE STATE

The National Army was the first instrument at the disposal of the Free State government to maintain law and order and to protect life and property. Army loyalty to the Treaty was thus paramount for the survival of the Free State.[101] Understanding the role of a fully functioning Irish army in protecting its own interests, the British government put its trust in the leadership of the Free State, backed up weapons, ammunition, and equipment. These capabilities, combined with leadership and expertise provided by veterans, allowed the National Army to maintain a favourable force ratio over the anti-Treaty IRA as the civil war progressed.

The integration of ex-servicemen from the British Army into the National Army proved to be an unqualified success. They offered steady leadership and specialist knowledge in transport and combat support, especially artillery. These veterans also provided the training expertise and important junior leadership at the squad and platoon levels and proved to be much more cohesive and responsive than the IRA.[102] By the start of the conflict, Free State soldiers (usually) wore uniforms, were armed with rifles that worked, and had ample ammunition they could trust. When fighting, they were supported by armoured cars, trucks, and artillery.¹⁰³ In time, superiority in arms, numbers, professionalism, and resources would pay off – as the British government regularly supplied the Free State with large consignments of arms, including artillery, that would prove crucial in the fighting.¹⁰⁴

Nevertheless, the formation of the National Army was not plain sailing. As Lieutenant General Collins Powell, a nephew of Michael Collins and Army Chief of Staff in the early 1960s, later commented, 'It would be wrong to accept the neat idea that the organisation went smoothly. The civil war disrupted many plans and the growth of the army was quite haphazard in 1922–23.'¹⁰⁵ But with the direct support of the British logistical supply system and the indirect support of British-trained combat veterans, the National Army evolved into a competent fighting force that was eventually disciplined, regimented, and well equipped. These were essential factors in ensuring that it was able to conduct the Clear–Hold–ReBuild counterinsurgency strategy that would subdue and ultimately defeat the IRA.

CLEAR

A tactical mission task that requires the commander to remove all enemy forces and eliminate organized resistance within an assigned area. The force does this by destroying, capturing, or forcing the withdrawal of enemy forces so they cannot interfere with the friendly unit's mission.

US Army Field Manual 3-90 Tactics, July 2001

4

SHAPING OPERATIONS: THE CONVENTIONAL PHASE OF WARFARE IN MUNSTER

> Never, probably, in the history of the world has a newly born army—hardly out of its swaddling clothes—achieved in such a short space of time, a series of sweeping victories comparable to those won up to date by Ireland's National troops.
>
> *Cork Examiner*, 14 August 1922

For the first seven months of 1922, the IRA constituted the only real authority in Cork and most of Munster, establishing what has already been described as the Cork Republic or Munster Republic.[1] The British government was concerned by these developments and keen to subdue this existential threat, but both the British and Free State governments agreed that the redeployment of British troops to Ireland to quell anti-Treaty sentiment or secession would be unwise. Such a move would be unwelcome by the local population and would help the IRA reunite the country against a common enemy. British assistance, therefore, remained indirect, primarily consisting of weapons, ammunition, vehicles and clothing.

On 30 June 1922, a few days after Free State artillery had shelled the Four Courts, Churchill rose in the House of Commons to confirm that Britain would support the Free State 'with such materials as they may require', while also noting that 'they have continued to decline any [direct] assistance of any sort from British troops, in which they are no doubt well advised, as it is undoubtedly an Irish quarrel, one [in] which the Irish Provisional [Free State] Government are acting in the sense of the mandate they have received from the Irish people'. At roughly the same time as Churchill was speaking in Westminster, Richard Mulcahy, the Irish Minister for Defence, made the following announcement: 'To maintain your rights, and to defend your liberties, the Government have been reluctantly compelled to take armed action against the elements of disorder' after it had 'exhausted every effort to prevent the necessity of a resort to armed force'.[2]

With a similar narrative on both sides of the Irish Sea, it became politically sanctioned for the Free State to clear the IRA from its strongholds, especially in the South and West. According to both Churchill and Mulcahy, this was done in order to uphold the Treaty, subdue the IRA, and cement the validity of the new Irish government.

The resulting clearance operations in Munster adhered to a progressive doctrine, demonstrating superior strategy, leadership, and tactical acumen on the Free State side shaped the battle space. National Army operational plans, maps, and orders are almost non-existent from this period because report writing, records, and filing were not fully institutionally conducted until 1923, when the army was run on a more professional basis.[3] Nevertheless, newspaper reports, archives, and available National Army documentation make it possible to examine the clearance operations, both shaping and decisive, conducted by the Free State in Munster. By clearing Munster of IRA resistance, the National Army set the context and conditions for follow-on hold and rebuild operations in the province.

IRA STRENGTHS IN MUNSTER

The size of active IRA divisions in Munster varied, but the vast majority of volunteers in the two largest, the 1st and 2nd Southern, supported the

SHAPING OPERATIONS: THE CONVENTIONAL PHASE OF WARFARE IN MUNSTER

anti-Treaty side as they were commanded respectively by two staunch Republicans, Liam Lynch and Ernie O'Malley. These two Munster-based divisions contained a third of the IRA's total force, meaning that most of its active, experienced troops supported the Republican cause.[4] Table 1 outlines the strength of the 1st and 2nd Southern Divisions on 1 July 1922.

Table 1 IRA 1st and 2nd Southern Divisions, 1 July 1922

	Cork	Kerry	Limerick	Waterford	Kilkenny	Tipperary	Total
1st Division brigades							
I	4,944	4,843					
II	2,318	3,033					
III	2,445	1,084					
IV	2,604						
V	2,701						
West			1,403				
Combined				1,897			
Total division strength							27,272
2nd Division brigades							
I					2,151		
II						601	
II						2,792	
East			2,003				
Mid			1,397				
Total division strength							8,944
Total							36,216

Source: Data from Military Service Pensions Collection, IRA Nominal Rolls, RO/1-611.

In addition to initial numerical supremacy, the IRA was much better off in terms of finances and equipment than they had been in 1919–21 and could meet the National Army on something approaching equal terms.[5] For example, both the Bandon and Ballyvourney battalions in Cork had doubled their stock of rifles since 1921.[6] Historian John O'Callaghan puts higher figures than I do on IRA strength in Munster, suggesting that it fielded 53,397 volunteers in 18 brigades organised geographically by parish.[7] These estimates may include parts of Munster not within the 1st and 2nd Division areas of operations.

However, figures can be deceiving and Borgonovo notes more widely, that most IRA members had probably never fired or even held a gun during the War of Independence, a point that Gavin Foster supports in reporting that 'a Free State correspondent confidentially claimed "to be in a position to know"' had suggested fewer than 200 of the IRA volunteers across the country had ever shot at the British forces.[8] Gerry White adds that although the IRA still included many officers and men who had fought in the War of Independence 'it also contained many others contemptuously referred to already as "Trucileers"' because they joined after the Truce had come into effect.' White surmises that the 'fighting qualities of these men were unknown and they lacked military experience.'[9] Diarmaid Ferriter disagrees, asserting that it was 'nonsense given that 75% of IRA members opposed the Treaty' and noting that the IRA had many experienced fighters – though not as many as in the earlier fight with the British. He draws on information from Tom Barry, a West Cork IRA commander who estimated that total anti-Treaty IRA strength did not exceed 8,000 men.[10] Michael Hopkinson, by contrast, puts the number of active IRA fighters across the country at the start of the civil war at 12,900.[11]

Regarding the IRA in Cork, Borgonovo asserts they accounted for 17,976, though I would revise that to 15,012 (see Table 1).[12] Nonetheless, he refines the figure by noting that the 'estimated strengths of all IRA flying columns and active service units in 1921 totalled 1,379 IRA full-time fighters of which 466 (34 percent) served in County Cork', adding that the 1st Southern Division possessed 26 per cent of IRA rifles, 25 per cent of its pistols, and 58 per cent of its machine guns.[13] By conducting various arms raids, the IRA in Cork hoped to have enough guns and ammunition to keep the Free State out of the county.[14] Without having the full details, Liam de Róiste in a 1922 diary entry agrees that the 'Irregulars [IRA] have got all the arms and ammunition there was to be had [in Cork], in their possession'.¹⁵

In contrast the composition of the National Army is clearer than these diverse figures for IRA strengths, composition, and experience. Maryann Valiulis reports that by August 1922, when Free State clearance operations were at their busiest, the National Army comprised approximately 14,000 regular soldiers and 5,000 reservists.¹⁶ As already documented, the British government had equipped most of the National Army before the conventional clearance phase of the fighting. But did they have the troop ratios to launch offensive operations southwards?

SHAPING OPERATIONS

> A shaping operation … establishes conditions for the decisive operation through effects on the enemy, other actors, and the terrain. Shaping operations may occur throughout the area of operations and involve any combination of forces and capabilities.
>
> US Army, *Field Manual 3-0: Operations*, 2017.

After being briefly detained but then allowed by National Army Chief-of-Staff Richard Mulcahy to leave Dublin in the hope that he would remain a voice for peace, Liam Lynch – the chief of staff of the IRA and former commander of 1ˢᵗ Southern Division – travelled south. Instead of being a peace advocate, Lynch set about organising IRA forces to challenge the Free State. The IRA hoped to defend a Republic south of a Limerick–Waterford line by demonstrating the limited authority of the Free State in the region.¹⁷ Nobody has ever questioned Lynch's selfless dedication to his cause, but his capacity to direct the Republican campaign has come in for criticism. Notwithstanding the aspiration for an independent Munster, Lynch lacked a definite policy or overall IRA strategy and according to Charles Townsend, 'seemed to reject the very notion of having one. He was an honourable person, but he did not have a revolutionary mind. He could not descend from the high ground of the Republic to the level of politics.'[18]

Florence O'Donoghue, a prominent IRA commander in Cork City who remained neutral during the civil war, states that from the start Lynch ordered his men to fight within their own divisional areas rather than to storm Dublin.[19] At the outset this may have been a wise decision because in the Munster area, the IRA had an initial advantage; only two posts were initially held by pro-Treaty forces, and these were immediately taken by the IRA. At that point in Munster, according to Townsend, the government's forces were outnumbered and outgunned by the IRA.[20] But the IRA made the strategic error of trying to fight the Free State conventionally, using up valuable manpower in order to position themselves in and around the main towns instead of utilising their familiar hedge-fighting tactics against semi-armoured Free State troops.[21] At the start of the civil war the IRA valued the support bases of urban centres rather than the countryside they had controlled in the previous conflict with the British.

NATIONAL ARMY STRATEGY

The clearance phase of counterinsurgency operations is often the most kinetic and the bloodiest.[22] Nevertheless it is strategically important because this phase removes the insurgents from key terrain. By assigning geographic areas of responsibility, the leadership of the National Army was formulating a strategic plan that included the capture of Munster and Cork.[23] The planning and leading of divisional-scale operations, the size of which had never been witnessed during the War of Independence, was crucial and indicated the ambition and strategic intent of the National Army. On 13 July 1922, an Army Council was set up, composed of General Michael Collins as Commander-in-Chief (C-in-C), General Richard Mulcahy as Chief of Staff (COS) and Minister for Defence, and

General Eoin O'Duffy as Assistant Chief of Staff (ACOS).[24] Centralised leadership permits centralised planning, and this gave the Free State a marked advantage over their IRA adversaries.

As Commander-in-Chief of the National Army, Collins set the government's overall strategy and guidance, but its implementation does not seem to have suited his skills. He certainly spent little time drawing arrows on maps or researching the art of war. His policy was simple enough – to win as quickly as possible 'but with the least possible nastiness'.[25] Collins became, in effect, a kind of generalissimo, combining military and political supremacy. Arthur Griffith, the President of the Executive Council, had no desire or capacity to dispute the day-to-day conduct of government with him, and while Mulcahy had greater administrative capacity, he sensibly deferred to Collins as a strategist.[26]

Fortuitously for Collins, the General Staff of the National Army contained experienced operational planners who could translate his guidance and strategies into a coherent framework. This plan, though hard to fully contextualise, is best summarised by an opponent who faced the Free State advances. IRA leader Frank Aiken describes the National Army strategy adopted in the southern province:

> The Provisional Government must inevitably succeed in advancing and conquering the South, even though it is quite possible to keep up guerrilla warfare for several years and thus make government and social peace impossible in large districts. Meanwhile, the Provisional Government will be hailed as saviours of the people, they will receive a great accession of power and authority. The national defences of Ireland will be handed over to those who are weakest nationally. The best fighters and strongest leaders will be killed, jailed and scattered; they will have lost all place in public life and all influence with the people. The greatest blow against the Republic is the coming exclusion of Republicans from what the vast majority of Ireland will regard as the Irish Army and the Irish Parliament.[27]

Free State planners determined that prior to a main strike into the heartland of Munster, the National Army would conduct shaping operations in northern and eastern Munster (see Map 1). From east to west, the IRA defensive line for the Munster Republic crossed the city of Waterford and the towns of Carrick-on-Suir, Clonmel, Fethard, Cashel, Golden, and Tipperary, and ended in the city of Limerick, where Lynch established his first headquarters. To the south lay the territory held by the 1st and 2nd IRA Southern Divisions.[28] In July 1922, seizing and securing Limerick and Waterford, which anchored the line defending the Munster Republic, became the focus of attention for the Free State leadership.

Gauging the situation from Cork City, de Róiste estimated that the IRA would have difficulty operating as a conventional force because, as an 'army they cannot hold out against artillery, which is being used by the Dáil Forces.'[29] In my professional opinion, positional (static) or delay (mobile) defence was futile because the IRA had few machine guns and no artillery.[30] Pat McCarthy characterises the IRA defences as grandiose, because the Republican forces did not have the manpower, equipment, training, or planning expertise to establish a cohesive defensive line. Instead, they concentrated in Limerick and Waterford and awaited the inevitable attack.[31] Ralph Riccio likewise believes that the IRA did not have the equipment to sustain a static or mobile defensive posture.[32] Without artillery support and facing overwhelming Free State artillery and capability for counter-battery fire, the defensive line established between Waterford and Limerick was more symbolic than operational.

SHAPING ON THE SOUTHEASTERN FRONT

Under the command of General John T. Prout, a US Army veteran of the First World War, a National Army force of 800 troops began shaping operations in southeastern Ireland.[33] Prout moved the National Army swiftly through Kilkenny and into Waterford by mid-July 1922.[34] Hopkinson asserts that IRA forces in Waterford City became isolated as a result of this rapid advance, with the Cork and Tipperary IRA units failing to give sufficient support to the Waterford Republican columns. Borgonovo differs, contending that up to 100 Cork City IRA volunteers supported the Republican defence of Waterford. McCarthy puts the total between 200 and 300, commanded by Pa Whelan with some volunteers from Cork No. 1 Brigade.[35] He further suggests that there was 'anarchy' in Waterford City prior to the National Army assault, and that ultimately IRA indiscipline fatally undermined any prospect of successfully defending it.

Among the National Army troops laying siege to Waterford was city son Lieutenant Colonel Patrick 'Paddy' Paul. Because Paul had served with the British Army in France and was used to planning, Prout asked him to submit a plan for seizing the city.[36] Paul had also commanded an east Waterford IRA unit during the War of Independence and knew the area very well. Importantly, the troops under his command also came from the southeastern counties of Waterford, Wexford, Kilkenny, and Tipperary, and so possessed similarly beneficial local knowledge.[37]

The plan envisioned by Paul, who was also a former gunnery officer, consisted of an artillery barrage. From the commanding heights of Mount Misery, indirect artillery fire was unleased onto the city by Free State gunners in order to prepare and subdue the city for a direct assault by the infantry.[38] The *Irish Independent* reported on 21 July that the use of artillery proved to be decisive as 'the deadly accuracy of the Irish gunners … compelled the irregulars to vacate their best positions. One shell exploded a mine in the infantry barracks, whereupon the occupants hurriedly left.' IRA 1st Division Commander Liam Deasy admitted that the Waterford columns broke up under the onslaught of shelling and made hardly any defence.[39] Townsend agrees, emphasising the importance of artillery when noting that 'Waterford was taken by Free State troops with a single field gun.'[40]

As the *Irish Independent* reported on the following day, at 9pm on Friday, 21 July 1922, pro-Treaty troops had lowered the bridge to volleys and cheers, and then advanced steadily along the quays to establish their domination. By then, the only centre of IRA resistance left in Waterford was the jail.[41] A significant victory in arms had been won, and the defensive line of the Munster Republic was now turned on the southeastern flank.[42] From there, the Free State could roll up the line through Carrick and Clonmel in order to link up with the forces moving south from the Thurles–Cashel–Roscrea area.[43]

To capitalise on their success, the National Army needed to reorganise, recruit, and reconstitute its forces, and a consignment of 500 rifles arrived on the gunboat *Helga* to re-equip them.[44] With local knowledge, an open advantageous road network, resupply, new recruits, and building momentum, the National Army fanned south in pursuit of the IRA.[45] Under Dinny Lacey, however, the IRA launched an immediate counter-attack. Three columns that had assembled in Carrick-on-Suir advanced on Kilkenny through Mullinavat but retreated again when Lacey thought he had lost the element of surprise.[46]

The *Irish Independent* reported on 4 August that the route to the next Free State objective, Carrick-on-Suir, was congested and the National Army had cleared Callan, Mullinahone, Ninemilehouse, Kilmogany, and Windgap. The London *Times* somewhat excitedly reported on 5 August that the anti-Treaty forces 'fought stubbornly to retain the position in Carrick-on-Suir and were dislodged only when shrapnel shells burst above them' – but not before unsuccessfully attempting to turn the right flank of the National Army. In retreat, they blew up all the bridges and cut off the water supply. Once the IRA had withdrawn, a National Army advance party entered Carrick-on-Suir at 2 p.m. on 3 August and were reinforced later that evening.[47]

The *Times* report concluded, 'The fall of the town of Carrick-on-Suir, announced today, is a serious blow to the Irregular leaders since the capture makes the evacuation of Clonmel almost certain.' Three days later, on 8 August, the paper analysed the battle for Carrick in the context of the larger South-East:

> The more one follows the operations in the field the more one realizes the difficulties against which the national forces have to contend ... The

SHAPING OPERATIONS: THE CONVENTIONAL PHASE OF WARFARE IN MUNSTER

fact this little town, some fifteen miles distant from Waterford, should have fallen a full fortnight after the capture of the latter place is the best proof of the resistance put up by the irregulars.

This resistance continued. Once Carrick-on-Suir was secured, the *Irish Independent* reported on 4 August, 'The irregulars, estimated at about 300, crossed the river and retreated hurriedly across the mountains towards Kilmacthomas and Dungarvan' and into the west of Waterford. As bridges over the southern river network of Munster became key terrain – Dungarvan soon fell to the National Army advance, and the *Independent* reported on 12 August that the remnants of the IRA forces had evacuated the town on the ninth, following the departure of nearly 300 men the day before. Despite stubborn IRA resistance, National Army equipment superiority had forced the collapse of the anti-Treaty forces in the Waterford area and the resultant retreat west.[48]

Having captured Waterford and cleared the southeast coast of the IRA, the Free State forces had seized many river crossings and opened the amphibious routes and sea lines of control to the more strategically important Munster cities and towns in the South. The way was now clear for land and maritime advances.

THE SOUTHWESTERN FRONT

Limerick City was strategically vital. It linked the South and West, and Republican control would make it possible for the IRA to consolidate its grip on the region. The capture of Limerick was also important for the Free State because the IRA plan had been to use the city as a staging base for clearance operations in Clare and Galway before linking up with Republican concentrations in Sligo and Mayo and ultimately marching on Dublin.[49] Bill Kissane asserts that if the Free State gained control of Limerick, it would be able to cut anti-Treaty forces in Connacht and Munster off from each other and use the city as a base from which to attack both areas.⁵⁰ IRA commander Tom McEllistrim later recalled his belief the civil war was over once its forces left Limerick.⁵¹ Liam de Róiste also emphasised the strategic importance of Limerick when he recorded that the IRA had gone in large numbers to defend it and left comparatively few behind in Cork City. Later historians have noted the rapid gathering of IRA forces to defend the city.⁵²

The first nine days of the battle of Limerick, in July 1922, involved intense street fighting that resulted in a stalemate. Similar to Waterford, the arrival of National Army artillery then swung the battle in favour of the Free State as they bombarded key IRA positions. When General Eoin O'Duffy, who was the operational commander of the National Army in the South-West, arrived with reinforcements and an 18-pounder gun, the four key Republican positions in the city were abandoned.⁵³ Lacking artillery of their own, IRA forces could not defend all the military barracks or key terrain in Limerick City. Instead, the demoralised troops set fire to the strand barracks, which had already been breached by artillery fire.⁵⁴ On the evening of 21 July, after burning their outposts, they retreated south towards the town of Kilmallock, near the Cork–Limerick border.⁵⁵ The next day the *Irish Independent* reported, 'Limerick has fallen and its long ordeal is at an end. The National Army is in full possession, and the Irregulars, who occupied so many strong positions, have either been made prisoners or have fled from the city.' In subsequent fighting in East Limerick on 28 July, O'Duffy faced what he described as the 'best fighting material the irregulars can muster ... having concentrated all their forces from Munster on the Kilmallock frontier.'⁵⁶

THE BATTLE FOR KILMALLOCK

As anti-Treaty Republicans from all over Munster evacuated their defences in Limerick City, resistance spread east and south across the county. The IRA forces that concentrated in the important town of Kilmallock were under the command of Liam Deasy. Located near the border with Cork, Kilmallock was one of the last towns on the south-western front for the National Army troops to capture before entering County Cork. Here, more than anywhere else during the civil war, the opposing sides faced each other in a conventional setting, as they both occupied clearly defined defensive front lines consisting of outposts in villages and towns and on the high ground.[57]

Traversing the *bocage* terrain around Kilmallock proved difficult for the pro-Treaty troops. Moreover, their tactical commander, Major General W.R.E Murphy, was fixated on his experience of trench warfare as a senior British Army officer in France. He inched along ponderously, relying on his map and ordering his troops to dig in the minute they came under sniper fire. By contrast, the leadership of Liam Deasy and Sean Moylan for the opposing IRA forces was outstanding.[58] Townsend calls Deasy one of the most able IRA commanders, suggesting that his tenacious defence of the Kilmallock front brought the National Army advance to a standstill and showed that Republican forces could fight positional battles in the countryside.[59] Deasy himself considered that the 'only fight was in Kilmallock area ... [with] Cork No. 3 Brigade.'[60]

Notwithstanding dynamic leadership capabilities within the IRA in Kilmallock, eventually the tide of battle turned in favour of the Free State. On Thursday, 3 August 1922, National Army forces consisting of some 2,000 troops supported by armoured cars and artillery began a steady advance on a wide front towards the town.[61] The *Irish Independent* captured this decisive moment a few days later when it reported that the armoured car *Danny Boy* had provided protection for the troops advancing onto the main road. The arrival of Free State reinforcements, armour, and artillery meant that Republican control of the area was only temporary.[62] By Saturday, Free State forces had encircled the town, and the artillery reinforcements had shelled Kilmallock Hill and the surrounding high ground. The National Army then advanced and, after some heavy fighting, occupied most of the high ground.[63] Deasy recorded that the IRA broke through the line on the Bruree side of the town, only to be driven back by National Army reinforcements. Eventually it took one of the 18-pounder field artillery guns giving covering fire and the 'dash of the crack Dublin Guards [Infantry] under Comdt Tom Flood' to penetrate the IRA defences. Kilmallock village was eventually occupied at 4 a.m. on 5 August 1922 after a fierce fight.[64]

Irish historian John O'Callaghan doubts the Free State victory was a result of brilliant planning by General W.R.E. Murphy. Rather, there was 'no final battle for Kilmallock, no all-out last stand' because the IRA had elected to abandon the town.[65] As its forces withdrew, they destroyed key infrastructure before it could be seized by the National Army. A disgruntled O'Duffy issued a proclamation giving his troops 'definite orders to fire on any person discovered in the act of (a) destroying bridges, railway lines, stations or signal cabins, canal locks, telephone or telegraph lines, (b) obstructing public roads, felling trees or cutting trenches, [or] (c) looting of private or public property.'[66]

On 8 August 1922, O'Duffy issued a review of the military situation in his area of operations that was reported in the *Irish Independent* the following day: 'The victorious march of the National troops in the South-Western Command continues from day to day. On 1st August we [National Army] held East and Mid-Limerick from the Tipperary border to the River Maigue. We have since crossed the Maigue and captured Adare, Rathkeale and Newcastle-West, 12 miles beyond the river.'

The success of Free State operations in the South-West represented a substantial setback for the IRA defensive line, as both flanks had now been captured. This seriously damaged IRA ambitions of defending the independent entity that was the Munster Republic. The strategic predicament was palpable. IRA men from Kerry and Cork who were fighting to prevent the National Army from advancing south were disillusioned when they subsequently learned that the Free State had encircled them by sea, landing a strong force in Fenit.[67] Calton Younger perhaps sums up the setback best: 'Allowing their front door to give so easily was the news that intruders had burst in the back.'[68] With Free State forces threatening from two fronts, the Cork and Kerry IRA withdrew to defend their own regions.

SHAPING OPERATIONS: THE CONVENTIONAL PHASE OF WARFARE IN MUNSTER

THE KERRY LANDINGS

While fighting was ongoing on the Limerick and Waterford fronts, supporting operations and subsequent concurrent amphibious landings of pro-Treaty forces were being planned for County Kerry. The south-western county had witnessed significant fighting during the War of Independence, and a large number of active IRA fighters were located there. But the local fighting strength was diluted as many experienced Kerry volunteers had been sent to support Kilmallock.[69] On 2 August 1922, a Free State force of 450 soldiers reached behind enemy lines in Kerry. Niall Harrington vividly describes the seaborne landing: 'With a roar the Vickers gun of the armoured car, together with Lewis guns and rifles, opened up from the deck of the *Lady Wicklow* with terrifying effect ... Within half an hour of the ship's berthing, the first important foothold had been gained in the south.'[70]

Four companies of the Dublin Guards Infantry under the command of General Patrick O'Daly disembarked from the chartered ship the *Lady Wicklow* and landed in Fenit. Once ashore and consolidated, the Guards moved on to the provincial town (and key terrain) of Tralee, which they captured after a short and bloody battle.[71] The London *Times*, reporting on 4 August 1922, gave an account of the meeting:

> A body of National troops landed last night at Fenit, some eight miles from Tralee ... The secret of their departure was not too well kept, and they were compelled to effect a difficult landing under machine-gun fire, in which they suffered three casualties ... The bald facts given above suffice to indicate that the [Free State] Government is determined to close in upon the Irregulars on all sides, and has no intention of allowing its opponents, as they fall back from Tipperary and Limerick, to find an unmolested haven in the rugged hills of the south-western extremity of the country.

The *Irish Independent* reported on 5 August that the incident had been 'the most dramatic coup of the present fighting', and declared that the

National Army had 'struck a deadly blow at the left flank of the position held by the irregulars.' The Free State soldiers 'quickly gained a lodgement in the costal port by using suppressive heavy machine gun fire to quickly silence the small IRA garrison at Fenit.' At the same time, the Fenit assault was supported by a landing at Tarbert, also in Kerry. Crossing the Shannon, the Free State force reportedly took the IRA by surprise and 'little opposition was offered to their landing'.

John Duggan suggests that the landing at Fenit produced a chain reaction. Not only did it envelop the rear of the Cork–Kerry anti-Treaty redoubt, but it also drew Kerry units away from the critical battle for Kilmallock, leaving the axis ahead clear for the pro-Treaty forces to advance.[72] From Fenit, the National Army secured Tralee and headed into the heartland of Kerry, where many prisoners were taken, including, according to a rather breathlessly excited *Irish Independent*, 'several leaders of the irregulars in the county.'[73]

Tom Doyle calls the seizing of Tralee 'a major blow in a powerful Free State punch combination intended to win the war in Munster'.[74] The landings sowed confusion and consternation among the rank-and-file IRA and precipitated the same domino collapse in Kerry as had happened in Waterford.[75] Exploiting the surprise, the National Army pushed on from Tralee to capture Castleisland and Farranfore on 5 August.[76]

Retreating from various former strongholds across the county, IRA volunteers then assembled in Killarney, one of the main towns of Kerry, and in the hilly country around it. From there, as the *Irish Independent* reported on 14 August, they turned their attention on the inhabitants: 'Scores of young men known to be loyal to the [Free State] Government were rounded up and brought out to trench roads and construct defensive works on the hills, whilst armed Irregulars stood over them giving instructions.'

On 11 August, a further 200-strong Free State invasion force under Commandant Tom O'Connor landed in Kenmare and went on to secure Rathmore and Millstreet on the Cork–Kerry border before doubling back to seize Cahersiveen. By mid-August, the National Army had taken most of the main population centres in Kerry, but the battle for full control of the county would take many more months as bitter fighting continued until the very end of the civil war in May 1923.⁷⁷ Nevertheless, the Kerry landings helped encircle the IRA in Munster and provided a very beneficial rehearsal for the main landings in Cork a few days later.

FROM SHAPING TO DECISIVE OPERATION

The end of Republican resistance in Waterford, coupled with the fall of Limerick, meant that by early August, both ends of its much-vaunted defensive line were in government hands.⁷⁸ The relative speed with which Free State forces had rolled up the anti-Treaty defensive flanks, and the success of their attacks on the Tipperary towns at the centre of the line, reinforced the perceptions of the anti-Treaty leadership that the main Free State strike would come from Dublin, through Tipperary, and eventually on to Cork. National Army leaders were content to reinforce these perceptions, but planners recognised that the fight to capture the decisive terrain of Cork City via land would be long and arduous, especially with the IRA preparing and reinforcing defences in North Cork. Speculation was rife about which axis of advance the National Army would take to seize the city and county and, indeed, whether the volunteers would make a stand in the city at all.⁷⁹

Over the summer of 1922, the IRA had sent many of its best fighters to the south-western and south-eastern fronts, leaving Cork exposed to a direct attack. This was an IRA vulnerability and a major advantage to the National Army, which was transforming into a competent and well-organised force as the fighting progressed. Improving organisational structures and reporting lines of communications within the Free State were captured in Cabinet minutes that highlighted the speed of advancement and identified the need for the government to be constantly updated and situationally aware.⁸⁰ The IRA had no such organisation in place and suffered as a result of the fighting encountered during the summer months of 1922. As John Borgonovo observes, the Republican forces were 'built for guerrilla operations, [and] the organisation of the IRA did not adjust well to conventional fighting'.[81]

As fighting continued, the Free State started to refine its tactics. It relied more on the fighting abilities of the National Army troops, especially the Dublin Guard, and the use of artillery. The southern advances of the National Army would have certainly focused the minds of the IRA men left to defend Cork, but De Róiste believed they had not yet definitely decided what to do about the city as only a small force remained.[82] Padraig O Caoimh goes further, suggesting that 'even though most of the best pre-Treaty fighting men had gone anti-Treaty, their hearts were not really in the struggle'.[83] The Battle for Cork would test the IRA resolve and ultimately prove to be the decisive operation for the National Army during the conventional phase of fighting. The capture of Cork would severely undermine the status of the Munster Republic.

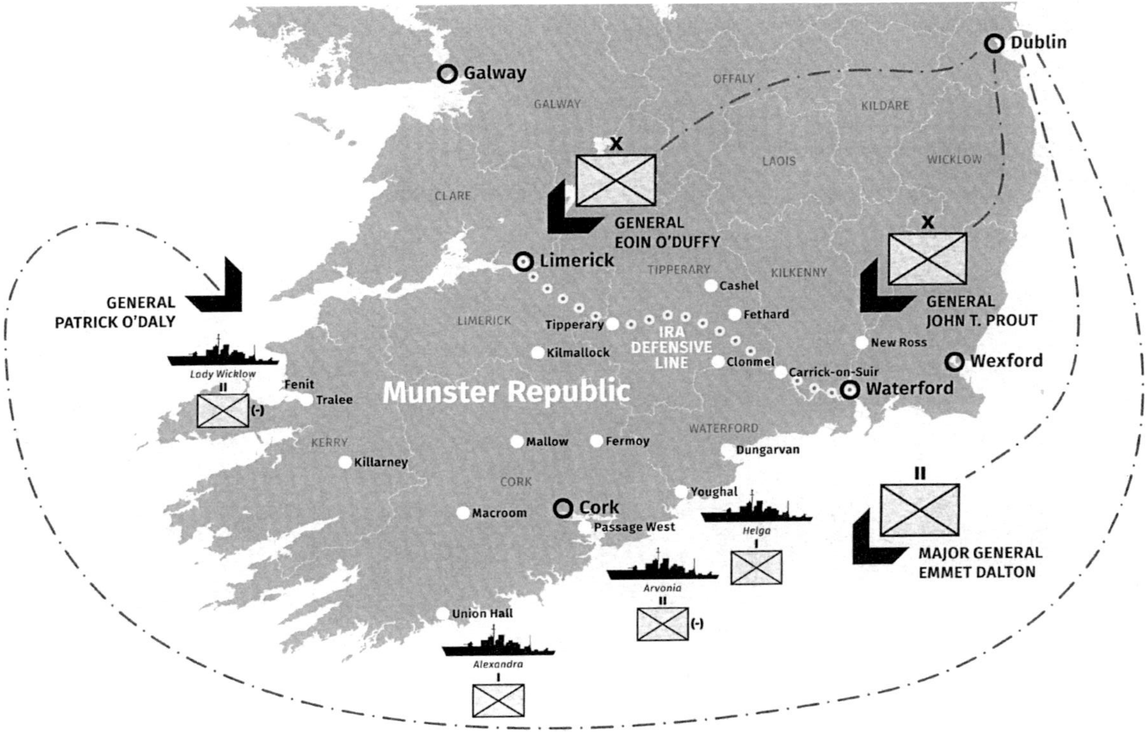

Map 1: National Army activity, 1922

5

THE CORK LANDINGS: THE DECISIVE OPERATION

The Decisive Operation is the operation that directly accomplishes the mission. It determines the outcome of a large-scale combat operation, battle or engagement.

> Turning Movement. A form of [offensive] manoeuvre in which the attacking force seeks to avoid the enemy's principal defensive positions by seizing objectives behind the enemy's current positions, thereby causing the enemy force to move out of his current positions or divert major forces to meet the threat. A major threat to his rear forces the enemy to attack or withdraw rearward, thus "turning" him out of his defensive positions.
>
> US Army, *Field Manual 3-0: Operations*, 2017

On 4 August 1922, Mulcahy assured Collins that the only 'definite military problem' was the Waterford–Cork–Kerry–Limerick area. Everywhere else the army could operate in support of the police.[1] Mulcahy believed the army had to take the lead in the turbulent areas of Munster where, he confidently stated, 'the establishing of ourselves in a few more of these positions would mean the resurgence of the people from their present cowed condition and the immediate demoralisation of the Irregular rank and file.'[2]

Cork City, and more generally the county, was among the more important of these positions because it had been cut off from much of Ireland and under direct IRA military rule following the outbreak of hostilities in June 1922. Cork was a main population centre, supply hub, and key industrial and communications centre for the South, but its population hadn't fully accepted the six-week-old Munster Republic, or Cork Republic. Successful amphibious landings could prove decisive by harnessing this ambivalence because, as Peter Hart suggests, during this period the IRA had assumed the role of an occupying army.[3]

In fact, Cork was a microcosm of the unhappy relationship between the civilian population and the anti-Treaty military administration during the civil war.[4] The people of Cork City were dissatisfied with the anti-Treaty regime, as growing unemployment was matched by rising taxes exacted by the occupiers.[5] Exacerbating local dissatisfaction was the IRA's seizure of every available motor vehicle and large quantities of food, while townspeople and farmers began sleeping in the fields to avoid the excesses of the volunteer forces.[6] De Róiste suspected that 99 per cent of the people of Cork would cheer the National Army forces if they did they come to the city, reasoning, 'Within the past few days, feeling has grown very strong here that the best chance for peace is the absolute defeat of the Irregulars… The people indeed object to the swaggering airs and the "Commandeering" and the threats and terrorism of the Irregular forces.'[7] The National Army would have been aware of these dissenting sentiments and sought to turn them into a vulnerability for the IRA.

CORK AS AN AMPHIBIOUS TARGET

As the summer fighting campaign intensified, the status of Cork city as the capital of the Munster Republic was waning. Once Waterford and Limerick had been captured by pro-Treaty forces, Cork was left open to attack by land and sea, and its status in the region and as a symbol of secession was undermined.[8] Imaginative sea landings at Westport had already clinched the takeover of Mayo in the West. Castlebar was taken on 25 July 1922, as a National Army division swept westward from Athlone practically unopposed.[9] Along with the successful Kerry landings, amphibious actions in the West and South-West acted as supporting operations and test cases for the more strategically important landings into Cork.

The Cork landings were planned for early August. Collins had been told by various sources, including family members, that if the National Army arrived in force inside Munster, it would be well received by citizens anxious to be relieved from the 'oppressions' of IRA rule.[10] As noted earlier, most of the experienced fighting men in Cork had, in fact, sided with the anti-Treaty IRA, but Free State reports indicated they might fight only half-heartedly because 'with such men it is a case of bread and butter. Many of those would have joined the National Army had they the opportunity of doing so.'[11] De Róiste recorded his findings from everyday conversations in Cork prior to the landings: although the IRA would be headquartered in Cork City, 'They will only conduct the guerrilla campaign from it, and still not fight in the city itself, but evacuate it without fighting and withdraw to the country westward and engage in guerrilla tactics.'[12]

Although the anti-Treaty side had defences along the south coast to pre-empt Free State amphibious actions, IRA defences of Cork had been based largely on the assumption that any attack would come from the north. The rolling up of the Waterford–Limerick line and the concentration of Free State forces on the Kilmallock, Tipperary, and Waterford fronts had certainly reinforced the assumption already held by the IRA leadership that an attack would come by land. The National Army did nothing to discourage this. On the contrary, it ordered diversionary attacks well to the north of Cork, which had the desired effect of employing the bulk of the IRA forces over a broad front.[13] Having experienced stiff IRA resistance in Kilmallock, Tipperary, and North Cork, the Free State leadership determined that a turning movement was the best course of action. Additionally, large parts of Munster were still under anti-Treaty control, especially the northern approaches to Cork city and county.[14]

A turning movement from the sea would also avoid the blockages and damage to transportation infrastructure that had been wrought in North Munster by the anti-Treaty forces. Jim Byrne, who served in the National Army and landed in Cork by sea, recalled later that 'there was no such thing as a railway or a road, they were all blocked or blown up.'[15] The blocking of routes and strong resistance by the IRA was a common theme in newspaper reports from the period. The London *Times* elaborated on 8 August 1922 that the Free State forces 'were constantly forced to turn back owing to obstructions ... dodging under telegraph wires stretched across the roads and wriggling through the debris of destroyed railway bridges', remarking further, 'The more one follows the operations in the field the more one realizes the difficulties against which the National Forces have to contend.' A land attack on Cork city would have been resisted by IRA forces in North Cork and slowed by the destruction of crucial transport infrastructure.

With these considerations, the Free State was aware that attacking Republican positions head-on would be slow and result in heavy casualties, so the National Army leadership devised a strategy to outflank the IRA by sea.[16] Seaborne landings first in Kerry and then in Cork would achieve several ends: they would allow National Army troops to capture large tracts of undefended territory; they would disrupt IRA lines of communication; and they would draw IRA forces away from their defensive line and allow pro-Treaty forces to continue advancing south.[17] A secondary and additional advantage would be to hasten the land advance southwards by the remainder of the National Army forces by forcing IRA troops to withdraw from the line in order to defend Cork city. Free State advances south would then permit link-up operations with troops who had been part of the seaborne landings into Cork and Kerry.

If successfully executed, the seaborne and land advances on Cork city had the possibility of entrapping and capturing many IRA fighters between National Army soldiers advancing on both flanks. To achieve this, the various Free State commanders had to ensure vital co-ordination and co-operation.

PLANNING THE ATTACK

The initial planning for the coastal landings in Cork was done by Major General Emmet Dalton and his staff. He was one of the finest field commanders of the Irish Civil War. Though still only twenty-four, he possessed extensive First World War combat experience, having won the Military Cross on the Western Front while still a teenager.[18] Not only had he commanded relatively large numbers of British troops but he had also learned guerrilla warfare during IRA service in the War of Independence.[19] Dalton had also served with the British Army during Edmund Allenby's advance through Palestine and Syria, where he would have witnessed first-hand how effective hybrid or proxy warfare could be.[20] His awareness of hybrid warfare doctrine cannot be proven, but he would have recognised the necessity for the support of a locally recruited force and local knowledge when dealing with complex operations in a hostile environment.[21] While serving as a member of the Royal Dublin Fusiliers and the 10th Irish Division, Dalton would also have been exposed to veterans who had participated in the British amphibious landings in Gallipoli.[22] Finally, while in the British Army, Dalton had also learned military planning and how to write operations orders.[23]

Within the National Army General Staff were other British Army veterans, including Major General Diarmuid McManus. Originally from Mayo, McManus completed a cadetship at the Royal Military Academy Sandhurst in 1910. He fought with the Royal Inniskilling Fusiliers during the First World War and was wounded during the Gallipoli amphibious landings. McManus joined the National Army before the civil war and helped plan the Free State landings in Cork and Kerry in August 1922. He was in charge of the successful amphibious landings at Tarbert on 3 August and Kenmare on 11 August.[24]

THE CORK LANDINGS: THE DECISIVE OPERATION

Alongside these planners with First World War experience was a cohort of pro-Treaty IRA leaders who had gained valuable combat experience and connections over the years fighting against the British. Major General Tom Ennis – who served as Dalton's second-in-command during the Cork landings and subsequent campaign in Cork – was one. He was a veteran of the 1916 Easter Rising and commanded the Dublin Brigade's 2nd Battalion during the War of Independence. Ennis was an intelligent and charismatic leader, considered by Ernie O'Malley to be the best officer in Dublin.[25] Reflecting his high level of competence, Ennis was charged with storming the Four Courts at the start of the civil war, and among the former Dublin Street fighters he enjoyed what Borgonovo terms 'perhaps the smoothest transition to a conventional officer'.[26]

The plan that Dalton chose was simple but audacious – the characteristics of most successful offensive operations. A large body of Free State troops would set sail from Dublin and then attack Cork Harbour from the open sea, make their way up the River Lee to land in the city centre, and capture crucial bridges intact before the Republicans could respond.[27] This was important for many reasons, including resupply, reinforcement and freedom of movement.

REQUIRED SHIPPING

When the Free State began planning the coastal landings in Cork, Kerry, and Mayo, it had no ships of its own with the capacity to transport an attack force. The former British gunboat *Helga*, used in 1916 to shell Dublin, was handed over to the Irish and would later support the landings at Youghal and subsequent operations along the West Cork coast in September 1922. The only additional option was to charter commercial services, and as early as 15 July, Mulcahy wrote to Collins with a list of vessels that could be made available as troop transports.[28] Two suitable ships were identified, the *Arvonia* and the *Lady Wicklow*. They were chartered on 20 July 1922 by the Free State government from London and North-Western Railways. The charter terms stipulated that 'the cargo shall be laden and discharged at all ports to which the vessels may be ordered'. The *Arvonia* was 'to be placed, with clear holds, at the disposal of the charterers at Holyhead, they being tight, staunch, and in every way fitted for service, and being maintained by the owners with a full complement of Officers, Seamen, Engineers, and Firemen necessary'.[29]

Jointness or cooperation at both the military and the civil–military level was required to ensure the successful execution of these plans. It would also be supported by crucial intelligence processed by the Free State.

INTELLIGENCE ASSESSMENT

Prior to any large-scale operation, the intelligence preparation of the battle space is a vital piece of the planning jigsaw. The National Army's intelligence department had been built during the War of Independence, essentially as a counter-intelligence organisation rather than a tactical intelligence one. It did not direct its efforts towards gathering and processing the basic intelligence data needed to support large-scale operations: information on the enemy order of battle and combat capabilities, the location of military and police installations, tide tables, offloading capabilities at ports selected for landings, and possible defensive measures, locations, and capabilities.[30] The lack of such tactical intelligence certainly hampered National Army planning, but it did receive intelligence assistance from sources that included ex-British Army servicemen living in Cork and residual British forces still in Ireland, especially the Royal Navy.[31] Borgonovo confirms that other Free State operatives were also active in Cork, and that the IRA arrested a number of them prior to the landings.[32]

Additional intelligence on the strength, location, and disposition of anti-Treaty forces in the area was obtained from other covert intelligence sources in Cork – including Michael Collins' own sister, Mary Collins Powell, who seems to have been very well-informed about the defences of Cork.[33] Dalton and his planners in other domains also received intelligence provided at the joint level by way of aerial reconnaissance flights carried out by the new Military Air Service in advance of the landings.[34] Also on board one of the Free State ships landing in Cork was Captain Frank O'Friel, who had spent his boyhood in the Cork Harbour area, where his father had served as a lighthouse keeper.[35]

By comparison, the IRA lacked intelligence resources, especially in the Free State staging area of Dublin. They may have anticipated Free State amphibious operations but they could not determine when and where they would occur, and were incapable of warning their Munster comrades about troops sailing south.[36]

EXECUTION OF THE PLAN

By early August 1922, the forces of the Cork Republic had fallen back as the Free State forces advanced from the north.[37] Meanwhile Dalton, as the operational commander for the amphibious action, set about planning to secure Cork city by using a three-pronged assault from the sea. The main force objective was Cork city, with supporting objectives at Youghal and Union Hall.[38] The plan was as follows. The main force, which Dalton termed Party A, was bound for Cork city and had a strength of about 450 men. The first supporting force, Party B, was to head for East Cork at Youghal with a strength of about 200. Party C was for West Cork at Union Hall with about 150 men.[39] In total, over 800 soldiers of the National Army would assemble at the North Wall Quay in Dublin to board the ships that took them down the coast to Cork.[40] Dalton and his second-in-command, Ennis, would take charge of the expedition from on board the *Arvonia*. On board the *Lady Wicklow*, which was to set sail for the main objective, were armoured cars and an 18-pounder field gun.[41] These combat support platforms represented a significant commitment of National Army assets.[42]

The port of embarkation for the entire landing force was Dublin due to the availability of shipping and the concentration of troops and equipment. The *Helga* and the *Alexandra* – chartered from Britain along with the *Arvonia* – departed for the supporting objectives of Youghal and Union Hall, respectively, in the late evening of 6 August; the ships bound for Cork City left a little after noon the next day.[43]

The captain of *Arvonia* had informed Dalton that his plan was impossible and that he and his mostly Welsh crew did not wish to become embroiled in a battle between Irishmen.[44] Once the operation was underway, however, the crews of all the ships involved proved to be extremely competent, as Dalton acknowledged to the chief of staff of the National Army:

> I AM WRITING THIS ABOARD THE ARVONIA JUST BEFORE I GIVE ORDERS TO SAIL.
> I think that in view of the tremendous difficulties that presented themselves to us on this expedition a word of thanks and appreciation is due to the captain and crew of the ship. They have really behaved very well and if they were a bit nervous and tense it is not to be wondered at.
>
> I would consider it advisable for you to write the ship's owners stating your appreciation of the work they have done.
>
> I have a special word for the captain who was really splendid.
>
> I have presented the Stewards with £20.
>
> Is mise [Yours sincerely],
>
> JE Dalton[45]

Facing the Free State Maritime Task Force when it landed was the Cork IRA. Anecdotal evidence suggests that the defending troops were not of the highest quality, as a good number of the best Cork troops had been sent to aid in the defence of Kilmallock and Waterford.[46] IRA rein-

THE CORK LANDINGS: THE DECISIVE OPERATION

forcements also came from other areas within the Munster Republic, which meant the units found themselves in totally unfamiliar territory at times.[47] On the Free State side were soldiers from the 2nd Eastern Division of the National Army's Eastern Command, most of them from the Dublin Guards battalion, which had participated in the recent Dublin fighting and was composed of former IRA veterans.[48] Not all the landing troops were veterans, however. Some had only just been recruited and had to be instructed on basic rifleman skills as they sailed for Cork.[49]

THE LANDINGS

Between 11 p.m. and sometime after midnight on 7–8 August 1922, a force of 200 men landed at Youghal and 180 (somewhat more than the original plan) disembarked at Union Hall. The IRA had mined the pier at Union Hall so the National Army troops rowed ashore with the primary objective of taking the larger town of Skibbereen in West Cork, which was vacated by the IRA on 8 August.[50]

Ted O'Sullivan, an IRA volunteer who was in West Cork, recollected that 20–30 men were at Skibbereen Barracks and that the IRA had complete control of the area from the beginning of July to mid-August. O'Sullivan speculated that behind his back 'the Free State crowd were quietly organizing all the time. Skibbereen sent most men to Dublin to join the Free State Army. And they got good men in Skibbereen.'[51] The IRA had a small outpost of coast watchers, who were cleared out when the National Army troops landed at Union Hall. O'Sullivan explains how the IRA 'rushed troops down, but they [the National Army] had already reached Skibbereen by moving across country for 5 miles, but it had been organized by the Free State before this. This was a strongly Free State area and our friends there were very few.'[52]

On the opposing side, Jim Byrne offers an eyewitness account: after the landing the National Army troops 'worked [their] way under fire, constantly being attacked, to Skibbereen and a short time in Skibbereen [they] started off to work [their] way further down towards Clonakilty … We were all the time on the go.' On the route, the troops passed a 'place called Sam's Cross where Michael Collins was born and reared, and we moved onto Clonakilty'.[53]

Meanwhile at Youghal a force of 200 men landed under the fire support of the *Helga*, along with two armoured cars and an 18-pounder field artillery gun. Dalton reported to Dublin that they had a heavy fight for the town. Eventually, after gaining a lodgement, the National Army troops posted strong guards on all the roads into the town and then fanned out to wait to conduct link-up operations with those landing in Cork City.[54]

In the early hours of Tuesday, 8 August 1922, the *Lady Wicklow* and the *Arvonia* entered Cork Harbour and made their way up the River Lee.[55] Contrary to popular misconceptions, the IRA did fear an amphibious attack and took steps to prevent it but did not have sufficient resources. IRA engineers had mined piers and approaches to likely landing spots, prepared bridges for demolition, and erected road barriers guarded by sentries.[56]

Dalton had initially planned to steam up river into Cork City as far as the Ford Factory Wharf and to disembark his main body there, but the plan was radically altered when he learned that the IRA had positioned two ships in Cork Harbour to act as a boom.[57] The Royal Navy was still occupying strategic seaports in Cork Harbour and its officers were taken by surprise by the arrival of Dalton's seaborne forces, but once communications had been established they advised the *Arvonia* captain that he needed a pilot to take him further upstream to Cork. The British summoned a pilot from Cobh, and he went on board the *Arvonia* to help the Free State landing force.[58] With his advice, the main landing force selected and successfully gained a lodgement in Passage West, a port town situated on the west bank of Cork Harbour and some 10 km southeast of Cork City.

Dalton recorded the hindrance in his after-action report: 'A' Landing had not taken place as arranged, but the alternative landing had been made at Passage West without loss.'[59] A correspondent for the *Irish Times* clocked the docking at exactly 2:20 a.m., 8 August, and the first troops

THE CORK LANDINGS: THE DECISIVE OPERATION

were ashore two minutes later.[60] Eoin Neeson contends that the IRA was taken by surprise.[61] Borgonovo believes otherwise, noting that 'within ninety minutes of the Free State army troops landing in Cork, a fierce cross-river firefight broke out and bridges began to explode around the City.'[62] The bridge on the road from Passage West to Cork City was destroyed and the inhabitants of the area thrown into confusion.[63]

Within 10 minutes of berthing at Passage West, 150 to 200 troops from the *Arvonia* had divided into three parties to form a protective screen half a mile inland.[64] The National Army also successfully disembarked an 18-pounder field gun and two armoured cars: 'a Rolls Royce Whippet known as *The Manager* equipped with the usual Vickers machine gun, and a Peerless, a much heavier vehicle with twin Hotchkiss machine guns'.[65] The disembarking of the heavy Peerless proved difficult, as no suitable crane was available and the National Army had to wait for low tide to offload it directly onto the dock.[66] Extra rifles were also disembarked because it was planned that each contingent would rapidly expand its strength with local volunteers from among pro-Treaty members of the IRA and ex-servicemen. Hundreds of these extra rifles were carried with the convoy into Cork city in order to arm any new recruits.[67]

The landings in Cork were a coup de force for the Free State, which was able to position approximately 830 troops behind the IRA front line in a turning operation that proved to be a major success.[68] The London *Times* on 9 August 1922 summarised the landings thus: 'The most daring stroke of the whole campaign has been struck by the [Free State] Government at the Irregulars. Four ships containing ... men, with artillery, having been sent from Dublin to Cork.' The *Irish Independent* of 12 August 1922 called the landings a complete shock to the IRA and 'the surprise created by the coup was only equalled by the successful, daringly brilliant manner in which it was accomplished'. On 14 August, the *Cork Examiner* similarly heralded the operation: 'In estimating this truly wonderful achievement the average civilian cannot thoroughly grasp the huge amount of work that has been accomplished. The mere recruitment, elementary drilling, training and equipping of so many men meant a fairly stiff proposition even if time was no consideration.'

Dalton reported to the National Army leadership that the expeditionary force consisted of three drafts: Party A, of 500 troops landed in Cork City, Party B, of 200 at Youghal, and C, of 150 at Glandore (in the vicinity of Union Hall).[69] With this considerable force now safely ashore, Dalton and his commanders set out to capture Cork City and the other urban centres close to the landing sites.

ADVANCING ON CORK CITY

After a successful lodgement was made and all of his men and equipment were put ashore, Dalton commenced his march on Cork City.[70] The dispersal of IRA forces between Monkstown and Passage West prevented the Republicans from easily concentrating their forces, and when news of the landings first reached Cork city, there was confusion within the anti-Treaty leadership. Most available IRA forces had to be rushed to unprepared positions at Rochestown, between Cork city and Passage West.[71] They took up positions on the hills overlooking the road towards Rochestown, maximising the advantage offered by the high ground to slow the progress of the National Army troops from the south. Peter Hart refers to a 'thin IRA firing line' that was assembled to block the advance.[72]

The IRA plan for defending Cork hinged on keeping the National Army south of the city until reinforcements arrived from North Cork and the Kilmallock defences. If they could hold a defensible line along the River Lee, Borgonovo suggests, the anti-Treaty troops could retain 'a sizeable portion of north and mid-Cork. This was mountainous country and included their bases in Macroom, Fermoy and Mallow.'[73] To counter this plan and gain the momentum, Free State troops advanced at a steady pace and on a wide front into Cork city over undulating terrain.[74] The two forces clashed in the suburban hills around Rochestown and Douglas, and some sharp fighting ensued.[75] Dalton recorded the progress in correspondence to the leadership of the Free State:

> Advance made on Cork City on a two-mile front—direction due west. Continuous Advance Guard action between Passage and Rochestown—two-and-a-half-hour engagement at Rochestown—Machine gun, rifle and shot gun resistance to my right flank ... [Troops] disobeyed orders by failing to close and enfilade. My right flank [was] assaulted and won the position.[76]

Hart summarises the Rochestown fighting, noting that although the IRA troops managed to capture quite a few unwary National Army soldiers, in the end they were 'outnumbered, outgunned, and exhausted'.[77]
Late in the evening of 8 August, some 140 Republicans from the Kilmallock and Waterford fronts arrived in Cork to support the city defences, but by the time they got there they were themselves exhausted and Rochestown was already in National Army hands.[78] A civilian witness, Olga Pyne Clarke, recalled the scene:

> They were tired, marching raggedly, no military precision about them. They probably had not been properly fed and had slept rough. Their trench coats were dirty and muddy, their faces hollow-eyed had a starved savage look in them ... at six pm they came from all directions ... They were a rabble and they knew it.[79]

The advance towards Cork from Passage West via Rochestown led to what John Duggan describes as 'bloody encounters in which both sides showed great bravery and resource.'[80] The most intense combat occurred on the following day, 9 August, when National Army troops attempted to turn the flank of the defenders, who had established a strong defensive line at Oldcourt, but this attack failed under the withering fire of the IRA. The fighting continued in the vicinity of Ballincummins Cross. Using field artillery, the National Army had advanced and by 10 August had captured the village of Douglas, south of the city. Tom Garvin contends that the junior leadership of the Free State officers and NCOs – most of whom possessed combat experience from the War of

Independence and the First World War – had to push some of the raw recruits on to Cork City over the unforgiving terrain and through the IRA defensive fire.[81]

SEIZING CORK CITY

In the end, the IRA simply did not have enough troops to hold the Limerick and Waterford fronts and prevent amphibious landings in Cork and Kerry.[82] The concentration of combat power on numerous fronts by the Free State proved too much for the conventional IRA. After scattered resistance from the suburbs, the IRA vacated Cork by 4pm on 10 August, leaving it open for the National Army advance.[83] Just before the Free State troops arrived, according to Borgonovo, 'the last IRA volunteers commandeered vehicles and sped out of the city at around 5 p.m., thus ending the Republican control of the city.'[84] Reporting on IRA activity on 16 August, the *Irish Times* special correspondent noted, 'The advance is becoming swift, but the retreat ... is swifter. Of the thousands of IRA who occupied Cork a month ago, there is no trace.'

After the ordered evacuation, the IRA set about the destruction of key infrastructure within Cork city before withdrawing into the surrounding countryside. The property damage was substantial.[85] John Dorney argues, however, that the destruction could have been far worse. The fact that IRA commander Liam Deasy declined to defend Cork city in the streets undoubtedly spared the city the inevitable destruction and civilian casualties that would have resulted.[86] Instead, Deasy gave the following order: 'As a result of the enemy invading the divisional area in numbers much larger than our available armed forces, verbal instructions to vacate all barracks and form into columns are hereby confirmed.'[87]

In its fight for Cork city, the National Army was assisted by locals and government supporters. At the Cork Ex-Servicemen's Association rooms, Republicans fired shots over the heads of Irish ex-servicemen of the British Army who were defending their headquarters from possible destruction, seemingly scattering them. Elsewhere, however, ex-British

Army soldiers managed to assist the approaching National Army troops. They sabotaged the Cork phone lines, making communication even more difficult for the IRA as they tried to counter the National Army advances.[88]

SECURING CORK CITY

The last of the IRA left Cork city an hour before pro-Treaty troops under Major General Ennis marched in.[89] The *Irish Independent* reported on 12 August 1922 that the troops were given 'a tremendous reception by the citizens', according to an official bulletin issued by National Army headquarters the day before. On arrival into Cork, Dalton sent the following report back to Dublin:

> From Arvonia
> We occupy Cork City. The reception our troops received passed imagination. The enemy evacuated the city before our arrival. They burned the following barracks: Union Quay, Empress Place, Cornmarket Street, Tuckey Street, Technical Schools, Victoria Barracks. The following bridges were destroyed: Brian Boru, Parnell, and Parliament. The enemy fled in disorder and threw their transport into the river.[90]

Borgonovo reports that 'Irish flags were hoisted on many buildings, and the troops quickly established outposts in key locations throughout the city. Most soldiers spent the night at the Cork, Bandon and South Coast railway station at Albert Quay. The Victoria Hotel delivered hot drinks and cigarettes to the victors.'[91] The *Irish Independent* noted on 12 August that the welcome came from all segments of society but that:

> it was not the rich, the big manufacturers, the merchants; it was not even the middle classes, the small shopkeepers, the commercial classes, but the very poorest of the poor, the working men and their wives—the labouring men, who were mainly responsible for the warmth of the reception given to the troops when they entered the city.

The British Army commander in Ireland, General Nevil Macready, noted the especially enthusiastic welcome 'from the young ladies, whose embraces considerably delayed the pursuit of the enemy'.[92]

Now secure in Cork, Dalton reported back to Dublin that 'I felt quite safe in saying that the morale of our enemies is practically broken. The impression one gets is that many of the people who were fighting were doing so more or less under a delusion.'[93] Once Cork residents were satisfied that the Republicans had gone, looting began. The burning barracks were the first targets, despite the heat and exploding ordnance. Furniture and fixtures were carried from the smoking buildings. One witness saw a piano being taken away by a donkey and cart. What's more, in the absence of any police authority, 'more useful booty was sought from shops that were neither abandoned nor burning'.[94] Dalton explained matters to HQ: 'Starvation has been staring a great many people in the face, and this horrible state of affairs has, to some extent, encouraged looting.'[95] In order to stabilise the situation and maintain popular support, it was necessary for the Free State leadership not simply to stop the looting but to provide immediate relief to the population of Cork.

INFORMATION OPERATIONS IN CORK

Forward-thinking Free State officers such as Dalton understood the significance of the press in warfare. They allowed members of the media to accompany National Army troops as long as they did not interfere with military operations and found their own accommodation.[96] This policy had been supported by Collins since the start of the National Army campaign, and signified the importance that public relations and information operations would play in the overall Free State strategy. This was especially marked during the amphibious landings in Cork, which were accompanied by a photographer and two newspaper correspondents.[97]

Publicising the Free State narrative was a priority for its leadership, and the national and international press trumpeted the victory in Cork.

In London, *The Times* hailed the landings, publishing a photograph on 12 August of Major General Dalton aboard ship under the headline, 'Irish Nationalists' Coup'. Presence, posture, and profile are vital components of an information operations campaign, a principle Dalton obviously understood. He ensured that his publicity officer issued statements to the press, organised photo opportunities, and sent reports to the publicity department at HQ. Throughout the war, Dalton consistently respected the press and in particular the *Cork Examiner* for its accurate reporting. This was important in a period when National Army report writing had not been fully institutionalised. Dalton even submitted a copy of the *Examiner*'s report on the 8 August 1922 landings to Free State HQ, observing that 'while inaccurate in some details, it was mainly correct.'[98]

THE CAMPAIGN FULCRUM

The landings in Cork could be described as the campaign fulcrum for the National Army operations in Munster and a culmination point for the IRA. IRA commander Liam Deasy stated that 'any possibility of our forces mounting a full-scale defence of Munster was by now discounted. The Free State forces were well organised and fully equipped with arms, armoured cars and transport.'[99] Dalton referred to the IRA exit from Cork city in amazement, proclaiming that 'it is hard to credit the extent of the disorder and disorganisation that was displayed in retreat'.[100] In a subsequent report to Mulcahy in September, Dalton reiterated that he had been surprised by the lack of resistance following the arrival of the pro-Treaty troops.[101] As for Dalton himself, the battle for Cork and the surrounding area highlighted his drive and ingenuity.[102]

Despite resounding victory, there were losses. On 12 August, the Office of Adjutant General of the National Army wrote to the Minister for Defence with the following details of casualties as a result of the fighting in Cork:

> He [General Emmet Dalton] instructed that I was to send up all my escort except six men and return to Dublin with bodies of eight of our men and thirty-six prisoners. The dead did not arrive until 3 pm on Friday and we sailed at 6pm. Arrived at North wall at 8 am today and brought dead men and prisoners to Portobello. One wounded prisoner, Frank O'Donoghue of the No. 1 Brigade [IRA], who was wounded in fight at Rochestown was sent in an ambulance to the hospital at Beggar's bush.
>
> P. Dalton, Capt.[103]

The casualty figures from the Cork landings are nonetheless hard to calculate. Dr. Lynch, a local doctor, reported 35 killed and 75 wounded in total. Borgonovo 'carefully' qualifies that with an estimate of 17–25 killed and 30–60 wounded, while the Cork Civil War Fatality Register lists 11 National Army fatalities.[104]

Perhaps the London *Times* best summed up the significance of the amphibious landings into Cork City, in the immediate aftermath on 11 August: 'The city was the last stronghold of the rebels before a retreat to the mountains. With Cork in their hands and their line pressing strongly southwards from Limerick and Kerry, the National troops will be able to harry the rebels both in front and rear.'

CONSOLIDATION AND CO-OPERATION

With the line pressing against the IRA from all directions, the National Army, if properly co-ordinated, could have inflicted serious damage to Republican resistance. But despite his progress, Dalton was still deeply concerned about his military position. On Friday, 11 August, he appealed urgently to Collins for reinforcements – he needed hundreds of extra men. 'I am at a standstill' he declared bluntly.[105] As an experienced veteran, Dalton expected the Republicans to respond with guerrilla warfare, and he wanted to be prepared. More troops arrived by sea in the fol-

THE CORK LANDINGS: THE DECISIVE OPERATION

lowing days. The *Lady Wicklow* had re-sailed from Dublin at about 1am on 11 August with 200 men and six officers. Also on board was another 18-pounder field gun, 100 shells of high explosive and shrapnel, two Lancias, six Lewis guns, and various kinds of ammunition and rations.[106]

After consolidating his gains, Dalton split up his forces to clear routes to the north and west of Cork.[107] His progress was greatly assisted by local pro-Treaty IRA leaders, such as Sean Hales, who deployed their own forces to help the National Army take control of various towns.[108] As centres across the county fell under Free State control, Dalton kept up the pressure. National Army forces pushed outwards from Cork city, clearing Middleton of anti-Treaty IRA forces on 11 August and linking up with those that had landed in Youghal on the same day.[109] By 15 August, the troops from the Youghal landing had even pushed out as far as Dungarvan in West Waterford to link-up with the National Army troops under the command of Prout.[110] The Free State then conducted three simultaneous drives to seize all the population centres of County Cork.[111]

On 12 August, Dalton stated that Cork city was entirely in his hands, although he thought there might be ambushing and sniping in a few days. He also reported, 'Trains to Thurles and Roscrea only.' In North Cork, the situation was more challenging, as National Army troops slowly advanced south from the Limerick front. Dalton noted on the twelfth that he had 'no information as to whether Limerick party reached Cork.'[112] This suggests that the planned link-up between Dalton's command and O'Duffy's forces advancing south from Limerick failed to materialise.

Sheila Lawlor points to that likelihood as an example of the lack of co-operation between various Commands in the National Army.[113] Other Free State correspondence suggests that O'Duffy's relationship with officers in adjoining commands, particularly Dalton, was poor.[114] Michael Hopkinson believes the link-up did not occur because O'Duffy became bogged down in the heaviest continuous fighting of the civil war as the IRA fought desperately to hold East Limerick road and rail routes necessary to defend Munster from a northern advance.[115] Lawlor suggests that the stiff IRA resistance in the South-West led the usually self-assured

O'Duffy to become hesitant, so much so that co-operation with Dalton's command was almost non-existent.[116] Lack of co-operation between the two generals and their commands certainly had strategic consequences; Dalton complained to National Army HQ that the war could have been ended by September 1922 if there had been proper co-ordination.[117]

As a direct result, the IRA forces in Cork managed to evacuate Buttevant and Mallow and then return to Dromcollogher for two weeks. From there they sent the columns home to reconsolidate, recuperate, and re-organise.[118] This undoubtedly prolonged the war, allowing the IRA to transform itself back into a guerrilla army and prosecute the type of campaign in which it was experienced.

LOCAL RECRUITMENT

Within two weeks of the landings almost all the towns of Cork were occupied and the IRA had retreated to the mountainous redoubts along the Cork–Kerry border. But the war had not ended. The National Army had taken towns, but it had not captured IRA troops and arms on anything like a large scale, and the Cork and Kerry IRA were apparently still more or less intact.[119]

The leadership of the National Army was improving as the fighting continued, however, and leaders such as Dalton and Ennis demonstrated this as they 'deployed their troops properly, kept them in hand, and adjusted and reinforced the advances when needed'.[120] Dalton expected that the anti-Treaty IRA would hold a line from Mallow to Millstreet, with Macroom and Bantry as bases. In order to prevent this, he undertook simultaneous operations, taking Fermoy, Macroom and Bantry and immediately following up by taking Clonakilty, Bandon, and Kinsale.[121]

As the fighting transitioned into unconventional warfare, new strategy, synergy, and additional resources were needed. In later life, Dalton explained part of his consolidation strategy. The use of new recruits from Dublin and former British Army veterans based in Cork was planned

THE CORK LANDINGS: THE DECISIVE OPERATION

prior to the landings. A local force of about 250 volunteers had been organised in Cork before the National Army arrived. They made contact with Dalton, who armed them with the rifles he had transported from Dublin aboard the *Arvonia*. He deemed them to be of considerable assistance to his campaign, and as giving a very good account of themselves in the subsequent fighting.[122]

On reviewing the new recruits, Dalton reported to Dublin, 'I am sorry and I am glad, that they [the former British servicemen] are conspicuous by their better discipline, deportment and efficiency than my other troops.'[123] The backbone provided to the National Army by Irish ex-servicemen of the British Army was extremely important, especially with respect to its overall fighting capabilities, as has been detailed earlier. Although its rank and file were relatively inexperienced at the start of civil war, they were soon trained by these veterans based on experience garnered from the First World War.[124]

It soon became obvious to Dalton that as he worked to increase the strength of his forces in the Cork region, he was finding no shortage of men willing to join the National Army and fight the IRA.[125] In comparison to British Army ex-servicemen, however, the local pro-Treaty IRA volunteers he assimilated did not meet his standards: 'These men are really almost out of control and only the most drastic action on my part is likely to have the desired effect.'[126] Cork IRA volunteers recruited into the National Army had more political importance than tactical merit. While local pro-Treaty IRA leaders such as Sean Hales were an excellent support to the National Army throughout operations in the region, their presence in the pro-Treaty forces also encouraged the population of Cork to accept Free State forces more freely.[127]

THE END OF THE CONVENTIONAL PHASE

The landings in Cork were an unqualified success, quickly driving the IRA defenders from the largest and most important city under their control. Although the fight for Cork city was brief, however, it was not without cost. The bodies of 18 Free State soldiers were sent back to Dublin to be buried in Glasnevin Cemetery: 10 from the Kerry landings, and eight from the Cork landings.[128] Overall, the conventional phase of the conflict was very costly for both sides, as nearly two-thirds of those killed in the war died in its first three months.[129]

To recover from the fighting, the National Army in Cork continued to make plans. In late August, a Free State memorandum outlined that the gunship *Helga* would travel to Cork to support Dalton through the now more secure sea lines of communication. Victoria Barracks was to be repaired in order to accommodate 600 men, with additional requirements in Cork for 1,000 rifles, 1,000 uniforms, 2 armoured cars, 12 Crossley tenders, 12 Lancias, and 50 Lewis guns.[130] During September 1922, the *Helga* helped Dalton circumvent IRA disruption of road and rail travel in West Cork, and on 7 September, the ship sailed from Cork to deliver troops and Lancia vehicles, under fire, at Courtmacsherry in an operation overseen by Tom Ennis.[131] After Courtmacsherry was secured in another operation along the Cork coast in September 1922, the *Helga* landed troops and armoured cars at Bantry.[132]

As the conventional phase of the war in Munster ended, it gave way to a guerrilla campaign waged by Republican forces that were far more effective than in conventional warfare.[133] The IRA returned to the tactics honed over recent years of fighting the might of the British Empire in order to fight their own countrymen. The volunteers returned to whatever safe areas and houses they could find and to their old routines of roadside ambushes, drive-by shootings, nocturnal raids, and sabotage. The first guerrilla attacks on National Army troops began a week after the capture of Cork city.[134] In response, the National Army took the unconventional fight back to the IRA, while making a genuine effort to hold the already captured and cleared terrain. This would afford the inhabitants protection from violence – which they were entitled to – by way of a national military which contained properly equipped personnel.[135] In addition to reinforcements, various government officials had

THE CORK LANDINGS: THE DECISIVE OPERATION

been sent from Dublin on board the *Alexandra* to assist with relief and reconstruction.[136]

The campaign conducted by the leadership of the National Army, in particular Major General Dalton, demonstrated how a newly constituted and generated force could become combat effective in a very short time. The seizing and securing of the flanks of the IRA defensive line at Waterford and Limerick set the conditions for a Free State strike south through Tipperary and onto Cork. Instead, by way of a turning movement, the main strike came in the form of Free State amphibious support landings in Kerry and the main effort, Cork. The clearance campaign conducted by the National Army in Munster set the IRA on the back foot, forcing it into an unconventional insurgency. Unlike in its successful guerrilla campaign against the British security apparatus in the War of Independence, the IRA could no longer rely on the complete support of the local population.

HOLD

After clearing the area of guerrillas, the counterinsurgent force must then assign sufficient troops to the cleared area to prevent their return, to defeat any remnants, and to secure the population. This is the hold task.

US Army Field Manual, M 3-24.2,
Tactics in Counterinsurgency, April 2009

6

ESTABLISH CIVIL SECURITY

> In Ireland the conventional phase of the civil war between June and September 1922 was less traumatic than what followed. Guerrilla warfare, terrorism, and systematic executions punctuated the last phase.
>
> Bill Kissane, The Politics of the Irish Civil War, 65

By mid-August 1922, conventional fighting was finished. The National Army had cleared most of the IRA fighters from the large towns and cities of Cork and the Munster Republic, and the war now developed into an insurgency. In order to win such a conflict, a counterinsurgent force must use holding operations to deny the insurgent the opportunity to return to former strongholds. These manpower-intensive operations involve securing both the terrain and the civilian population. Thus, the key to a successful counterinsurgency operation lies in holding not only the physical terrain but also the moral high ground through confidence-building operations. By actively patrolling and establishing bases, counterinsurgent forces become aware that they need to win the support of the population, realising instinctively that their own safety depends on good relations with the local people.[1] When counterinsurgent forces are firmly embedded with the local population, they can provide the required all-round protection. They become the holders and builders.[2]

Civil security operations are labour intensive, demanding concurrent processes of continuously securing the population, separating them from the insurgents, and establishing terrain domination. Firm government control over the area is required, and is accomplished by recruiting, organising, arming, and training local forces for use in operations against the insurgents.[3] Civil security is thus an inherent part of holding operations that predominantly involves complex kinetic and non-kinetic processes.

The National Army was faced with the task of establishing its authority across Munster and Cork in order to protect civilians and restore civil security. It did so by securing key terrain, building operating bases and providing freedom of movement within the region.

FREE STATE COUNTERINSURGENCY

> Counterinsurgency is 20 percent military and 80 percent everything else—political, economic, and information operations.
>
> John Nagl, *Knife Fights: A Memoir of Modern War in Theory and Practice.*

From the top down, the National Army had a considered approach to its goals and methods during the Irish Civil War. As Chief of Staff, General Richard Mulcahy had an impeccable dedication to duty because, as Charles Townsend notes, 'he had a clear-eyed view of what could and what needed to be done'.[4] Mulcahy and most of the other Free State generals understood the nature of the war that had to be prosecuted in Munster, and the real positives of his leadership were evident on this operational level, in contrast to his IRA counterpart, Liam Lynch. The Free State government also fundamentally understood that it had to win the civil war not only on the battlefield but also in the minds of the Irish people. Its strategy had to respond to the security needs of the country.

AN IRISH SOLUTION TO AN IRISH PROBLEM

Before the fighting had even begun, in April 1922, General Michael Collins summarised the strategic policy of the Free State government: 'We may be depended upon to deal with the disorder in our midst just as effectively, and just as thoroughly, as those several [other European] governments dealt with it in their sphere. Our methods may be different, but the results will be equally satisfactory.'[5]

Collins advocated an Irish solution to an Irish problem, in which the National Army would be more clinical and precise in its actions than the British Army had been during the War of Independence.[6] The *modus operandi* of the National Army would be different to that of the British Army. The more local soldiers one can incorporate into the counterinsurgent force the better, as they bring with them better situational awareness and intelligence gathering. Because locally recruited units operate in areas where they live and among people they know intimately, they have access to information.[7] Further, local recruitment helps to support the legitimacy of the government forces.[8]

As a native Irish force, the National Army instinctively understood the Irish population and social infrastructure, both apparent and hidden. It recognised how Irish people think and react to certain provocations and encouragements.[9] As Florence O'Donoghue noted, it had an intimate knowledge of IRA volunteers, which the British lacked, and inevitably knew all their trusted haunts. The IRA itself faced two serious disadvantages that it had not encountered in the earlier fight against the British. First, most people were no longer on its side, and second, its opponent had detailed knowledge of its personnel.[10] These are the key factors in an unconventional war, not armaments or supplies. And as Townsend remarks, the IRA Republican leaders showed little sign of understanding this.[11] Evidence indicates that the Free State government and the National Army did.

HARASSMENT POLICY

Emmet Dalton understood from his previous military experience the importance of critical thought as a combat multiplier, especially when dealing with the unknowns turned up in a counterinsurgency.[12] Through its information and intelligence services the Free State worked on answering the unknowns, and had already identified areas of local dissent from the IRA. Dalton needed to exploit this and take advantage of the successes already achieved, as a pre-invasion report outlines:

> In the south, the immediate military problem that confronts us is not so much the military defeat of the Irregulars in that area as the establishing of our Forces in certain principal points in the area, with a view to shaking the domination held over the ordinary people by the Irregulars ... [This would lead to] the realisation by the Irregulars that they had lost their grip on the people and that they could not hope to last.[13]

By supporting the population and putting pressure on the remaining Republicans, Dalton hoped to prevent them from re-organising in the countryside after the surrender of Cork city, a strategy he explained to Mulcahy and the higher HQ staff:

> In view of the fact that their numbers must be in the vicinity of four or five thousand, taking into account the poor nature of the country and knowing that all communications, roads, railways, etc., were broken, it will be seen that their position was next to hopeless. There was one obvious course for us to take and that was to *harass* them, keep them moving.[14]

Dalton's strategy can best be described as co-ordinating and exploiting National Army momentum in order to discommode the IRA. This would be achieved by the constant harassment of IRA fighters in the South. He, therefore, set about securing the population by establishing bases throughout County Cork, while advocating a less static version of a holding operation that required the National Army to be more offensive. The policy underlying the ensuing conduct of numerous searches, patrols, sweeps, and round-ups in the countryside can be summarised as follows:

- intelligence-led patrolling, harassment, and round-up operations to cordon, capture, or kill IRA fighters, especially leaders
- the occupation of bases throughout County Cork in order to dominate the terrain, protect the local population, and ensure freedom of movement, while denying safe areas and key terrain to the IRA
- augmenting troop levels by recruiting local soldiers to increase the combat power and intelligence capabilities of the National Army in Cork.[15]

The execution of this policy would be challenging for Dalton. It relied heavily on continued recruitment, the maintenance of discipline, and improved logistical support to increase the footprint of the National Army in Cork. Free State troops also had to keep up the pressure on IRA volunteers to prevent them from consolidating. Co-ordination, communications, and liaison with neighbouring friendly forces and commanders would prove to be determining factors.

EXECUTION OF THE FREE STATE STRATEGY

Dalton set about recruiting from the local Cork population, especially men with previous military service. The initial National Army force that landed in Cork numbered 850 men across the county, but that strength was almost immediately nearly doubled, to 1,600. In Cork city alone, 700 British ex-servicemen had secretly been sworn into the army before the invasion, and in Youghal another 500 were ready to join. Dalton observed that in C Company of 1st Battalion alone, about 100 new recruits had military experience.[16] The training, discipline, and combat experience of these former British Army recruits was a significant force multiplier for the Free State and gave them a distinct advantage. They needed only minimal induction training and could almost immediately be operationally deployed to locations where they were most needed.

The Free State needed these additional numbers of combat-ready troops because its troops would face a more resolute IRA within the villages of rural Munster than they had encountered in Cork city. By mid-August 1922, Liam Lynch had ordered the formation of IRA flying columns and assigned them to defined operating areas, thus allowing the Republicans to launch the kind of guerrilla operations at which they excelled.[17] As counterinsurgency theorist David Galula explains, government forces must prevent the main body of the guerrilla forces from returning to insurgency tactics by installing garrisons to protect the population, and by tracking their remnants.[18] The National Army now had to demonstrate its security presence in the Munster countryside in order to signal that it was the dominant force and there to stay.

POLARISATION

Dalton wanted to pursue the IRA volunteers into their safe havens, where he believed they were 'crowded into positions of a barren nature without a base for supplies'.[19] But he had to be vigilant, constantly assessing the situation, cautious about the prospect of being isolated, and aware of enemy fighters re-grouping to threaten his forces.[20] This was a major concern because at the start of his campaign, Dalton had reported to Dublin that 'one may travel 70 to 80 miles in part of the county [Cork] without meeting even one Free State soldier.'[21] With additional troops recruited and newly-established bases in the towns and villages, Dalton pushed out into the countryside.

He did so not only for security reasons but also because he feared that the lack of observable pro-Treaty progress would reflect badly on the Free State government.[22] A military stalemate would allow the insurgent forces to capitalise on a prolonged conflict and perceived lack of government progress. Dalton's strategy had to correspond with the strategic intent advanced by Mulcahy and the National Army HQ. They wanted to avoid leaving National Army posts isolated and at the mercy of IRA forces: 'It is absolutely necessary to have at our disposal central force enough to allow elasticity in our plans' – or in military parlance, a flexible and mobile reserve.[23]

To garner support for the push out into the countryside and counter IRA propaganda, Dalton had to generate positive media coverage of National Army activities and advances. On 15 August 1922, the *Cork Examiner* – a firm advocate for the Free State once its forces had secured Cork city – reported on the situation:

> The National troops, having taken undisputed possession of Cork City and the eastern area of the county, Cobh and Youghal and Midleton areas are apparently arranging concentration camps in these districts.
>
> On their arrival at Midleton from Youghal last night at 10.30 p.m. the National troops were the recipients of a very enthusiastic welcome from the townspeople.

At the national level, the *Irish Times* on 23 August 1922 quoted General Michael Collins' satisfaction with the initial 'progresses of the Free State troops since landing in Cork, and the effective consolidation of the important positions they held throughout the county'. Collins had in fact been killed the day before in an IRA ambush at Béal na Bláth in his native West Cork.[24]

The death of its leader nonetheless did not interrupt the measured advances of National Army troops into the rural environs. On 11 September 1922, Dalton reported to Mulcahy on the deployment of his forces in bases for the subsequent counterinsurgency operations in Cork:

> 'A' Party [Cork] reinforced City positions occupied Cobh, Douglas, Blarney.
> 'B' Party [Youghal] occupied Youghal, Killeagh, Carrigtwohill, Midleton, and gained touch with Cork City.
> 'C' Party [Glandore] occupied Skibbereen and Roscarberry.[25]

The Free State government policy was to support Dalton's requirements in order to expand the National Army presence. He received a cipher message on 19 September 1922, stating that 350 reinforcements would set off for Cork from Dublin.[26]

Yet the ambush in Béal na Bláth had strategic consequences. With the death of Collins, the guerrilla phase of the civil war began in earnest, as the Free State absorbed the influence of those 'determined to exclude the Republican viewpoint entirely from the chambers of power.'[27] This marked a turning point in the civil war and polarised the opposing sides. All hope of an early cessation of violence disappeared into the grave with Collins. Dalton expanded his operations progressively in order to counter any potential swing of momentum in favour of the IRA. The number of Free State forces in Cork rose, and the continuous harassment of Republicans in their strongholds began to have a telling effect on their numbers and morale.[28]

Essentially, the National Army was able to exert pressure on the IRA because by holding the towns it held the country.[29] In September 1922, Dalton wrote to National Army HQ, re-advocating his policy of pressurising and harassing the IRA and outlining how he was going to utilise Free State reinforcements. He also used the letter to formally announce his intention to get married in October 1922 – but before that he expected 'to do a big round-up with 800 men in west Cork' in order 'to hand over a more or less quiet area to Colonel Comdt Byrne to look after in my absence.'[30]

SPREADING OUT FORCES

As their numbers increased, Free State forces spread into the Cork countryside to establish forward operating bases. From these the National Army attempted to concentrate on the primary purposes of counterinsurgency: 'to disrupt, identify, and ultimately eliminate the insurgents, especially their leadership and infrastructure'.[31] Success in a counterinsurgency environment requires a military to focus on the population and its security, establish and expand secure areas, and create a preponderance of smaller bases in key population centres rather than concentrating in large bases for protection.[32] By September 1922, some 1,620 Free State troops were garrisoned throughout Cork County within the largest towns and villages:

Cork City	600
Fermoy	100
Lismore	40
Cappoquin	30
Kilworth	40
Youghal	80
Middleton	50
Carrigtwohill	30
Castlemartyer	30
Killegh	20
Kinsale	50
Passage	30
Waterfall	50
Bantry	100
Skibbereen	60
Rosscarbery	50
Clonakilty	50
Bandon	60
Dunmanway	50
Macroom	100.[33]

Establishing security forces in these bases facilitated the National Army's attempts at countering the IRA insurgents. It also demonstrated the presence of a growing armed force, reassuring the population and allowing normality to return to the urban centres of the county. On 5 October 1922, Dalton communicated to National Army HQ that he had advanced on Ballyvourney and National Army troops were engaged 'in a vigorous campaign in the Inchigeelagh-Ballyvourney area of County Cork. There has been quite a battle around the village of Ballingeary.'[34]

As part of Dalton's harassment policy, the National Army continually tried to isolate the IRA insurgents from the population. Without barracks or bases, the IRA, out of necessity had to revert to guerrilla tactics. As in the War of Independence, the volunteers were again totally dependent on their supporters in their areas of operation.[35] But the loyalty of the local population was no longer assured, especially as the IRA had to commandeer everything they needed from civilians and local businesses in order to survive the economic hardships imposed on them.[36] The process was even regularised though notifications such as this: 'Warning is hereby given that seven days after the date of this notice … any of the above-mentioned forms of Motor transport or Push-Bicycles being used for which a permit has not been obtained after the date mentioned are liable to be confiscated by the forces of the Irish Republican Army.'[37]

The upheaval the volunteers caused to civilian life damaged the standing of the IRA, and Liam de Róiste believed that the unarmed community came in for the greatest suffering in the armed conflict.[38] IRA forces paid scant attention to bad publicity, however, citing the needs of warfare and the chance to get back at some of the wealthier factions of society, as IRA West Cork commander Ted O'Sullivan emphasises: 'All roads were cut by us and provisions were scarce in the houses. We commandeered a boat of flour in Castletownbere and we took cattle from the big shots.'[39] By big shots, he is talking about community members with wealth and standing, and they became a particular target for IRA economic retribution. De Róiste elaborates:

> In letters that were captured by the National Forces recently—dated 25th and 26th Oct 31st Oct 1st and 2nd Nov—the following ideas for action are expressed by the … Irregular army for approval by De Velera [sic].
>
> (1) Collection of money by forcible seizure of publicans' licences fees.
> (2) The burning of the private houses of the proprietors of the *The Freeman* and *Independent*.[40]

For some IRA units, commandeering and survival took precedence over their republican ideology and the needs of the local population, isolating them from their original support base and undermining their cause.

QUARTERMASTERING AND SUPPORT

While the IRA resorted to commandeering to survive, the Free State put a proper logistical organisation in place. Quartermastering and accommodating nearly 2,000 (and rising) officers, NCOs, and soldiers in County Cork was a very challenging proposition as the IRA had destroyed barracks and other army premises at the outset of the conflict. As the civil war progressed the difficulties were gradually overcome, however, as the civil board of works pitched in and army works companies were established. A Quartermaster General's report indicates that large-scale billeting was being undertaken 'at the discretion of local officers.'[41] Similarly, feeding the troops was a monumental task. Dalton at one point noted that 'it would be easy to get the dietary scale of the British Army and model ours.' [But] some wouldn't like it, complaining as well about 'the price it costs the army … Where possible the army should have issued stores … [to avoid] enormous retail profit charges. It's monstrous.'[42]

Despite the hurdles, the garrisoning of the Free State troops allowed the National Army to spread its influence throughout Munster. Free State troops with local knowledge were able to make use of advantageous connections, and the bases also brought with them trade and military commerce to the impoverished towns and villages of Munster and Cork. This proved to be very beneficial, influencing and popular.

LACK OF CO-OPERATION

To the advantage of the IRA, the Free State leadership apparatus in Munster continued to experience problems of co-operation and mutual support, especially between O'Duffy's and Dalton's command areas. By early September 1922, collaboration between some commands in Munster had ceased, permitting many IRA fighters to escape into ungoverned spaces, often along the boundaries between the National Army command responsibilities.[43]

To address the problem, southern and western Munster were divided into extended command areas primarily under the control of O'Duffy in

Limerick and Dalton in Cork. National Army HQ tried to improve the dysfunctional relationship, directing O'Duffy, 'Arrange for closest possible cooperation of your troops at Mallow ... Lombardstown, Banteer, Millstreet and Rathmore with Major General Dalton. Cooperation between Millstreet and Macroom very important. I propose to divide the southwestern command forthwith making Dalton responsible for the Cork Kerry area.'[44]

But the required improvements took time to materialise, and the IRA continued to exploit this Free State vulnerability. Colonel Commandant Charles Russell from the Irish Military Air Service reported on 12 September:

> In conversation with General Dalton yesterday in Cork, he explained the position with regard to the mountainous area immediately south of the towns—Mallow, Banteer, Millstreet, Killarney, as follows: The irregulars are occupying this ground because of lack of cooperation between the forces on either side of them. This lack of cooperation is the result of the dual command of this area.[45]

A South-Western Command Report from 8 September reports that 'about 60 of the most dangerous Irregulars are situated in the area [between both Command Areas] around Dromina, S.W. of Charleville [near Kilmallock]. These Irregulars were dominating the rural countryside.'[46] Their presence created major difficulties for the pro-Treaty forces. On 20 September, the *Irish Times* reported that the National Army was finding it hard to strike 'any blow of immediate effect' and that without quick improvement in the army and more troops, the conflict would be protracted.

An anonymous report from autumn 1922 indicates that the National Army had begun to lose its organisation and direction.[47] The isolation of its troops in rural Munster certainly contributed to the disorder. A few years after the war, the initial decision to deploy Free State troops to remote bases was questioned by General Seán Mac Mahon in a statement to the Army Inquiry Committee:

> The Irregular columns were moving around attacking our troops, looting, and destroying property. During the winter months the conditions under which our troops worked proved to be demoralising and the form of operations which had to be carried out was very severe on both officers and men. We had occupied numerous towns and villages and established small posts in them in order to try and prevent Irregular columns from swooping down and looting such places. These small posts had a very demoralising effect on our men.[48]

Without proper support, manpower, and logistics the IRA turned Free State isolation and vulnerabilities into weaknesses, susceptible to attack. The National Army needed to improve its co-ordination and reinforcement capabilities.

IRA COUNTERSTRATEGY

> However desirable for the insurgent to possess territory, large regular forces, and powerful weapons, to possess them and to rely on them prematurely could spell his doom.
>
> David Galula, *Counterinsurgency Warfare*, 7

Prior to August 1922 and in defiance of the Free State government, the IRA freely controlled the towns and cities of the Munster Republic by being better armed and equipped than they had been during the previous war against the British.[49] As described earlier, the IRA had to shift hastily back to guerrilla warfare after the initial conventional fighting. It was what they did best, and Liam Lynch believed it would defeat the National Army in a war of attrition, just as it had defeated the British Army.[50] The IRA for its part thought that prolonged conflict would wear down a spread-out National Army discouraged by the cost of fighting.[51]

Ultimately the IRA strategy was to prevent the Free State from governing, in the expectation that popular opinion would force their abdication and that elements in the National Army would revolt.[52] The volunteers returned to whatever safe areas and houses they could find and resumed roadside ambushes, drive-by shootings, nocturnal raids, and sabotage. They quickly adapted, and unconventional attacks against the National Army and vital infrastructure began to ramp up.[53] But the IRA made the mistake of taking local public opinion for granted, overlooking that most of the population questioned its leaders' views on what was best for the country.[54] Tom Garvin puts the matter baldly: 'The civil war was fought over an issue that most people cared little about.'[55] Without the moral support of their communities, armed struggle was always going to be a difficult proposition for the Republican forces.

Another determining and detrimental factor was the capture of nearly 2,000 IRA fighters during the summer months of 1922, seriously degrading the organisation's combat power.[56] Nonetheless, some 4,000 to 5,000 IRA volunteers were still active in Cork by September, in Dalton's assessment.[57] Reconstituted and corralled into a co-ordinated campaign, these fighters started to exploit the vulnerabilities of the National Army.

To seek refuge, consolidate, and support their reconstitution, IRA forces moved farther north and west to mountainous countryside, to the Comeraghs of Waterford, the Galtee Mountains of Tipperary, and the MacGillycuddy Reeks in Kerry.[58] They were determined to use these operating areas to regroup and launch an offensive against the National Army. Bridges were blown up, railway tracks were sabotaged, roads were mined or destroyed, and defensive positions were prepared.[59] From its staging points, the IRA formulated a policy of attacking small Free State outposts. The insurgents concentrated on destroying National Army intelligence services and rail and road communications and intensifying the campaign in cities and towns.[60] West Cork IRA Commander Ted O'Sullivan explains: 'We cut their communications in the towns, and we isolated them as much as we could.'[61] Recognising the significance of National Army bases as a symbol of its presence in rural Munster, IRA fighters also made them a target. The idea was to prolong the war by disorder and exploit the Free State government's lack of practical authority in the ungoverned spaces throughout the state.[62]

As the IRA once again became a very effective fighting force, casualties started to increase on the Free State side. At one point in September 1922, Dalton reported 26 casualties in 22 hours and ruefully noted an irony: 'They [IRA fighters] now operate over territory which they know. They are now better armed and better trained than they were against the British. In short, they have placed me and my troops in the same position as the British were a little over a year ago.'[63]

IRA documents captured in Cork give an outline of the pattern of the evolving guerrilla tactics. IRA flying columns normally consisted of 35 men, including engineers, signallers, and machine gunners, subdivided into squads of five men and a leader.[64] O'Sullivan notes that his flying column was larger than this, however, with a more amalgamated character: 'The 5th Brigade IRA column in Cork—was from 96 to 120 men. We had 3 Machine Guns, 1 Hotchkiss, and 2 Lewis, which we got from division during the truce.'[65] A preponderance of these weapons were obtained from the raid on the *Upnor* in March 1922, and as a result most IRA flying columns were broken into self-sufficient squads to ambush Free State supply lines and communications.[66]

Movement between towns became hazardous for the National Army and IRA raids on towns became frequent. The interference with communications undermined confidence in the Free State government's ability to govern.[67] Constant sniping at Free State positions, trenching and blocking of roads, destruction of bridges, localised attacks on Free State patrols, and larger-scale ones on Free State garrisons in the bigger towns all had their intended result.[68] As the conflict entered the winter months, National Army resolve began to weaken.

ANALYSIS OF THE IRA OFFENSIVE AUGUST 1922-JANUARY 1923

At 1.30 a.m. on 30 August 1922, the IRA attacked the Bantry Free State garrison. Bantry is a key provincial town in West Cork and was of major strategic interest to both sides. The engagement was one of the first IRA mass attacks on a Free State base and involved between 400 and 500 fighters, according to an article in the *Irish Independent* the next day.[69] O'Sullivan gives more moderate figures: 'We mobilized all our men for an attack [on Bantry] for they couldn't up to this [point] show their noses … We had roughly 90 men … [but with the combined figure] we would have had 120 all told.'[70] The *Irish Independent* article gives details of the well-co-ordinated, complex attack, including preparations beforehand: 'Irregulars started tunnelling operations with a view to attacking our [Free State] people from strategic positions—from 1.30am machine-gun and rifle fire was kept up continuously until 6pm.' O'Sullivan claims that the IRA captured the first few National Army billets at about daybreak and had taken about eight or ten by the time they decided to retreat because four of their members were dying and had to receive the last rites. At that point, he recalls, they had captured 22 prisoners with their rifles and ammunition. The *Irish Independent* article contests this account, asserting that the National Army eventually repelled the attack after intense fighting, naming four IRA volunteers killed, with several more wounded, and one National Army soldier killed. The Cork Civil War Fatality Register confirms the newspaper report of fatalities on both sides.[71]

After the attack, the Free State reinforced Bantry from the sea and from Cork through Clonakilty.[72] Although it was ultimately unsuccessful for the IRA, the Bantry action did demonstrate the fighting prowess and determination of the reconstituted flying columns and established a precedent for activities against the National Army in North and West Cork in the months that followed.

On 11 September 1922, the IRA attacked a Free State patrol on a bridge near Carrigaphooca, three miles from Macroom. Eight soldiers in the patrol, which was travelling between Macroom and Kerry, were blown to pieces by a road mine laid beside the bridge.[73] Among the dead was a high-ranking Free State officer, Colonel-Commandant Tom Kehoe, who had been a prominent member of Michael Collins' squad during the War of Independence.[74] In retaliation, Dublin Guards troops shot dead a Republican prisoner.[75] On 27 October, three IRA volunteers were killed by Free State forces as they returned from a funeral in Castletownroche in North Cork, near Mallow, and a further nine were wounded.[76]

Gaining momentum, the IRA increased the size of its mass attacks. On the morning of 5 November 1922, at least 200 volunteers stormed the Free State garrisons of Enniskean and Balineen, adjoining villages near Bandon in West Cork (see Map 4). The National Army defenders comprised 'one officer and 25 men at Enniskean and two officers and 38 men and Ballineen', according to an *Irish Independent* account on 7 November 1922. Demonstrating their complexity and command-and-control abilities, the IRA seized control of both villages at approximately 10 p.m. but withdrew on the arrival of National Army reinforcements at 11 p.m.

As the evenings grew shorter with the approach of winter, an increasingly confident IRA ratcheted up the pressure on the National Army: 'Up to close on Christmas of 1922 there was no other Free State post in our area save Bantry and Skibbereen. We had a good column, and we raided these towns at times, and they sallied out, but we beat hell out of them each time they came out.'[77]

Compared to other regions in Ireland and to the losses of the National Army defenders, however, the IRA took a considerable number of casualties during these complex attacks in Cork. Various factors could explain this, but certainly one is the large proportion of the National Army soldiers with previous military experience deployed in rural outposts in in the county. With that experience came the ability to deploy soldiers into adequately defended localities and positions and basic tactical knowledge such as how to defend a village and how to conduct ambushes.

This ability to protect its force and minimise casualties enabled the National Army to persist in the fight over the 1922–23 winter, but the leadership in Cork was concerned about the increase in IRA activity. In November, Dalton complained that his freedom of movement was being hampered not only by the IRA but also by 'a horrible lack of transport, competent drivers ... a lack of spares for motors' and was exasperated as he saw Republican support begin to seep back into popular opinion.[78] As 1922 came to a close and the new year turned, IRA fighters concentrated on using explosives, holding up and looting trains, and burning down houses – forms of warfare that General Seán Mac Mahon later noted had been 'very difficult to counteract but steps were taken to deal with it'.[79]

A prolonged war, with its deepening erosion of public confidence, is exactly what National Army HQ wanted to avoid, and the Free State government was coming under increasing pressure to bring an end to the conflict.[80] The situation appears to have taken a personal toll on Dalton. In December, he was replaced by Major General David Reynolds as the commander of Free State forces in Cork. Minutes of a Free State Cabinet meeting on 5 December 1922 note that Major General Emmet Dalton had returned from 'active duty in Cork and was appointed to be the Clerk of the Seanad', though he continued for some weeks in his military post and was on the army payroll until 9 December.[81] A letter written by Dalton in November gives an insight into his state of mind, perhaps indicating that frustration was a deciding factor in his decision to leave the Cork command. 'I am beginning to lose hope,' he declared. 'I believe the lack of transport – cohesion – organisation are creating the necessity for the soldier, particularly in Cork, to find some means of occupation, they naturally choose the fascinating one.'[82]

Before Dalton resigned, he made a speech in Fermoy to loud applause. As the *Freeman's Journal* reported on 9 November 1922, he issued a ringing declaration that 'the army was the army of the people: they were not the dictators of the people; the people were their master. The army was there to protect and to help the people in maintaining their rights and their property, and to carry out their wishes.'

A FINAL MASS ATTACK

The IRA conducted one of its final mass attacks in early 1923. Millstreet is a small town in northern County Cork (see Map 4). In January 1923, it was occupied by a platoon of approximately 30 Free State soldiers who faced an attacking party of at least 400 IRA volunteers, not counting the number they used to hold the roads and approaches to the town. The IRA first captured the National Army outposts on the periphery of the town, then launched its main attack on the Free State HQ at the end of the town known as Carnegie Hall. The volunteers used six machine guns and concentrated heavy fire on the building from various vantage points. The 23 Free State troops in the HQ had only one Lewis gun in the building and replied vigorously to the attackers, who advanced under cover of machine-gun fire as far as the entrance of the hall but were then forced to withdraw. The main body of the IRA then retreated in the direction of Kerry and Ballyvourney.[83]

The *Cork Examiner* reported that the doctor in attendance put the Republican casualties at seven killed and 19 wounded, though these figures appear to be inaccurate.[84] The IRA reported that 65 Free State soldiers had been in Millstreet, and that they had captured 39 prisoners, 38 rifles, and one Lewis gun.[85] This claim is not validated, but the Cork Civil War Fatality Register lists three National Army soldiers killed and no IRA fatalities.[86] The *Freeman's Journal* of 6 January described the Millstreet action as a 'thrilling story of gallant defence by a small National Army force against great odds.'

The failure to capture Millstreet – and the determined resistance put up by the National Army defenders – was a serious setback for the volunteers, especially as the mass attack column had been led by legendary IRA man, Tom Barry. Michael Harrington believes it struck a commensurate blow to their morale.[87] And along with the disappointment of Millstreet, the leadership of the IRA was concerned about the effectiveness of their volunteers and how long they could sustain such tactics against a National Army that was now growing in strength in Cork.

Although initially effective, the IRA policy of attacking and isolating National Army bases had not driven the Free State out of the small towns and villages of Cork or created ungoverned spaces in which the IRA could operate freely. Dogged resistance and a continual ability to reinforce rural garrisons paid dividends to the National Army, facilitating an improvement in strategy, tactics, and surge capacity across the county.

A return to guerrilla warfare did have rewards for the IRA from September to December 1922, but the National Army was a different foe from the British: it had nowhere to go and was fighting for basic survival.[88] Liam de Róiste, remarking in his diary that the IRA failed to realise it was not in a war with the British, came to a logical conclusion: 'It is therefore, a 'war' against the Irish people, and for what?'[89] That was perhaps the most important question of the conflict. What was the IRA's war about? What did it want to achieve?

The Four Courts on fire after National Army assault 28 June 1922. NLI Ref: Hog 57.

National Army soldiers advancing south. NLI Ref: Hog 124.

National Army Soldiers recuperating and reorganizing during clearance operations in Limerick.
NLI Ref: Hog 133.

National Army Officers pose for photograph outside the Royal Hotel Limerick.
NLI Ref: Hog 133.

Photographs of Generals (Eoin O'Duffy, Michael Brennan, Fionan Lynch, WRE Murphy) during clearance operations in Limerick
NLI Ref: Hog 128.

National Army Troops Preparing for the Decisive Operation of Landings in Passage West in Cork.
NLI Ref: Hog 79.

Republican Prisoners Captured during the landings and seizure of Passage West.
NLI Ref: Hog W12.

Major General [Tom] Ennis with Thompson [Machine] Gun and Comdt. McCreagh. Location Passage West Cork.
NLI Ref: Hog W96.

Armoured Car on Henry Street, Dublin. NLI Ref: Hog 134.

Priest giving General Absolution to National Army Soldiers. NLI Ref: Hog 137.

Republican Prisoner under Control of National Army Soldier. NLI Ref: Hog 106.

Railway Protection Corps up-armouring a specially adapted National Army Armoured Car for railway security.

7

A LEARNING ORGANISATION

> Adaptive military organisations must be able to react positively to the unexpected, adjusting their methods of operation rapidly to the circumstances actually prevailing.
>
> <div align="right">British Army, <i>Design for Operations:
The British Military Doctrine</i>, vii.</div>

Wars fought over a prolonged period become contests in organisational learning and adaptation that can make the difference between winning and losing. Because victory is gained through a tempo of adaptation that is beyond the other side's ability to achieve or sustain, counterinsurgency should emphasise learning and adaptation.[1] As the National Army expanded it had to be aware of an additional responsibility not to alienate the population by acting like a force of occupation. Whatever their informational benefits, using mass detentions, cordon-and-search, collective punishments, or property destruction as intelligence collection tactics typically estranges the people affected.[2]

Conventional military forces have historically struggled to display common sense and defeat insurgencies; those that succeeded did so by being adaptive.[3] The structure of military organisations, and the ability to develop new organisations or other institutional responses to deal with new or changed situations, reflects learning.[4] Adaptive learning organisations can react and change in order to rectify setbacks, giving them an advantage in counterinsurgent warfare.

The Enniskean and Millstreet complex attacks proved to be a wake-up call for the National Army, as were evolving IRA tactics. The National Army and Free State government had to transform their efforts in order to counter IRA momentum and tactics and regain the initiative. On 12 December 1922, General Richard Mulcahy suggested to General Seán Mac Mahon that despite their widespread unpopularity, former British Army officers should be enlisted into a technical committee so that 'their ideas would … provide a base line against which we would compare what we're actually doing ourselves'.[5]

At the political-strategic level, the Cabinet (or Executive Council) also wanted to fight the war in a different manner. To that end, on 11 January 1923, each minister submitted a memorandum of personal opinions on military, economic, and political developments throughout the country. After pooling these opinions, the government provisionally agreed on certain lines of policy in consultation with the Army Council.[6] With new political guidance, the leadership of the National Army understood it had to change in order to counter the developing IRA tactics and bring the civil war to a swifter resolution for political expediency. This led to a restructuring and realignment of the overall Free State strategy in early 1923.

The evolution of the National Army progressed steadily. By early 1923, the Free State strategy had responded very well to the continually changing situation, proving that adaptive military organisations are, as British Army doctrine describes, 'able to react positively to the unexpected, adjusting their methods of operation rapidly to the circumstances actually prevailing.'[7] Analysis of the enemy threat is vital when developing a capability, whether organisational, doctrinal, or material, and the Free State developed four policies, or capability improvements, based on its assessment of the IRA:

- National Army bases were expanded and additional troop surges were undertaken.

- National Army mobility and armoured mobility was dramatically improved in order to bring the fight to the IRA and secure freedom of movement.
- Counter columns of the most experienced soldiers were established within the National Army to counter the IRA flying columns.
- Infantry battalions were battle grouped to make them more self-sufficient and deployable. These units were used at the end of the civil war to target the IRA in their last safe havens using overwhelming National Army combat power.

EXPANDING THE NATIONAL ARMY

In his later writing on counterinsurgency, Roger Trinquier advocates making the expansion of bases and freedom of movement priorities and emphasises that the network of roads must be kept open to allow the movement of troops specialising in offensive operations.[8] An enhanced recruitment policy now meant that the National Army was able to deploy more troops to rural outposts in the Cork countryside. Prior to the Free State expansion the IRA had, as Ted O'Sullivan explains, 'burned all our barracks before we cleared out so that the Free State had to billet their men around town'.[9] Although that caused significant inconvenience to the army it also indirectly helped it by forcing the troops to live more closely with local people, building up confidence and better relationships. This working relationship was further strengthened when the IRA took the unpopular decision to threaten townsfolk who co-operated with Free State forces, issuing a public notice: 'Warning is hereby given to all such civilians who continue to work or reside in premises which are at the same time occupied by Free State forces, that after the date of the publication of this notice they will do so at their own risk.'[10]

By April 1923, the situation had changed dramatically from the one Emmet Dalton reported in September 1922. With the additional troop surges, the National Army was over 5,000 strong, with its largest bases in Cork as follows, counting all ranks:

Free State HQ (Cork City):	594
Michael Collins Barracks (Cork City):	214
Bandon:	202
Macroom:	336
Mallow:	171
Kanturk:	215
Youghal:	315
Fermoy:	145
Bantry:	213
Kinsale:	162.[11]

Over the course of the war the National Army established 64 bases in Cork – nearly 18 per cent of the 367 that were scattered across the country – and these were occupied by 220 officers and 5,219 other ranks.[12] Cork was second only to Dublin in number of bases, and soon became the main effort for the National Army. It was also the centre of operations for the IRA, as it was the location of Liam Lynch's HQ. Because of this Cork had to be secured, occupied, and the insurgency defeated.

National Army troops in the Cork posts were actively living within the community, aggressively patrolling contested spaces and reassuring the inhabitants. They provided the safe and secure environment that was keenly sought by the local traders and population, and is a crucial element of an effective counterinsurgency campaign.

IMPROVING MOBILITY

As pro-Treaty troops occupied the various small towns in Cork, they established forward operating bases, or combat outposts, to hold the key terrain.[13] The Free State realised that the soldiers in these bases had to bring the fight to the IRA, but various pro-Treaty sources admitted that throughout the second half of 1922 in many areas, National Army troops controlled little more than the towns in which they were based.[14] A dedicated strategy was required to provide the bases with more secure transportation as the IRA continued to trench roads.[15]

The US Department of Defence defines counter-mobility operations as 'the construction of obstacles and emplacement of minefields to delay, disrupt, and destroy the enemy by reinforcement of the terrain … [or] to slow or divert the enemy'.[16] Since the fight with the British, the IRA had become adept in such tactics, but the National Army adopted various ideas and methodologies to counter them, proving itself to be a learning organisation.[17] It also needed knowledge of mechanised warfare and an additional supply of armoured cars and motorised transport.[18]

Mobility was important for the National Army because isolating the insurgents required its troops to be thoroughly familiar with the terrain over which they repeatedly travelled.[19] Armoured mobility would enable the army to protect its own forces and harass and round up the insurgents, keeping them constantly on the move and on the defensive. Mobile light infantry forces with light armoured vehicles make the best counterinsurgency soldiers. Because of this, Dalton's harassment strategy was to be underpinned by mobile columns, especially in the more remote and dangerous parts of Cork. These columns could enter IRA safe areas, seize arms, and safeguard the National Army lines of supply.[20] They also provided brute force to break the insurgents' will and capability to fight on.[21] Additional mobility, especially armoured mobility, also corresponded to Richard Mulcahy's intention to have a flexible reserve that would allow plans to shift and respond to circumstances.[22]

Achieving this level of mobility was nevertheless a constant struggle for Dalton and his successor, General David Reynolds. In November 1922, Dalton complained to Mulcahy about the lack of suitable transport in Cork, warning of the consequences if deficiencies were not addressed: 'Transport continues hopelessly impoverished down here and unless it is immediately attended to the garrisons must continue as they are—comparatively ineffective.'[23] Eventually, after much encouragement, HQ started to make more transport vehicles available to troops in Cork, allowing them to extend their operational reach throughout the county in a safer and more robust manner.

At the start of the civil war, over 395 former British vehicles were handed over to the National Army. These vehicles included three-ton trucks, touring cars, armoured Lancia trucks, and armoured and unarmoured Crossley tenders.[24] The British Army also supplied seven Peerless armoured cars and, most importantly, 13 Rolls-Royce 1920 pattern armoured cars.[25] These vehicles, especially the armoured ones, gave the National Army a marked advantage over the IRA as they allowed aggressive patrolling and the re-supply of outlying garrisons.[26] This permitted the National Army to discommode the IRA and keep its own lines of communication open. By the end of the civil war, almost all the National Army posts in Cork were supplied with an armoured car or armoured Lancia.[27] Improved mobility had another consequence. As Dalton noted, the solution to low morale among National Army soldiers was 'plenty of transport and no excuse [to avoid] plenty of work, which will keep them [from] brooding over their 'cups' of imaginary wrongs' and encourage 'sterner conduct' towards their foe.[28]

As their experience grew, Free State troops also became more adept at using armoured mobility. On 8 December 1922, the National Army cornered IRA troops and a noteworthy armour-versus-armour conflict ensued in the Bantry–Dunmanway–Drimoleague region. Ted O'Sullivan describes how the National Army discovered an IRA column and:

> pasted at us from across the river [in the vicinity of Kealkil] and Mossy [Donegan] went off to get the armored lorry [given to Cork 5 Brigade by Cork 1 Brigade] and with it get close to them. To counter this the Free State got their armored cars across the river and got behind the IRA armored lorry. The IRA armored lorry escaped but they burnt the engine to prevent its capture intact by the National army.[29]

This was a significant clash for both sides, and IRA reports suggest that eight of its sections were surrounded by 2,000 Free State soldiers with eight armoured vehicles, all out searching for *Slieve na mBan*, a Rolls-Royce armoured car that had been captured by the IRA and was a valuable National Army asset. According to Sullivan, the IRA was trying to get the car to Bantry but the heavy vehicle kept sinking in the soft terrain. His assessment of troop numbers may have been an overestimation, but National Army forces did converge on Kealkil in order to retrieve *Slieve na mBan*, and multiple columns were deployed from Free State bases in Clonakilty, Kinsale, Skibbereen, Ballineen, and Bantry.[30]

DEVELOPING COUNTER COLUMNS

Evidence that the National Army was transforming its organisation to counter IRA developments can also be seen in the formation of Free State counter columns to fight the effective IRA flying columns. Essentially this meant taking on the anti-Treaty forces at their own game. The ability to use small, mobile columns in intelligence-led operations to raid specific areas was already substantiated before the January 1923 re-organisation. In a test of new tactics and procedures on 28 November 1922, mobile columns of 15 National Army soldiers proceeded from Charleville to Dromina, where they rounded up nine Republicans.[31] Similarly, a system was developed in Donegal whereby large National Army columns would guard the mountain passes while smaller mopping-up columns searched the interior for IRA volunteers.[32] This became a very effective tactic for harassing and tiring out the insurgents, forcing them to rediscover 'what it means to pass several nights hungry, tired and cold … [because] the plan has been to allow no rest.'[33]

US Army Field Manual 3.24.2, published in 2009, states that small, well-trained units should be used in search operations, since they can move quickly and quietly among the population regardless of the size of the area they are covering and then, once insurgents have been located, strike or fix them for a larger attack force.³⁴ As previously described, the use of local forces supported by specialised troops dramatically increases the capabilities of the counterinsurgent force, especially in cordon-and-search operations.³⁵

By early 1923, specialised Free State search units countered the IRA flying columns operating in isolated parts of Cork. These units usually contained experienced soldiers, and as the fighting progressed the need for them became more pressing because even the sweeping movements of large Free State forces had failed to envelope or even contact IRA columns working in the mountain regions of Munster. Defeating the flying columns would take 'dogged, drawn-out manoeuvring', a December 1922 army report described, adding that 'the most successful way has been to operate against them with counter columns moving quietly and surprising them in their haunts.'³⁶ Free State counter columns also deployed a light horse scouting capability to counter an IRA cavalry unit. The *Irish Times* reported as early as 2 October 1922 that some Republicans were on horseback, 'having commandeered hunters in the Muskerry foxhunting district'.

The exact composition of the Free State counter columns is unknown, but their strength can be determined from newspaper articles and official documentation as approximately 15 to 20 trained soldiers. A National Army after-action report on a major operation conducted in West Cork and South Kerry in late-April and early-May 1923 explains how the Railway Corps established billeting centres at Loo Bridge, Morleys Bridge, and Kilgarvan, and then conveyed stores to these points that could be used to feed soldiers in the columns on the following day.³⁷ More significantly, it outlines efforts to discommode IRA flying columns operating along the mountainous Cork–Kerry border. On 30 April 1923, it reports, 'All columns moved as per operation order, but the weather was entirely against the operation and it was very difficult for columns to keep in touch … This in no doubt greatly facilitated Irregulars in the area in making their escape through the cordon of columns which was closing in on the railway line.'

Nevertheless, the establishment of the counter columns demonstrates the ability of Free State HQ to think critically and arrive at feasible solutions. By 3 May, the columns were having more success as operations were refocused and better administrated. Supplementary operation orders instructed the columns to move back over the same ground because of better weather conditions, and the after-action report noted that 'this day's operation was very heavy on the troops and … some columns had to operate a distance of 35 miles.' The same report commends the co-operation between the sweeping new infantry battalion battle groups and the newly developed counter columns. While the counter columns in the first line captured very few prisoners, they captured quite a number of dumps, as well as motor cars concealed in dugouts. Counter columns would become a very successful and adaptive capability for the National Army, especially when they worked alongside the newly re-organised infantry corps.

BATTLE-GROUPING INFANTRY BATTALIONS

By early-1923, the National Army had recognised that counterinsurgency is primarily a war of infantry, and that it would benefit from having a smaller logistical tail and being more combined.[38] This led to a strategic and organisational transformation from a conventional to a non-conventional force. The Free State also understood that a significant combat advantage was obtained by deploying forces to a specific area in the quickest time possible in order to overwhelm the IRA forces through a concentration of superior combat power.

Deployment and organisation are vital factors in a counterinsurgency operation. A concentrated population is easier to protect; an infantry company of 100 soldiers can easily control a small town of 10,000 to 20,000 inhabitants, short of a general uprising. On the other hand, it would take a much larger unit if the same population were spread throughout the countryside.[39] Ireland had numerous rural and urban centres, especially in Munster, and holding operations were consequently manpower intensive. Trinquier suggests a possible solution: that a counterinsurgent force can be supported when the population is allowed to participate in its own defence.[40] To do so, the population needs continual military and civil police protection, along with a sense of security provided by the counterinsurgent force. That requires a consistent military presence comprising mobile, self-sufficient infantry forces actively patrolling the area of operations and unsettling the insurgent force.

As more transport became available and mobility increased, the National Army transformed itself into a self-sufficient and effective force capable of supporting isolated outposts. The reorganisation of January 1923 transformed the infantry into 65 battalions, abandoning divisional organisation structures inherited from the British Army and helping to stabilise the Irish countryside by bringing the fight to the IRA.[41] The entire infantry force was established at 32,304 all ranks, and independent units were battle-grouped into self-sufficient entities that were easily deployable with combat support.[42] Units became more robust and better able to stand up to mass attacks, while also providing greater protection to the towns and villages of Ireland. This new strategy also allowed the National Army to mass forces quickly to specific locations in order to overwhelm the IRA defenders.

A National Army organisation report explains the composition and taskings of these battle groups in Cork, whereby the new infantry battalions were led by the General Officer Commanding (GOC) of the command in which they were stationed.[43] The battalions would be predominantly mobile and deployed to areas where the IRA was most active. They had no territorial area, but centres were fixed for battalion HQs for purposes of organisation and control. There would be seven headquarter towns in Cork, predominantly in the northern and western parts of the county, where the fighting was most intense at the end of the war. Mobility and flexibility became key principles for the newly re-organised army as it actively patrolled in order to hold the towns and villages and bring a focused fight to the IRA in the isolated hills and countryside.

A National Army report from April 1923 highlights the ability of the army to concentrate its forces to overwhelm the IRA in locations they had once dominated: 'Operation reports show that all battalions are working hard, continual sweeping and searching is weakening enemy morale and preventing any attempt at concentrated activity.'[44] Operations carried out in West Cork and South Kerry over a week in April and May seriously degraded the IRA, and an after-action report from West Cork states that the Free State was able to mass approximately 2,500 troops.[45] The operation covered almost 500 square miles, or 1,300 square kilometres, of difficult mountainous terrain. At the outset, National Army intelligence indicated that at least four IRA columns were operating in the area, numbering 30–50 fighters. By the end, only about a dozen remained. Even more intensive efforts were made in the southern counties. In one of the biggest operations of its kind during the war, the whole of South Tipperary was combed by battle-grouped National Army troops, leading to the capture of the important Republican political leader Austin Stack.[46]

An interesting parallel tactic was also developed to exploit the success of these large, co-ordinated operations. The National Army acknowledged in the April–May report that numerous small posts had been established 'in order to clinch the operation, and with a view to picking up stragglers and discovering dumps and dug-outs.' These posts were temporary but allowed the army to hold, consolidate, and secure the terrain, while also accommodating specialised troops such as counter columns. They also helped to reassure the local population and support future exploitation operations. By May 1923, the outright defeat of the IRA had become the ultimate objective of the National Army.

IMPROVING FREE STATE MORALE AND PERFORMANCE

> It is quite clear that the battalion organisation is working well, and each battalion is beginning to feel that it is the best ... It is agreed by those

who have had experience in other armies that in no Army could the same amount of work be got out of the troops as we got out of our men last week.

National Army Report on Operations, 29 April–5 May 1923

The new task organisation of the infantry into independent and mobile battle-grouped battalions allowed the National Army to bring the fight to the IRA in overwhelming numbers in even the most isolated areas. The newly-adopted leadership format, streamlining of command-and-control, and breakdown of territory for these units allowed them to co-operate and operate cohesively and effectively. It also gave the units the 'elasticity' advocated by Mulcahy as early as August 1922.[47]

In conventional warfare, it is important to hold the high ground as the key terrain. A counterinsurgent force must also occupy the moral high ground in order to build the legitimacy of the government that sends out that force. The fact that the Free State government had been democratically elected strengthened its legitimacy as well as its resolve to defeat the IRA, whose own legitimacy ultimately waned as the civil war progressed. Modern counterinsurgency discourse contends that government legitimacy is constantly questioned by those who oppose it. Whether that is so – or functions as a determining factor – is debatable, but the testimony of Captain Joseph Lawless of the National Army shows that the perception was significant to some of those involved in the fighting: 'Although I had no heart in the fratricidal struggle, I realised that I must make my contribution towards the supremacy of the Government of Dáil Éireann as representing the democratic majority of the people of Ireland.'[48]

Occupying the moral high ground also depends on discipline. Undisciplined behaviour can antagonise the population and feed negative propaganda fostered by the insurgent side. At the start of the fighting, Free State Army discipline had been poor but it steadily improved.[49] With better discipline, better tactics, and better organisation, General

Michael Costello stated in 1924, every officer admitted that the army underwent extraordinary improvement between December 1922 and April 1923. Costello put much of that down to the re-organisation and re-structuring that occurred in January. General Mulcahy agreed, commenting, 'We are getting some strength and discipline into the Army.'[50] This was a marked change that improved National Army morale and performance whilst effecting the ability of the IRA to prosecute its insurgency against the Free State.

CULMINATION POINT

A key factor in a successful counterinsurgency campaign is the ability to take advantage of favourable conditions. Such opportunities are often ignored by non-local troops but local soldiers are more apt to notice them. The National Army troops deployed in Cork and Munster were more culturally aware than the British security forces had ever been during the War of Independence, with a better feeling for the prevalent atmosphere and the society in which they were operating. Various reports make reference to a steadily improving relationship between the army and the people, especially in Cork.[51]

By contrast, Liam Deasy, Officer Commanding the 1st Southern Division IRA, reported that 'in many instances ASUs [Active Service Units], are not properly staffed, receive no regular directions, are not supplied with the necessary local or other intelligence, carry out no systematic method of attempted ambushes, or other forms of attack.'[52] In guerrilla warfare it is such factors, more than armaments or supplies that can determine success or failure.[53] Some IRA brigades started to lose their combat effectiveness as the Free State forces improved. Ted O'Sullivan admits that the IRA 5 (Cork) Brigade 'fell asunder quickly … There was no real brigade column to hold them, and the Free State had the towns around them held. Towards December they [Free State soldiers] occupied Castletownbere, and they always recruited local fellows to guide them.'[54]

This was an extraordinary turnaround considering the performance of many of the same IRA Cork units in the fight against the British.

In early January 1923, the 1st Southern Division of the IRA held a meeting. O'Sullivan recalled, 'At that time the Staters [National Army] were giving us the full whack. I had said that if … the other areas in Kerry and in Cork 1, 2 [and] 3 Brigades didn't work harder I could not hold out.' In response, the other IRA units promised to 'intensify the war', but this support did not materialise. By the spring of that year, the National Army had the upper hand. IRA Chief of Staff Liam Lynch commented on the large enemy presence around the boundary between the IRA Cork 1 and 2 Brigades, commenting that Mulcahy 'has realised the importance of initiative and his forces are continually on the move, following up our men to our safer areas.'[55] The number of Republican safe havens – so important during the War of Independence – substantially decreased as the civil war progressed. As the ungoverned spaces shrank, so too did local support for the IRA.

Ernie O'Malley agreed with Lynch that the essential differences between the British and the Irish National Army during this period was that the British 'did not know our [IRA] officers personally. We were an invisible army who melted away when they tried to steam-roll. Now the people, on the whole, were against us, they were willing to give information.'[56]

THE NAIL IN THE COFFIN

The IRA 1st Southern Division met again on 26 February 1923, and representatives from all the brigades agreed that only small operations were now possible. The officer commanding the Cork 3 Brigade stated that in a very short time he would have no men left 'owing to the great number of arrests and casualties.'[57] Moreover, the cumulative effect of peace moves by influential civic groups and senior representatives on both sides inevitably weakened Republican resolve. The National Army had the support of the majority of the population and of the Catholic Church, along with the backing of the press and a government with substantial resources and outside support.[58] The will to resist in arms and the fighting resolve eventually deserted the anti-Treatyites, 'especially after the death of Liam Lynch on 10 April 1923, and the subsequent capture of key leaders during large-scale National Army operations.'[59] Their overall military position was bleak, their war materials and essential supplies were steadily diminishing, and many had to take refuge high in the hills and in well-concealed dugouts to avoid capture.[60] Already, on 31 March, the National Army reported, 'These areas, with a little more pressure, will be cleaned up in the course of a few weeks, providing that we can come into contact with the Irregular forces operating.' As for IRA prisoners, they were 'fed up.'[61]

Additional National Army troops were locally recruited, gaining in effectiveness as they acquired combat experience. By April, they had detailed knowledge of the topography of the areas used by IRA Republicans and of their regular billets, which they used to meticulously plan searches.[62] Supported by supplementary orders and detailed terrain analysis, operation orders were now the remit of Free State tactical and operational planners.[63] Co-ordination between command areas had improved and internal communications had been enhanced, ensuring unity of effort and economy of force. A National Army report of 28 April stated that 'the army's grip on the situation is daily becoming stronger and better, while within the army itself a healthy spirit of confidence, discipline, and a very real soldierly outlook is growing to a very appreciable extent.'[64]

But the National Army also had to make it difficult for IRA flying columns to gain or regain traction with the population or to operate safely. They could not be allowed to recruit locally, and a dedicated rebuilding programme was required to subdue the anti-government cause. As counterinsurgency theorist David Galula explains, 'Complete elimination of the guerrillas by military action being practically impossible at this stage, remnants will always manage to stay in the area, and new recruits will join their ranks so long as the political cells have not been destroyed.'[65] Key areas of Cork County were flooded with Free State resources and troops to deny them to the IRA.

By this stage, any armed IRA action won little sympathy from a population eager for a more settled economic and social environment. The *Irish Times* was able to report, 'The National Army has now a position of overwhelming superiority in the field. The militant Republicans have lost their most active leaders … The hour is ripe for peace. The whole country seeks it.'[66]

MOMENTUM SWING

By the end of the civil war, the morale of the IRA in Cork was at an all-time low. Senior IRA leader Pa Murray bemoaned the fact that the National Army could now concentrate its forces at will and overwhelm the insurgents: 'The Staters [National Army] have all areas overran [sic] and … columns cannot exist except in small parties … Killing a few of the other side does not count as they can be easily replaced.'[67]

Although the IRA had not been defeated outright, the pro-Treaty forces had progressively worn down their will to continue the struggle.[68] Flying columns still in the field were harassed without rest by superior Free State forces. Republican fatigue was rampant, supplies were scarce, clothing and equipment were unobtainable, and the organisation was in disarray.[69] A National Army report from 4 May 1923 notes the capture of 60 IRA prisoners in Cork over previous week, by far the largest number taken in the country.[70] Another report from 5 May 1923 describes IRA policy in Cork as 'waiting for some kind of settlement at the same time letting it be known that they are still around.'[71] Following the disintegration of the anti-Treaty war effort over the first four months of 1923, large-scale IRA military activity became impossible; columns could remain in existence only if small, while arms and financial resources were extremely limited.[72] Mick Murphy recalls that 'Republicans resembled wandering sheep.'[73]

As spring drew to a close and the days lengthened, many IRA leaders doubted their battered and weary troops could face a summer campaign.[74] They put their weapons away on 24 May 1923, as O'Sullivan describes: 'We dumped our arms and we ran through the country, and they caught men wholesale. Up to that time they had taken a lot of our combatants and they filled the gaols with them.'[75] A National Army report confidently asserted in mid-June, 'The Irregulars have no intention of resurrecting the vicious aggressive campaign out of which the country has just emerged.'[76]

The IRA had also lost the goodwill of the people by their heavy-handed tactics of destroying infrastructure and railways.[77] This seriously inconvenienced the rural communities whose backing they sought and isolated their own forces from the very lifeline they needed to prosecute the insurgency. Further, the burning of buildings and commandeering of goods – activities that had been deemed tolerable in the War of Independence against a common British enemy – seemed to have been adjudged as futile in an internecine struggle and cost the IRA the support on which its cause depended.[78]

During the War of Independence, the IRA had numerous safe havens in which to shelter from British security forces. During the Irish Civil War, these safe areas became scarce. As the prominent IRA leader Ernie O'Malley remarked, 'In the Tan War [War of Independence], you would be received into any house you went into, but in the civil war you had to be very sure of your house.'[79]

The co-ordination between National Army commands in Munster also improved, allowing the troops to gain and move into the ungoverned spaces previously controlled by the IRA. On 10 September 1922, the government announced that the appointment of General Eoin O'Duffy as chief commissioner of the Civic Guard had been approved.[80] In other words, O'Duffy was out of an army command, a shift that ultimately helped to reduce the personality clashes between Free State commanders that had hindered operations in Munster.

A LEARNING ORGANISATION

With re-organisation and the adoption of a new strategy, including using local troops supported by specialised troops, the Free State eventually broke the IRA network and fighting spirit. IRA hopes that 'the decent elements' of the National Army would revolt and the people would come to its side never materialised.[81] Instead, the National Army learned from its mistakes and brought the fight back to the IRA by improving tactics and strategy.

The army leadership recognised the consequences: 'Events of the past few days point to the beginning of the end so far as the Irregular campaign is concerned … The general feeling of the people seems to be that Irregular organisation, as a whole, is doomed as a result of the recent operations and captures of leaders.'[82] To ensure that the pendulum wouldn't swing back, the Free State had to replace the civil security imposed by the National Army with civil control that would be enforced by a newly established civil police force and would uphold a newly constituted rule of law.

8

ESTABLISH CIVIL CONTROL

> O'Higgins had no doubts. Although a virulent critic of the army on grounds both of inefficiency and ill-discipline, he told Cosgrave in April 1923 that it was up to the military to restore order.
>
> O'Halpin, *Defending Ireland*, 40

In April 1922, an Irish Ministry of Home Affairs report outlined a breakdown in law and order following the withdrawal of the British security apparatus:

> The peace of the country is at present menaced by the operation of armed bands engaged in robberies of Banks and Post Offices; armed interference with public meetings, suppression of free speech, and of the press. Trains are being held up and goods stolen; business premises are being raided and large quantities of goods removed by force; and large money levies are being made on proprietors of business premises ... Order should be restored, and life and property respected.[1]

Defeating an insurgency requires a joint civil–military security force. Working in conjunction, the military provides civil security while the police force provides civil control. The military actions of the National Army had helped to restore a semblance of order in the Free State that had shaped the initial environment, setting the conditions to facilitate a transition to civil power. At the start of the fighting in June 1922, the army was one of the few functioning Free State organs of power and, therefore, tasked with providing civil control and civil security in most areas. Civil control is primarily a civil police function because it supports the rule of law, channelling the population's activities to permit the provision of security and essential services while co-existing with a military force that conducts operations.[2]

A timely transition to using civil police was important, because using soldiers as police diverts them from their core mission, undermines military professionalism, and can erect a barrier between the population and the guardians of the peace by unduly politicising the military.[3] The gunman had to be removed from Irish politics, Irish society, and everyday Irish life, and replaced by a functioning, regularised police force. A civil police force needed to be locally recruited, trained, and deployed throughout the state to provide an impartial and legitimate alternative to army provision of civil control. The new force also had to differ from the previous British police force, the RIC, in order to be accepted.

Replacing the RIC was a necessary process to restore a safe environment and release National Army resources. It was also a difficult one. Establishing civil control led to the restoration of the rule of law, but it also entailed the passage of the Public Safety Bill – also known as the Execution Policy – with notable effects on the outcome of the conflict.

AN IRISH CIVIL POLICE FORCE

The Civic Guard was officially launched in February 1922 in Dublin at the Royal Dublin Society (RDS), Ballsbridge, under Michael Staines, its first commissioner. Staines was an active IRA officer from western Ireland, and coincidentally the son of an RIC officer. He would later state that he viewed the appointment as temporary as he had little interest in staying on in the long term.[4]

On 25 April 1922, an estimated 1,100 police recruits were transferred from the RDS to a new headquarters in a former British Army barracks in Kildare. Accompanying them was an arsenal of 200 rifles and 1,000 revolvers for use in training and arming the new force.[5]

THE KILDARE MUTINY

On arrival in Kildare Barracks, the recruits became disgruntled to learn that most of the 12 most senior positions in the Civic Guard had been bestowed on former RIC members.[6] On the morning of 15 May 1922, training came to an abrupt halt following an official announcement that additional (disbanded and experienced) RIC officers were to be promoted to superintendents.[7] This proved too much for the new recruits. A disenfranchised protest committee was formed under Thomas Daly, a recruit who helped lead an anti-Treaty faction within the Civic Guard. He directed the committee to issue Staines with an ultimatum demanding 'the immediate expulsion of certain ex-RIC men', and threatening drastic action if the demand was not complied with.[8] Dissension and division spread throughout the Kildare police training depot against a backdrop of Treaty-related tensions that still simmered among the rank-and-file recruits.[9]

National Army units were dispatched to Kildare to quell the disturbance, but a stand-off ensued at the main gates of the barracks on the arrival of the troops. Army officer Captain Corry told the guards inside the gates that he had been instructed to take over the camp, by force if necessary. The guards inside responded by pointing 'in the direction of the avenue, from which three hundred rifles were trained on the gate'.[10] After a brief exchange between Corry and those inside, one of the recruits telephoned the captain's superior officer and 'convinced the military that the 'Irregulars' were not in control of the camp and that the dispute was an internal issue.'[11] Eventually the situation calmed down, order was restored, and training resumed.

But the purported mutiny contained another significant and ominous development. Evidence given at the subsequent inquiry alleged that

Thomas Daly had supplied the password and led a convoy of anti-Treaty IRA trucks into Kildare Barracks. These were filled with weapons and driven away for later use by the IRA, possibly in the Four Courts.[12]

THE COMMISSION OF INQUIRY

The decision of the recruits at Kildare Barracks to openly challenge appointments and arm themselves against the military provoked the government to seriously reconsider policing policy, with lasting consequences for Irish policing. A Commission of Inquiry into the mutiny produced some key recommendations: each police station was to have at least one former police officer, although he would not necessarily be in charge of the station; the main body of the new force would be unarmed in order to facilitate public acceptance; and it should be deployed in stations around the country.[13]

The commission also noted the desire of many Civic Guard recruits to differentiate themselves from their predecessors – as well as their belief that using RIC training methods merely created a new Irish police force that was a second edition of the earlier constabulary.[14] This issue needed to be addressed in order to uphold the impartiality and legitimacy of the Civic Guard, and to encourage its acceptance by a population that would not only be policed by the new force but would also provide its pool of recruits.

On 17 August 1922, senior civil servants Kevin O'Shiel and Michael MacAuliffe presented the findings of the commission to the Free State government. The commission asserted that the original organising committee had made a mistake in its decision to arm the Civic Guard, 'thereby creating a militaristic instead of a peaceful outlook in the minds of the officers and men, and not tending to assure the public that the day of militaristic and coercive policemen was at an end in Ireland.'[15] Staines predicted that the new force would succeed on the strength of its 'moral authority as [the employer of] servants of the people', not by force of arms or sheer numbers.[16]

As a direct consequence of the Free State government's new policy of an unarmed police force, all 14,744 RIC rifles that were no longer needed by the Civic Guard were handed over to the government to support the arming of the National Army. This was a substantial force multiplier and combat advantage for the Free State soldiers over their IRA adversaries.[17] The initial proposal of an unarmed police force became a political matter. Ernest Blythe, the minister for local government and later for finance, remembered that some ministers believed that the police would be hunted out of their stations within a few days if had no guns to defend themselves. The government nonetheless remained steadfast in its resolve to remove the gun from Irish society – and to promote *policing by consent*.[18]

On 22 August 1922, O'Shiel wrote to Michael Collins to summarise the recommendations and urge him to dispatch the new guard on police duty as soon as possible.[19] Collins never received the memorandum; he was killed on the same day. Only days later the Civic Guard made its first public appearance, in his funeral cortège.

According to James Donohue, the Kildare mutiny had the significant outcome of diffusing a potential conflict between two newly formed institutions of the Irish government: 'Had the discharge of a single firearm occurred it might have altered the course of events, not only of that day and of the formation of a police force, but of the future politically.'[20] Instead, the Free State established an unarmed civil police force that was free from colonialism and hoped to be free from political interference.

IMPLEMENTING THE RECOMMENDATIONS

The Free State government immediately set out to implement the commission's recommendation to push the police force out into the countryside as soon as possible. It was convinced that an unarmed force interwoven with the community would be the safest and best way to gain public acceptance, and that keeping the guards defenceless against armed attack would win them public sympathy.[21] From the outset, the Free State strategy was to establish sufficient police and military barracks throughout the state to break the hold that local IRA brigades had on public perceptions.[22] The guards would live within the communities they hoped to police in order to provide the all-encompassing and ongoing security required of a successful counterinsurgency.[23]

Diarmaid Ferriter suggests that Staines resigned from the force in the aftermath of the Kildare mutiny because the commission recommended against politicians serving in the Civic Guard.[24] General Eoin O'Duffy replaced Staines as commissioner, inheriting what historian Brian McCarthy characterises as a largely untrained and disgruntled force.[25] Minister for Justice Kevin O'Higgins believed that only a figure of O'Duffy's stature could 'redeem the force which had been paralysed by indiscipline since its formation.'[26] As a result, the new commissioner needed to secure the loyalty of the new police force and quickly demonstrate its capabilities to both the Free State government and the Irish public it hoped to secure.

DEPLOYING THE CIVIC GUARD

Shortly before his death, Michael Collins reported to Cabinet that only four IRA units presented a problem in western Ireland. He recommended that the Civic Guard be introduced to restore law and order outside the Waterford–Cork–Kerry–Limerick area.[27] As the initial roll-out of the new force began in earnest, it met varying degrees of success, but the ungoverned spaces of the Free State needed to be policed and the Civic Guard needed to establish a firm presence countrywide. Mulcahy told O'Higgins in September 1922 that he was gradually evacuating government forces from many of the more peaceful districts in order to surge them in the more dangerous regions of Munster. Therefore, he urgently required the Civic Guard to take up duties in Limerick, East Cork, and Waterford, as 'there is danger in some places that barracks that we evacuate in this way will be burned.'[28]

To comply with Mulcahy's request and to foster public confidence, O'Duffy quickly allocated recruits to unoccupied police stations throughout the country, and especially Munster – sometimes without the assistance of experienced police personnel or even manuals.[29] Realising the dangers but also the political-strategic implications and advantages of this policy, Commissioner O'Duffy paraded guards deploying to former RIC barracks, declaring in ringing tones, 'You are going out unarmed into a hostile area. You are the first to be sent out. You may be murdered, your barracks burned, your uniform taken off you, but you must carry on and bring peace to the people.'[30]

With these words of somewhat unnerving encouragement, the Civic Guard was deployed throughout the newly established Free State. Between September and October 1922, an estimated 1,700 officers took up duty at police stations around the country.[31] With many being deployed to the less hostile areas within the province of Munster.

Cork was a battleground county and soon became an important area for recruitment and deployment of the new police force. Before the Civic Guards official deployment, Cork public bodies, desiring civil control had already made plans for civil and local policing, and published the following advertisement in the *Cork Examiner* on 14 August 1922:

> The Civic Committeee representing the Corporation and other Public Bodies have instituted a Provisional Civic Force for the Policing of the City. About one hundred men are required … Applicants must be of good height and physique, of Irish nationality, of good education and reliable character.
>
> J. MURPHY (Provisional Organiser).

After initial difficulties, Civic Guard recruitment and deployment started to spread in Cork and Munster. By early 1923, due to National Army actions, the area was more amenable to policing by consent. A confidential report in January 1923 indicated that Republicans had moved on from attacks directed chiefly against the army and army posts and were now focused on creating economic damage.[32] In March, a Civic Guard report detailing activities over the month before highlighted the differences between regions within Cork where the guards could operate alone and regions where they still needed army support:

Cork East: This is an area in which the Guards have recently taken up quarters in some of the more important towns, and in which it cannot at present be said that they are absolutely familiar with all the currents of life in the areas to which they have come. This difficulty is, however, being rapidly overcome.

Cork West: [The Superintendent] states that many people who were apparently cold, if not hostile, in their demeanour, are now inclined to be friendly and … it can be gathered that the hostile elements are anxious to terminate hostilities.[33]

THE IRA RESPONSE

The IRA response to the Civic Guard was summed up in a general order issued in November 1922, in which the Republican leadership dismissed the new force as a mere continuation of the RIC and accused it of masquerading as a purely civic body while functioning as an arm of the Free State government's intelligence service.[34] That was a textbook Republican position, one of consistent attempts to brand Free State security forces as an outgrowth of the former British security apparatus. It also justified the concerns of Civic Guard recruits who wanted to distinguish themselves from their RIC predecessors.

Yet the IRA did not envision deploying lethal force against the guards, presumably out of concern for the public response. IRA headquarters explicitly ordered its fighters not to fire on any unit or individual of the Civic Guard as long as they remained unarmed. The overall policy was to harm but not to kill, thereby forcing the guards either to leave the area or to arm themselves.[35] The latter would confirm the status of the force as a successor to the RIC and, thereby, damage its legitimacy.

Notwithstanding prevailing IRA threats, the vast majority of Civic Guard members stayed resolute in their duty, including by resisting IRA harassment and intimidation. Additionally, high levels of unemployment made it unlikely that many guards would simply walk away from new and potentially lifelong careers in the state's employ.[36]

Initially, the IRA attacked the new police force using small bombs, mines, and sledgehammers to break barrack doors and windows. The property inside – uniforms, bedding, furniture, files – was periodically looted, and arson then used to prevent the posts from being easily re-occupied.[37] The IRA also attacked the Civic Guard indirectly through a boycott, a tactic it had already successfully used against the RIC. Traders and contractors who serviced guard (and army) barracks were threatened with the confiscation of all goods and services that could be intercepted. The IRA also planned raids on factories that produced police and army uniforms.[38]

Over the winter of 1922–23, the IRA destroyed 485 police stations across the Free State, including many in Cork and Munster. The unarmed guards could not always resist their armed attackers, and some 400 police officers were beaten, stripped of their uniforms, and robbed of their personal possessions.[39] In many areas where the IRA operated freely, the police were at the mercy of the local Republicans.

But despite – or possibly because of – their helplessness, the guards won public support.[40] By 1923, reports from across the country reflected a favourable attitude towards the Free State security forces.[41] A government doesn't have to win over the broad mass of people; the people who matter are the local inhabitants who constitute the neutral majority and want peace and security.[42] Public acceptance through public influence can be transformed into popular support. That trajectory allowed policing by consent to develop in Ireland, which ultimately entrenched overall legitimacy for the police and the Free State government.

RESTORATION OF LAW AND ORDER

By early 1923, the Free State believed its position to be as follows:

> The effective Irregular war has definitely taken the form of a war ... with no common basis except this—that all have a vested interest in

chaos, in bringing about a state of affairs where force is substituted for law ... Trains are attacked; post offices robbed; banks raided ... [and] men are murdered for personal reasons or in the name of the Republic.[43]

The Civic Guard clearly had to become a noticeable security presence and a building block of the new Irish state.[44] Charles Townsend contends that from the start, the public attitude of the Irish to the Civic Guard was different from feelings about the RIC.[45] Monthly reports from Cork outline a growing process of acceptance as the Civic Guard stations became more established in communities.[46] As they did so, public co-operation gave government security forces preferential access to information in areas they controlled.

A local Irish police force was perfectly situated to maximise the advantages of this situation. Strong connections, good actions, and growing acceptance afforded the guards near immunity from assassination by the IRA. Only one member of the Civic Guard was killed in the course of the civil war, although many were assaulted and their stations ransacked and burned.[47] Similar to the National Army, the Civic Guard demonstrated remarkable resilience in occupying their posts and barracks, establishing a presence that undoubtedly helped to normalise local communities.

Minister O'Higgins was clear about the roles of the Civic Guard and the National Army – and the difference between the two of them. He told W.T. Cosgrave, the president of the Free State Executive Council, in April 1923 that it was up to the military to restore order.[48] At that point, the Civic Guard would become the primary security agency. In May 1923, a National Army after-action report stated that the guard should be established throughout Munster because 'the pioneering work has been done by the soldiers and ... the possibility of a recurrence of armed Irregulars is practically negligible.'[49]

As more and more IRA volunteers were taken out of the fight, and more regions became relatively secure, the Civic Guard opened police stations in most parts of the country.[50] As they spread their influence and dedication, the guards gained a firm footing within the state, within Munster, and within Irish society as a whole.

THE SPECIAL INFANTRY CORPS

Although they were unarmed, the civil police were not totally defenceless. Kevin O'Higgins consistently sought to establish a generic force to support the Civic Guard in some of its more robust civil control taskings. His demands materialised when the Special Infantry Corps (SIC) was formally set up in January 1923. Under the command of Patrick Dalton, the SIC consisted of roughly 4,000 soldiers in eight companies or units (later battalions) stationed semi-permanently in strategic locations across the country.[51] They acted as an additional security force to exert civil control but on occasion ventured outside the realms of civic policing. The SIC sometimes acted in conjunction with unofficial groups organised by farmers, making vigorous and partisan interventions in agrarian and industrial disputes.[52] It also operated as an outside armed security force to deal with potentially delicate and unpopular activities such as strike breaking, land clearing, process serving, and evictions.[53]

In April 1923, O'Higgins told Cosgrave that with the prevailing 'revolt against all idea of morality, law and social order', no greater disaster could overtake the country than to be overtaken by a peace that would leave conditions such as these to be dealt with by a novice unarmed police force and in the courts.[54] Through the National Army and the SIC, the government had to shape the conditions that would allow the Civic Guard to take control, maintain policing, and uphold law and order.

THE FREE STATE EXECUTION POLICY

Because the National Army had an intimate knowledge of IRA personnel and knew all their trusted haunts, it was able to capture more and more prisoners: over 1,800 in Cork and nearly 12,000 more widely by the end of the war.[55] This was the majority of active IRA fighters taken out of the fight, due to intelligence-led raids and a relatively secure prison system. What happened to them?

No work on the Irish Civil War can be written without mention of the Free State government's Public Safety Bill. After Michael Collins was killed, an attempt was made to shorten the war by introducing a form of martial law. On 15 September 1922, Richard Mulcahy asked Cabinet to introduce emergency powers of arrest, detention, and capital punishment.[56] The Public Safety Bill, or Execution Policy, was introduced in the Dáil almost two weeks later, on 27 September. The legislation established military courts with punitive powers, including that of execution, for sundry offences such as possessing arms or aiding attacks on government forces.[57] The policy understandably drew immediate scorn from IRA leaders, who perceived it as a means to set up secret military courts that would give Free State officers in command of districts the power to inflict the death penalty on any IRA volunteer captured with arms.[58]

Whether legal or not, the Free State government persisted with the policy in order to break the morale of the anti-Treaty Republicans. The government adjudged that some form of coercion was a necessary evil to convince targeted individuals to cease their subversive actions against the newly-formed state. Conflict studies scholar Stathis Kalyvas perceptively remarks, 'We must remember that the main purpose of the trial and execution is not to save the soul of the accused but to achieve the public good and put fear into others.'[59]

The Public Safety Bill certainly put fear into many on the anti-Treaty side, especially their supporters and family members. Simultaneously, the civilian Free State leaders believed that the unpopular policy was necessary because those carrying out armed resistance to the government should be made aware that 'they shall forfeit their lives if they continue to do that work ... [and the army] is prepared to do the work of executing these people ... It is the servant of the Government.'[60]

The first executions caused IRA leaders to formulate reprisals against the Free State political leadership. On 28 November 1922, Liam Lynch addressed a letter to the Ceann Comhairle (Speaker) of Dáil Éireann threatening 'very drastic measures' against those who had voted for the bill. Two days later, a general order was sent out to all IRA units to kill listed categories of government supporters.[61] Lynch argued that up to that time, the IRA had abided by the rules of warfare but that now it had to respond to the ultimate provocation.[62]

On the government side, Cosgrave noted his prior opposition to the death penalty but affirmed he could now see 'no other way … in which ordered conditions can be restored in this country, or any security obtained for our troops—or indeed to give our troops any confidence in us as a Government.'[63] The policy was to proceed, but the Free State could not afford the risk of its soldiers refusing to carry out the order to open fire: 'It was decided that the first firing squad would be picked from the men of the best unit we had in Dublin and that proved successful.'[64]

Whereas the British authorities had executed 24 IRA volunteers before the truce, the Free State executed at least 77, and probably four more, for political offences during the civil war.[65] The pace continued into 1923 and began to intensify, with 34 executions in January alone.[66] At the height of the policy, Cosgrave turned down any peace or reconciliation moves by the IRA. He was adamant that a minority had provoked the conflict and 'it is easy for them to try and win the peace now when they have lost the war.' It was time for them to 'act like men and admit the authority of the ballot box.' If not, he declared, 'they will have to submit to stronger force.'[67]

The Execution Policy had its opponents within the Free State establishment as well, those who feared the adverse effects on the population. General W.R.E Murphy of the Kerry Command wrote to Mulcahy in December 1922 that although the handful of executions already carried out were having a 'salutary effect' on public opinion, conducting too many would backfire.[68] Certainly, the executions produced a toxic legacy.[69] A Free State soldier serving in Cork during the period, Jim Byrne, was forthright about his disillusionment with the policy in later life, asserting that 'an awful lot of great men' had been executed but would not have been if Collins had lived. It's interesting to note that Byrne also admits, 'We let it be known that there was to be no firing parties from our crowd … If there was any prisoners brought into where we were to be shot ... the British ex-soldiers [within the National Army] would do it ... We wouldn't do it.'[70]

Cork was one of the busiest areas of operations in the war, yet only one of the 77 official executions took place there.[71] An explanation may lie in the high numbers of locally recruited Free State soldiers deployed in the county, which may have caused the National Army presence to be less oppressive than it was elsewhere.[72] This familiarity might have underscored the reticence of the Cork command from proclaiming a death sentence on a fellow county man. In one letter to Mulcahy, Emmet Dalton pointed out that he had 1,800 prisoners in Cork caught in the possession of arms and asked if he was expected to execute them all.[73] Dalton was perhaps being facetious, but although Mulcahy replied that this was not required of him, the government had got to the point of deciding that 'strong action would have to be taken.'[74]

The contentious policy had a seriously detrimental effect on IRA morale, as Republicans worried that if they intensified the war some of their best men would be executed: 'It was no good carrying out an operation ... for our prisoners ... would have been taken out and shot.'[75] In Limerick, IRA prisoners issued an appeal to their comrades still fighting that a continuation of the present struggle was a 'waste of blood and [had] developed into a war of extermination.'[76] Supporters and their family members lived under the cloud of potential death sentences being imposed upon imprisoned volunteers, bringing pressure on the IRA to suspend or conclude hostilities.[77] Thus the threat of executions was perhaps the most effective psychological tool available to the National Army during the counterinsurgency phase of the conflict.

In February 1923, after various peace proposals had been spurned, Cosgrave made it clear that he would accept no result other than the complete defeat of the anti-Treaty forces: '[We will not] hesitate if ... we have to exterminate 10,000 Republicans' because 'the 3 million of our people is bigger than this 10,000.'[78] Cosgrave also declared that Éamon de Valera's followers were scarce throughout the country, and his cause had not a ghost of a chance of succeeding.[79]

The execution of former comrades during the civil war was a draconian measure that undoubtedly caused friction and hatred. It also shortened the war considerably. Along with harassing, capturing, killing, and executing IRA volunteers during the civil security and civil control phases, the Free State successfully utilised non-kinetic measures such as psychological warfare and information operations. In combination, these actions were essential weapons in the National Army arsenal.

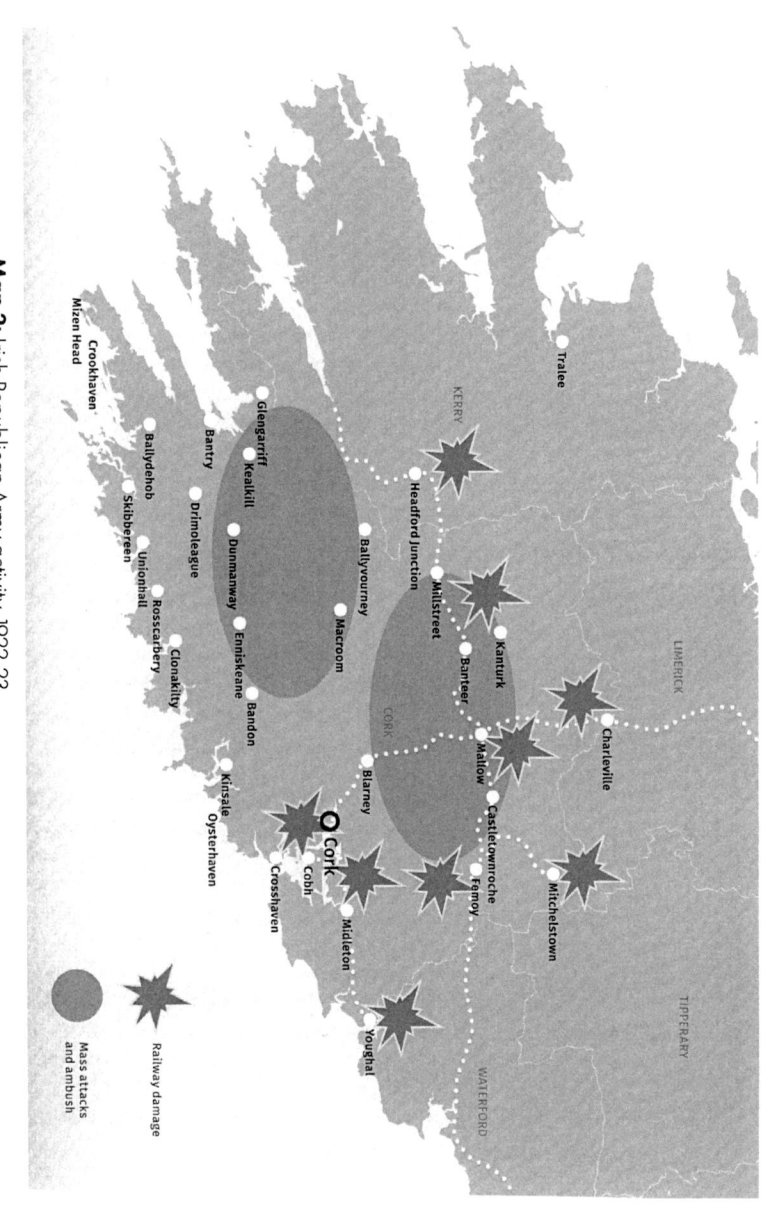

Map 2: Irish Republican Army activity, 1922-23

9

INFORMATION OPERATIONS

If they had wooed public support instead of flouting it, the outcome of the war might well have been affected.

Neeson, *The Civil War in Ireland*, 97

Any counterinsurgency campaign depends on gleaning intelligence from the local population to identify the enemy.[1] The Free State intelligence services were brought to a high pitch – unmatched by British security forces during the War of Independence – in the later phases of the civil war.[2] By early 1923, under the implacable effects of the Free State information machine, IRA resistance and optimism started to fade. 'In the past [we hoped] that we could prevent their governing, that popular opinion would force their abdication', IRA man Tom Barry told the IRA Executive Council, 'but none of these things happened.'[3]

As others have pointed out, holding territory is not enough to secure victory.[4] The side that dictates the narrative generally wins the conflict. An insurgency requires a popular cause, one strong enough that both the insurgents and their support base are willing to endure prolonged hardships and subsequent repercussions. A counterinsurgency campaign discredits the insurgent and the insurgent's cause, turning popular support in order to win the middle ground and deny the insurgent physical, mental, and moral sanctuary within the population. Counterinsurgency also requires an acceptable counter cause that strengthens government legitimacy and helps to marginalise the insurgent force. Popular support is hard to quantify, but spontaneous information is a key metric. When the population sharply increases its provision of intelligence, a breakthrough has occurred.

Sinn Féin had formed a powerful information arm during the War of Independence and waged a successful propaganda war against the British government between 1919 and 1921 that took advantage of the openness of the British and American press.[5] Those on both sides of the coming civil war were experienced in information operations. An appreciation of the significance of information warfare is evident in a 1923 National Army report urging an imperative: every man in uniform should understand that the slightest suggestion of 'Black and Tan methods' would be tangibly harmful.[6] The Free State government realised it had to discredit an IRA counter narrative that characterised it as a replica of, or proxy for, the previous British administration.

As part of its information operations campaign, the Free State used both internal and external communications to expound its narrative and ensure its legitimacy. *An t-Óglách* was the internal instrument to communicate the desired message.[7] The Catholic Church and the Free State–supporting press were the key external organs of influence. Both were considered to be reputable sources of information, and both had access to the all-important local population.

THE ROLE OF THE CHURCH

The Catholic hierarchy was attached to the institutions of the new state; many senior clerics excused the excesses of the state security forces and blamed the IRA for all the evils of the civil war while actively using their influence to garner public support for Free State government.[8] Even before the civil war had begun, the Irish bishops issued a stinging condemnation of the IRA, calling its rejection of civilian authority both 'a sacrilege against national freedom' and 'an immoral usurpation and confiscation of the people's rights', as the *Freeman's Journal* reported on 27 April 1922. The bishops demonised the IRA volunteers: 'When they shoot their brothers on the opposite side they are murderers; when they commandeer public or private property, they are robbers and brigands ... all sins and crimes of the most heinous kind.'[9]

Liam de Róiste, a prominent pro-Treaty Sinn Féin TD in Cork, supported the bishops. He pointed out that since the Catholic Church had declared the Free State government to be lawful, from the moral point of view it was, therefore, entitled to obedience.[10] The government actively encouraged this perception. In early August 1922, Cosgrave addressed a letter to each parish priest, outlining how they could help the government and the army in what he called the 'present crises.'[11]

The National Army certainly received religious support in Cork, and not only from the Catholic side. Shortly after Emmet Dalton's arrival, the Protestant Bishop of Cork, Cloyne, and Ross visited 'to assure him of the loyal cooperation of the clergy and members of the Church of Ireland.'[12] Dalton also received a visit in his initial Command HQ in the Imperial Hotel Cork from the Most Reverand Dr Cohalan, the Catholic Bishop of Cork, who publicly welcomed pro-Treaty troops to the city.[13] This interaction soon paid dividends. Within weeks, Cohalan had essentially ex-communicated IRA volunteers in Cork and ordered the Cork Diocese to support the new state.[14]

Priests had a firm control over their congregations. They spoke of young minds being poisoned by false principles, falling into cruelty, robbery, falsehood, and crime, and warned that 'any priests who approve of this Irregular insurrection were false to their sacred office.'[15] De Róiste, a devout Catholic, echoed their moral argument: 'The taking of life by the Irregulars is *murder*: the taking of property *robbery*: destruction a grievous crime. Thus the sacraments cannot be administered to those who persist in these crimes.'[16] The Catholic hierarchy went further, proclaiming it every citizen's duty to support the civil and military authorities 'by every available means.'[17]

On 10 October 1922, the Catholic bishops issued a pastoral letter to be read from the pulpits. The letter declared that the IRA's war lacked legal justification, and should, therefore, be morally regarded as a system of murder and assassination of the National forces, 'for it must not be forgotten that killing in an unjust war is as much murder before God as if there were no war.'[18] For maximum effect the pastoral letter, which was also published in local and national newspapers, coincided with an amnesty period and the application of the Execution Policy.[19] It stressed that the public had a clear duty to support the government, and that continued resistance to the Free State government would result in excommunication.

On the Republican side, Seán O'Faoláin asserted that outrages committed by the Free State under the auspices of the pastoral letter were 'perpetrated by those that forgot God.'[20] According to de Róiste, however, any criticism of the Catholic hierarchy by the IRA was 'the height of arrogance', and he noted that the 'churches are thronged these days while the novena of prayer for peace is being offered.' In his view, the October pastoral letter seriously undermined Republican claims of 'upholding the moral right.'[21]

Exclusion from absolution and the last sacraments was now the fate for IRA members who fell in action or were executed. According to Florence O'Donoghue, the Catholic Church's hostility was devastating for the IRA volunteers and their families.[22] Ernie O'Malley remarked on the contrast between the treatment volunteers had experienced during the War of Independence, when the clergy had tacitly supported them, and the current edict against them: 'It crystallised the random fulminations of the great majority of the priests who were in favour of the Treaty. Sunday after Sunday their sermons had degenerated into essays of political abuse.'[23]

To counter the damage being inflicted by the clergy, the IRA sent a delegation to Rome in January 1923 to try to convince the Vatican to lift the excommunication order on its members. In response, the Vatican sent papal envoy Monsignor Luzio to Ireland. The Free State government complained bitterly, especially as Luzio expressed Republican sympathies, and he was later recalled.[24] The faithful de Róiste declared, 'There can be an appeal to Rome: but until Rome declares to the contrary, the Bishops' voice is the authoritative voice of the Church.[25]

Some in the Republican leadership, such as Austin Stack, dismissed the issue: 'The stories of all these periods in history are simply the telling of how the church's heads helped the oppressor against a people... Their influence in politics is not what it was.'[26] IRA handbills questioned the relevance of the Catholic Church: 'Ghosts—Other Ghosts or the Priests and the Republic.'[27] Although some hard-line anti-Treaty activists did not care much about the influence of the Church, most volunteers commented that the social ostracism had its effect on their families.[28] Soon, IRA volunteers felt that they could no longer attend mass. In the sermons, 'We were looters, robbers, and murderers. The Hand of God was against us.'[29]

Free State military efforts were thus supplemented by an intensive psychological offensive against the guerrillas. Propaganda and pressures have always been powerful tools to influence public perceptions.[30] The actions of the Catholic Church reached deep into the Irish psyche to discredit the insurgents and erode their support. Sean Gaynor from the IRA's 2nd Division in Tipperary found that in many cases, the clergy's refusal to give them absolution was turning men from the anti-Treaty ranks.[31] Some IRA leaders decried what they saw as hypocrisy: 'Prisoners who die whilst in military custody in the Kerry Command shall be interred by the troops in the area in which the death has taken place. The thundering religious pulpits were strangely silent about what the crows ate in Kerry.'[32]

THE FREE STATE PRESS

At the start of the civil war, the IRA made a fundamental mistake in leaving Dublin and all its instruments of power, including most of the national press, in the hands of its adversaries. This allowed the Free State to present itself to the country and wider world as the lawful government and in overall control.[33]

INFORMATION OPERATIONS

The Free State government had an early and inherent understanding about the power of the press to influence national and international audiences. Government legitimacy, as communicated by the press, became a crucial weapon in its information armoury. For that, it needed good publicity and strong press relations. Michael Collins stated that reporters 'may be allowed to photograph at the discretion of the Officer Commanding operations in any particular area. They will, of course, be asked to undertake that they obey censorship rules issued or to be issued.'[34] Measures to influence and control the press were thus implemented to ensure its support, along with rigorous media censorship, including a prohibition against screening certain films. As early as 29 June 1922, it was decided that newspaper references to the military situation in Dublin would be censored.[35]

On 6 July 1922, a government notice appeared in the *Freeman's Journal* describing the IRA campaign as 'a conspiracy to override the will of the nation and subject the people to a despotism based on brigandage ... regardless of the people's inalienable right to life, liberty and security.' On 11 July, the Cabinet minutes refer to an 'interview with the editor of the *Freeman's Journal* and the *Irish Times* that had produced a good effect', adding that 'these papers had shown a considerable improvement on previous issues.'[36] Not all newspapers were fully compliant; it was observed in the same minutes that 'the attitude of the *Irish Independent* is still unsatisfactory ... The publicity department of the Free State Government should prepare a full statement of the case for Mr. Collins, who will see the proprietor, Mr. Lombard Murphy, on the matter.'

On 12 July, Collins wrote to Desmond FitzGerald, who was in charge of publicity, encouraging him to emphasise the economically destructive nature of the IRA campaign.[37] This became a Free State mantra throughout the civil war, as a National Army report advised: 'Propaganda should be taken now, so that the people will be in no doubt as to what the issue was.'[38] The goals of the Free State were to divide the ranks of the insurgents, to stir up opposition between the mass and the leaders, and to win over the dissidents – classic counterinsurgency tactics described by David

Galula.³⁹ The IRA had to be discredited, undermined, and marginalised in the eyes of the Irish people, because the feeling that 'the poor boys put up a good fight, anyhow' would grow if it were not stamped out. Through the individual soldier and the press, pride in the army should be inculcated in every citizen.⁴⁰

OFFICIAL CENSORSHIP

Censorship policies and measures don't spring fully formed from the state but must be developed and honed. Early in the summer of 1922, a Cabinet meeting revealed dissatisfaction with the manner in which censorship was being conducted. Desmond FitzGerald was instructed to draft a letter to the Army authorities to address the issue.⁴¹ To formalise and regularise censorship procedures, pro-Treaty TD Piaras Béaslaí, a former editor of *An tÓglach* and eventual National Army Major General, was appointed the official military censor. A number of Irish and British publications had their circulation temporarily stopped until a clear press censorship policy had been developed; after a re-alignment, most publications followed Béaslaí's rules and were allowed to circulate.⁴²

Free State censors did not permit the publication of any information about the movements of troops, foodstuffs, trains, transport, or equipment for army purposes. Articles or letters concerning the treatment of the IRA prisoners were suppressed. Government policy insisted on the use of a highly specific vocabulary to subtly undermine the IRA cause and its status as a military force. The volunteers were *Irregulars*, not *Republicans*, who *seized* private property rather than *commandeered* it and *kidnapped* their opponents rather than *arrested* them. Their members were *enrolled* in an organisation, not *enlisted* in a force, and they *fired at* Free State soldiers rather than *attacked* them. The ranks of IRA officers were also not mentioned.⁴³ In contrast, the pro-Treaty forces were to be called the *Irish Army*, the *National Army*, *national forces*, or *troops*, while the *Provisional Government* was the *Irish Government* – or simply, *the government*.⁴⁴

As the Free State forces spread security throughout Cork and Munster, the press followed to counteract the IRA narrative. Their influence was necessary. Once the town of Sneem, in South Kerry, had been secured, for example, the National Army made a discovery: 'There were miles of country between that point and Killarney where the people had not seen a paper for months and were fed solely on Irregular propaganda.'[45]

IRA COUNTERPROPAGANDA

Exasperated by Free State censorship and propaganda, the IRA tried to counter with its own. They initially used coercive methods against the press. In Waterford, an IRA gunman threatened a local newspaper office: 'Your paper has got to be produced as I say, not as you say.'[46] In Cork, the press reported that soon after the National Army's successful landings:

> about forty IRA men with sledgehammers and revolvers entered the *Examiner* office. When the staff refused to leave, shots were fired over their heads to force them outside. IRA Volunteers then systematically smashed up the printing presses, causing £39,000 worth of damage. A similar group went on to the *Constitution* and created another £23,000 worth of destruction.[47]

The IRA issued handbills and press releases to undermine the Free State press. One handbill exclaimed, 'The newspapers can provoke a war, but they cannot win it.'[48] Another handbill from the period informed people that 'the Free State have borrowed British soldiers, British guns, British munitions and British methods. Look around for yourself and see what their denials are worth.'[49] Erskine Childers, the main IRA propagandist, produced pro-Republican press releases and sporadic newsletters complaining that 'the British press of Ireland refuses to publish any of the successes of the Republican troops.'[50]

The IRA consistently re-affirmed its loyalty to the Irish Republic and questioned British support and the partition of Ireland: 'The army of the South is united under Liam Lynch in the defence of the Republic. Men of Dublin where do you stand? With the English allies or with a united South of Ireland?'[51] The *Irish Independent* reported on 10 August 1922 that other IRA slogans were being publicised to question the allegiances of the Free State: 'Collins is marching on Cork—Why not Belfast?'

As well as claiming that the Free State was a proxy for the British establishment, IRA propaganda described the national government as a 'colonial junta' deriving its powers not from the people but from the British. It emphasised the 'mercenary nature of the National Army, which is carrying out a war of re-conquest on the part of the British.'[52] Attempts were made to compare Free State propaganda to the British press: 'Read what the Free State leaflets are saying about Republican soldiers and Republican Prisoners. Remember what the British Press said about Terence MacSwiney.'[53] But handbills and posters had limited success, and the IRA tried other propaganda methods. A National Army report from 15 April 1923 described an increasingly prevalent IRA tactic of serving civilians threatening letters to stop them supporting the Free State.[54]

Without the backing of the mainstream press, however, most IRA statements did not receive wide circulation, and in an already challenging information environment, activities such as commandeering goods and destroying infrastructure significantly reduced support for the Republican cause. IRA West Cork Commander Sean Lehane told Ernie O'Malley that the civilian population was 'practically 90% Free State.'[55] Lacking the support of the Church, the press, or the people, it was very hard for the IRA to counter the Free State information operations campaign.

FREE STATE INFORMATION OPERATIONS IN CORK

Beyond the strategic level, information operations were conducted locally and tactically. Just before the amphibious landings in Cork, Cabinet Minister Desmond FitzGerald made new arrangements for the 'distribution and dissemination of propaganda literature [because previous methods were] unsatisfactory. An aeroplane for use in this connection was now ready, and under control of the civil aviation authority.'[56] A Bristol F.2 fighter was tasked with observing conditions, strafing Republican formations, and dropping thousands of National Army leaflets.[57]

After the National Army secured Cork City, the IRA lost control of its last major media outlets and with them the ability to reach a wider audience. And although the insurgents attempted to deny the attacking force media access by ransacking Cork newspaper offices and wrecking the machinery, the owners of the *Cork Examiner*, the Crosbies, demonstrated remarkable entrepreneurial ability and got the newspaper back onto the streets quickly.[58]

Emmet Dalton understood the importance of maintaining high levels of public support and issued the following edict to his troops operating in Cork: 'It should be remembered that the vast majority of the civilian population is friendly, and that discourteous treatment is likely to alienate their sympathy and friendship.'[59] He further urged his men 'to display discipline through our actions and smartness of dress.' The Free State strategy of portraying its troops as the liberators of Cork City and continued focus on popular support for the army paid off. By September 1922, Dalton declared, 'there are two outstanding points in my favour. I have the good will of the people. They [IRA volunteers] have poor morale owing to the indefiniteness of their objective and owing to the lack of confidence in their leaders.'[60]

This Free State interest in self-promotion continued into 1923. The National Army produced another internal magazine, this one called *The Cap Badge*, to document the actions of its soldiers during the fighting and get the message out.[61]

DIRECTING THE NARRATIVE

With control of the press and Catholic Church, the Free State government dictated the narrative during the civil war, further marginalising and isolating the IRA. Because Republicans abstained from the Dáil, they had no public forum for the views of their political leadership.[62] And once their occupation of provincial towns ended – and with it control of the *Cork Examiner* and other newspapers – they had no hope of seeing the IRA cause represented in the Irish press.[63]

A successful counterinsurgency campaign must be supported by an effective publicity campaign, as Dalton and the National Army understood from the early stages of the civil war. Too late, the IRA leadership recognised the consequences of a failed propaganda strategy: 'increasing support for the F.S. [Free State] Government, consequent on our failure to combat the false propaganda.'[64] IRA leader Harry Boland remarked on the telling effect, that 'the people in the main' undoubtedly blamed the Republican side for the state of the country's affairs.[65]

The Free State leadership had its own clear view: 'Our propaganda should be on a more solid and permanent basis even if what may look to be advantages have to be sacrificed.'[66] Solid propaganda combined with good press relations were essential. A National Army report from April 1923 states that 'spectacular show, parades, route marches, etc. and all other methods of indirect propaganda produce very good results here and should be concentrated on.'[67] The army found that the indirect propaganda of such displays prompted a 'most gratifying' response from the citizens.[68] The reaction to these shows of force was closely monitored, and command reports noted that 'our own people are taking up the proper attitude in relations with the army.'[69] The people of Cork were 'beginning to see light, [being] quite friendly towards our troops and [it is believed that] most of these men will one day join either the Army or Civic Guard.'[70]

The posture and profile of the National Army thus paid dividends throughout the civil war. As the war concluded, even the most stridently Republican areas became more favourably inclined to the Free State. On 5 May 1923, a National Army report observed that 'in West Cork it is altogether untrue that the people were really hostile to us ... People seemed glad to have our troops in their locality and treated them in most cases without reserve or suspicion. In some cases, they gave information more freely than has been experienced in any other part of Ireland.'[71] This was an important consequence of the effective information operations campaign.

Hunted and harassed, the IRA faced increasing difficulties. By March 1923, its fighters could put up armed opposition at full column strength in only a few more mountainous areas.[72] As the remaining fighters did their best to evade capture, morale was sharply wounded when several iconic Republicans were killed in action, taken prisoner, or surrendered. Dinny Lacey was killed on 18 February 1923 and a seriously injured Con Moloney was captured on 7 March. Dan Breen capitulated without a fight when discovered in a dugout on 17 April 1923.[73]

The capture of Liam Deasy proved even worse. Deasy was tried by court martial on 25 January 1923, and found guilty of 'having in his possession, without proper authority, one long Parabellum revolver and twenty-one rounds of ammunition.'[74] He was duly sentenced to death. The Free State decided not to create a martyr, however, and instead struck another blow in the psychological war. A stay of execution was ordered and, following negotiations, Deasy signed a document agreeing to aid in an immediate unconditional surrender of men and arms, and stating that he would appeal to Liam Lynch and the Republican executive to do likewise.[75] The statement shattered IRA morale.

In a letter to Liam Lynch on 11 February 1923, Frank Barrett, an IRA officer from Clare, wrote that until Deasy's declaration, 'I had no doubt but we could have defeated the Free-State army, and compelled the Free-State government to capitulate. My hopes of ever doing this now are not all bright. Anyhow to do so will exhaust our last resources and England is there always.'[76]

THE TIDE OF PUBLIC OPINION

The combination of limited popular backing and National Army military success forced the most ardent Republicans to accept that the Free

State policies were defeating the IRA. As 1923 progressed, most of its leadership and fighting cadre were dead, injured, imprisoned, or in hiding, leaving very few men in the field to question state authority. The Free State continued to detain IRA prisoners for a time after the civil war, until it was clear that the fighting was over. Up to 90 per cent of them remained in detention until the end of 1923, and all were eventually set free before the autumn of 1924.[77]

The substantial support of the Catholic Church and press proved to be hugely significant in the information battle, helping the Free State control the narrative, undercut the IRA cause, and mobilise popular support. Because the government was Irish and had popular approval, the Church could enthusiastically endorse the established order.[78] In Cork, Dalton immediately shaped the information narrative by securing the support of both the Catholic and the Protestant bishop.

As Roger Trinquier argues, any propaganda that weakens the state's morale or causes it to doubt the necessity of its sacrifice is to be immediately repressed.[79] Throughout the civil war, targeted information operations led the Irish population to believe that supporting the IRA would lead to more commandeering and infrastructure damage. The Free State put forward a compelling message that economic prosperity and peace were best achieved by betting on the government.

BUILD

The build phase of clear–hold–build operations consists of carrying out programs designed to remove the root causes that led to the insurgency, improve the lives of the inhabitants, and strengthen the host nation's ability to provide effective governance.

US Army FM 3-24.2,
Tactics in Counterinsurgency (April 2009), 3–21

To rebuild is to do it all again.

10

THE RESTORATION OF ESSENTIAL SERVICES

> The construction of a new state with enduring democratic institutions, an army subservient to the civil power, an unarmed police force and a meritocratic civil service free from political interference are seen rightly as the great achievement of the treatyite regime between 1922–32.
>
> J.M. Regan, "The Politics of Utopia", 32

As part of an overall strategy to destabilise the Free State government, the IRA conducted an extensive and systematic campaign to destroy the essential services and railway infrastructure of the new state. Nearly a fifth of Republican operations in Munster took the form of railway sabotage of some kind. The objective was not just to deny the railways to government forces but to paralyse the whole system.[1] Essential services were in danger of collapse and in desperate need of repair.[2] Kevin O'Higgins assessed that the 'wheels of administration lay idle, battered out of recognition by the clash of rival jurisdictions.'[3] If the Free State wanted to win the war, it would have to rebuild the capacity of the state – and in the process dig up and destroy the roots of the insurgency.[4]

Phase Four of combat operations involves capacity building and returning stability to a conflict zone. Capacity building is a process of creating an environment that fosters institutional development, community participation, improved governance, and the development of the economy and infrastructure.[5] The Free State government would have to make a cohesive and all-encompassing effort to rebuild Irish capacity by re-establishing and co-ordinating the institutions that facilitated such basic functions as civil participation, livelihood, and the well-being of citizens and the state. A co-ordinated approach is vitally important to any government operating in a counterinsurgency. It must co-ordinate all the instruments at its disposal and empower its citizens – thereby, making them more willing to provide support – to avoid working in a vacuum. The government achieves this by delivering services and demonstrating the value of a joint civil–military organisation that can control this space.[6]

Capacity building and the restoration of essential infrastructure constitute one of the most effective strategies in a counterinsurgency, and it is, therefore, instructive to analyse how the Free State rebuilt essential services and railway infrastructure of Ireland in a co-ordinated manner at both national and local levels.[7] That analysis must be preceded, however, by an examination of the extensive damage to infrastructure caused by the IRA and the ramifications of these actions for both the IRA and the National Army.

THE IRA CAMPAIGN OF DESTRUCTION

> There never has been a case of any country in which such a fierce attack was made on its railway system.
>
> Notes for a speech, possibly by Mulcahy, in the Mulchahy Papers

Ireland in this period relied on the railway and road system. When this network was incapacitated, freedom of movement, social interaction, trade, and development ground to a halt, literally and figuratively. After Republican saboteurs had inflicted massive damage, prominent national-

THE RESTORATION OF ESSENTIAL SERVICES

ist Mary Spring Rice noted in her diary 'This is the end of the first phase' and asked 'What will the second be?'[8]

The effect of the IRA campaign was profound, yet many Republicans displayed a remarkable indifference to the problems posed to the population. Con Moloney, the adjutant of the IRA 2nd Division in Munster, demonstrated a characteristic attitude when he suggested in correspondence with Ernie O'Malley that the inhabitants of local communities would eventually 'settle down to the inconvenience of rail and road destruction.'[9] He expected them to get on with life.

THE FIRST ATTACKS ON CORK INFRASTRUCTURE

Disorder is cheap to provoke and very costly to prevent.[10] After the IRA had lost the conventional warfare phase, road and rail disruption may have been the best-organised aspect of its defence of the Munster Republic. As noted earlier, bridges began to explode around Cork within 90 minutes of the National Army landing.[11] As fighting continued and the IRA withdrew from the city, the cantilevered railway bridges spanning the River Lee were in line for destruction. On Tuesday evening, 8 August 1922, as the army advanced on Cork City, the railway bridge outside Rochestown shattered in a deafening explosion, cutting the road from Passage West to the city centre and causing panic among city residents.[12] Their fear intensified as the Douglas Channel bridge was brought down, rupturing the railway line and blocking the electric tramway to Cork. In the early hours of Wednesday morning, IRA engineers blew up the Fota railway bridge, severing the Cork-to-Cobh rail line as part of what John Borgonovo refers to as a preconceived defensive response to the anticipated landings.[13] Once Cork was no longer defensible, the IRA dumped its trucks, cars, and motorcycles into the river rather than letting them fall into Free State hands.[14]

IRA engineers were also busy across Cork Harbour. The 9th IRA Battalion destroyed the piers at Ringaskiddy and Currabinny by setting them alight.[15] The *Irish Times* reported on 12 August that in the early morning of the tenth, IRA engineers had blown up part of the Chetwynd railway viaduct, about two miles south-west of the city on the Bandon road, and wrecked the Rathpeacon viaduct north of Cork, severing the Great Southern and Western Railway. Frank Brewitt provided an eyewitness account: 'There were huge explosions during the early hours and these were the viaduct on the Bandon and South Coast Railway and the Rathpeacon Viaduct on the Great Southern and Western Railway, thus stopping every railway and closing 5/6 of our business down.'[16]

IRA efforts to destroy the city's essential infrastructure prior to the arrival of the National Army were both comprehensive and deliberate. On 13 August 1922, the National Army conducted an aerial reconnaissance to ascertain the scale of destruction. The pilot reported, 'The main road from Kanturk to Charleville via Freemount was apparently clear. Bridges were observed to be blown up including the railway bridge crossing [the River] Blackwater at Mallow.'[17]

Even after the IRA withdrew from Cork City, the *Cork Examiner* carried multiple reports of 'wanton destruction' conducted in August and September 1922.

> MORE DESTRUCTION—Bridges Destroyed near Cork
> During Monday night the Irregulars were very active close to the city, on the Western and Northern sides, and the wanton destruction of bridges continued.[18]

> DRIPSEY BRIDGE BLOWN UP
> During the early hours of yesterday morning the Irregulars blew up Dripsey bridge and now people of the Macroom area have to come to Cork by Berrings and Clougduv as other bridges in the same area had previously been removed by explosives.[19]

> DESTRUCTION OF PROPERTY
> Midleton, Thursday—The loss of the East Ferry floating bridge which was destroyed or nearly so by the Irregulars is causing serious inconvenience to passengers and traffic from Cobh.[20]

TELEGRAPH WIRES CUT—YOUGHAL TRAINS DELAYED
Owing to the cutting of telegraph wires during the night.[21]

RAILWAY POSITION REPORTS IN CORK

Cork is a good case study of the IRA campaign, as some 32 bridges were damaged or wrecked in the weeks following the landings.[22] A series of reports filed by the Ministry of Economic Affairs in 1922 vividly describes the systematic destruction of the county's railway network and the initial efforts of the National Army to protect and restore these essential services:

24 August	Chetwynd viaduct, 5 miles from Cork, is very badly damaged. The company has had over from England representatives of the firm who constructed the bridge and it will take considerable time before necessary repairs can be affected.[23]
24 August	Ballymantle Bridge, 17 miles from Cork on line to Kinsale, is small and can probably be repaired in a few days.[24]
24 August	Cork and Muskerry Railway, A three arch span masonry bridge four miles from Cork over the River Lee has been seriously damaged. In this case perhaps you could use your influence with the authorities responsible so that repairs may be proceeded with at once.[25]
25 August	GSW Railways: The viaduct at 91½ miles between Wellington Bridge and Ballycullane was almost completely destroyed by explosives on the night of 23/24 Augustust 1922.[26]
26 August	GSW Railways: Bridge No. 4 near Glanworth Station was burned, Bridge No. 7 between Glanworth and Ballindanger was damaged by explosives. Bridge No. 36 between Fermoy and Clondule was damaged by explosives.[27]

26 August	Bridge No 4 near Glanworth station was burned. Bridge No 7 between Glanworth and Ballindangan was damaged by explosives. Bridge No 36 between Fermoy and Clondulane was damaged by explosives.[28]
29 August	A bridge between Barna and Devon Road was blown up.[29]
30 August	GSW Railways: The company report that Carrick Bridge between Mallow and Castletownroche was blown up.[30]

Other Free State reports from September 1922 indicate that the widespread destruction was seriously affecting routine life: 'Communications stopped to Killarney and all beyond, to Bandon and all west, to Fermoy and Mallow.'[31] By late 1922, the railway routes to the south and west had ceased to function.[32]

OUTLINE OF THE IRA UNITS COMMITTING THE DAMAGE

The IRA was split into five brigade areas in County Cork.[33] As the active fighters battled Free State forces, inexperienced newer recruits were disarmed and re-designated into next-best, or Y Class, units. These volunteers were sent back to their own areas with instructions to organise, do intelligence work, destroy roads and railways, keep up sniping operations, and remain in a position to co-operate with the flying columns in their areas.[34]

The Y Class IRA men were the primary conduits for the assault on the essential services and infrastructure of Munster during this period. Their units were equipped with high explosives that had been taken from the *Upnor* as the raw materials for landmines and explosive devices.[35] As a result of this and other high-explosive seizures, the trail of destruction continued. Most IRA operations took the form of railway sabotage of some kind, denying the rail routes to government forces and destroying the system.[36]

Cork No. 4 Brigade, operating in North Cork, was one of the busiest units involved in the destruction of infrastructure. Its operations

THE RESTORATION OF ESSENTIAL SERVICES

for October 1922 give a sense of the scale of damage caused in a single month:

2 October	3rd Battalion, 4th Brigade, destroys 10 bridges in the vicinity of Charleville and Liscarroll. Charleville–Buttevant and Charleville–Doneraile roads blocked, all roads in the area trenched.
5 October	5th Battalion, 4th Brigade, destroys 15 bridges in the vicinity of Mallow. Roads in the area blocked, telegraph poles cut between Mallow and Lombardstown and between Mallow and Buttevant. Railway signal cabs at Mourneabbey and Lombardstown destroyed.
17 October	3rd Battalion, 4th Brigade, cuts poles and wires on railway line between Charleville and Buttevant. Trenches created on the Charleville–Dromina and Milford–Drumcollogher roads.
20 October	3rd Battalion, 4th Brigade, causes serious damage to the railway line between Ballinguile Bridge and Shannagh. Poles and wires cut.
21 October	3rd Battalion, 4th Brigade, fires on breakdown gang repairing the railway line.[37]

A WINTER OF DISCONTENT

> Making government impossible is your only chance of success and for the past month it has been more effective than for the six months prior to that.
>
> Letter to Pa Murray, 13 February 1923, Mulcahy Papers

As the fighting progressed, preventing the Free State government from functioning became one of the IRA's main purposes. On 17 August 1922, the *Cork Examiner* declared that 'the damage suffered by the Cork Harbour Commissioners as a result of the Irregulars using and destroying part of their plant and property is estimated to be at least £14,000.' A month later, on 27 September, the paper reported that IRA volunteers had destroyed the telegraph office at the General Post Office and the telephone exchange on MacCurtain Street. While it may have been tactically astute, however, the damage was strategically unwise. It compounded Cork's economic woes during harvest time, provoking strong animosity among civilians.[38]

Not all Republicans supported the policy. Shrewder IRA commanders, such as Ernie O'Malley, protested the destruction of communications as an end in itself: 'I thought the policy a fatal one, giving an excuse to men in some areas who would not fight. If such tearing up of rails and roads was to be a prelude to good fighting, then it was justified, otherwise not.'[39] According to the Cork Chamber of Commerce, the common perception throughout this period was that if Republicans wanted to understand their growing unpopularity 'they needed to look no further than the nearest collapsed bridge.'[40]

Local community leaders pointed out to the Republican leadership the disastrous social and economic consequences such actions were having for the state. Éamon de Valera responded that it was a military necessity, a view stemming from the idea that Republicans had a 'vested interest in disorder, whether or not they inspired it, because it underlined the government's lack of practical authority.'[41]

As 1922 drew to a close, the destruction of the Cork railway system, therefore, remained an IRA priority. On 29 December, the organisation's Director of Engineering emphasised the goal of 'bringing railways to a standstill, as on this to a great extent depends the success of our campaign.'[42] By January, the monthly report by the Civic Guard for Cork East Riding indicated that while Republican activity had been 'formerly chiefly directed against the army and army posts ... it is now concentrated with a view to ruin on the economical side ... [including the destruction of] railways and all sources of revenue for the state.'[43] A National Army report from the Charleville area on 21 January stated that a 'large force of Irregulars have been operating in this area and traces of their activity are shown in the blocking of roads and railways. Shinana Bridge came into the line of destruction.'[44] Map 5 indicates the scale of widespread and indiscriminate destruction in the county up to the start of 1923, especially in North Cork, the No. 4 Brigade area. The policy of trying to make governance impossible was having the desired effect.

As the IRA continued to train its attention on undermining Free State authority, it also imposed compulsory levies on the population and employers. Its fighters robbed post offices for funds, interfered with newspaper distribution, and disrupted transport. These activities continued throughout the civil war: 331 raids on post offices between 23 March and 19 April 1923; and 319 armed attacks on the Great Southern and Western Railway between 1 March and 22 April 1923.[45]

Frustration deepened among Free State politicians, who saw that the growing toll on property and communications threatened effective governance across the country. Constant reports of burned-out railway stations and bombings hurt the economy by discouraging both external and internal investment in the new state.[46] The Free State leadership had to stabilise the situation and restore infrastructure and essential services. Solutions would have to be innovative and systematic.

NATIONAL ARMY ACTIONS AND POLICY

> As early as 5 August 1922, General Eoin O'Duffy had found it necessary to issue a proclamation stating that troops had been authorised to fire on persons committing a variety of offences such as destroying bridges and railway lines, blocking roads, felling trees and looting.
>
> *Irish Independent*, 5 August 1922

By 22 September 1922, the *Irish Independent* was reporting that local authorities were overwhelmed. With respect to the southern railway system, it noted, 'the damage in practically every direction is so serious that in some cases years must elapse before a complete service is attempted.' A National Army report published in January 1923 was staggering; over the previous 12 months, railway lines had been damaged in 375 places and 42 engines had been derailed, while 51 over-bridges, 207 under-bridges, 83 signal cabins, and 13 other buildings had been destroyed.[47] In Cork County alone, the IRA destroyed 211 bridges and 301 railway buildings between 1917 and 1923; most of the damage, especially to bridges, occurred during the civil war.[48]

In times of conflict, a counterinsurgent force can, if necessary, establish or restore the most basic services and protect them until a civil authority can provide them, thereby, helping to meet the population's basic needs.[49] But transportation infrastructure underpins that process. As one of the few instruments of power operating during the early stages of the Free State, the National Army had to reverse the momentum of destruction and provide a safe environment to permit normal life to continue.

At both the national and local levels, Irish military forces played a significant role in stabilisation and also infrastructural development. Restoration of essential services included protecting, repairing, and reconstructing state infrastructure. It complemented Free State efforts to stabilise the economy by focusing on the physical elements that make a state economically viable.[50]

THE RESOLVE TO REBUILD

The National Army had to demonstrate its resolve to the Irish public and show it was capable of rebuilding the country after years of warfare and division. Rebuilding the railways would also demonstrate the futility of the IRA sabotage. Michael Collins was aware of this; his notebook entry of 20 August 1922 records the need 'to send Engineering help to Mallow' when the bridge crossing the River Blackwater was blown up.[51] Emmet Dalton would also recall in later life how Collins had told him of the need to capture Cork City intact because disruption of road and rail links would leave the Republican forces in full control of Munster.[52]

Efforts to rebuild started early and in earnest. The *Cork Examiner* reported on 12 August, just after the Cork landings, that 'taking advantage of the darkness, National Army soldiers cleared away some of the wreckage and made the Rochestown bridge, previously damaged by the IRA, accessible to foot traffic'. At a national level, a tentative reconstruction policy was formulated. Acting Minister of Labour Patrick Hogan reported to the government that railway lines would 'be repaired for the period 21st August to 3rd September inclusive, to the following sections of the Great Southern & Western Railway: Mallow to Waterford (excluding Waterford), Mallow to Kilmallock.'[53]

The Free State government also focused its propaganda on what it called the 'campaign of destruction' being waged by the IRA, taking particular note of interference with railways, roads, and bridges, injury to industries, and destruction of property.[54] W.T. Cosgrave believed that the best way to stop a campaign of outrage and destruction was to let it be seen for what it was, remarking that it was 'rousing the people to opposition.'[55]

THE NEED FOR OUTSIDE SUPPORT

Pro-Treaty sources nonetheless admitted that the IRA tactics were threatening to undermine confidence in the government's stability.[56] Definite actions needed to be taken, but the situation was something of a vicious circle; stability was threatened while at the same time, as Donal Cororan notes, 'money was scarce and difficult to borrow due to the state's instability and fears that it might be unable to repay.'[57] Initial efforts by the National Army to restore essential services were admirable but inadequate owing to the sheer scale of the destruction.

The repair of railway bridges and the protection of those carrying out the work was a particular priority for Dalton and the National Army, and he and other Free State generals quickly ascertained that they would need additional support.[58] Dalton asked General Headquarters to send aircraft pilot Colonel Charles Russell to conduct aerial reconnaissance.[59] On 19 September 1922, Dalton told Mulcahy, he was starting to restore the bridges that the IRA had destroyed in August: 'Protection for Rathpeacon and other bridges arranged, work about to go ahead.'[60]

The government decided to provide external and expert support at national and local levels in the form of civil engineer expertise – crucial professional assistance, especially in repairing the all-important railway system. In a letter to the General Staff of the National Army, Mulcahy announced the appointment of a government consulting engineer, a Dr J.F. Crowley of 16 Victoria Street, London, who would have offices in Merrion Street and would 'especially control and advise in connection with our present railway work.'[61] The repair work was also decentralised. Cork Corporation took responsibility for the administration of funds for rebuilding and 'ensuring payments were made only with engineering certificate of work done.'[62]

External expertise was utilised by the Free State throughout the country, but the task of rebuilding was extensive, and the National Army was required to support the strategy. For that, it had to find the capacity within its own organisation to load and spread resources and reduce the costs.

THE RAILWAY PROTECTION CORPS

The railway engines and tracks became essential assets for the Free State and protecting them was an important element of the army's campaign. The army leadership, in conjunction with the Great Southern and Western Railway Company, considered how to best to do so in the summer months of 1922. Both sides understood the requirement for a coherent strategy in this regard. The National Government wrote to the railway manager about:

> the vital necessity of maintaining as far as possible on your company's system a service of trains adequate not only for military requirements of the Government but also for the distribution of food supplies to the population and the maintenance of trade generally. To effect this every

THE RESTORATION OF ESSENTIAL SERVICES

effort should be made to have any obstacle to traffic caused by the breaking or obstructing of the lines removed at the earliest possible moment.[63]

In late July 1922, the Ministry of Economic Affairs wrote to the Minister for Defence:

> I am informed that if the government wish to complete immediately the armoured train there will be no difficulty in getting volunteers from men employed at Inchicore and the Great Southern & Western Railway generally to work day and night to complete it at very short notice. I think also that the time has come to urge Portobello to put a guard on all trains.[64]

Great Southern and Western Railways management was aware that the Ministry of Economics needed to be 'appraised immediately of any interruption of traffic and should be kept constantly informed as to the progress made with works of repair.'[65] By early August 1922, Mulcahy had issued General Order No. 12, outlining the importance of the issue:

> It is desired to give some protection to those goods trains, with a view of preventing interference with them by Irregulars, and, at the same time, keep in touch with the general conditions of railway traffic along the routes mentioned. To this end it will be arranged that as far as possible use will be made of those goods trains to transport military stores, and a suitable guard will be sent with those stores.[66]

The practical need to formalise arrangements with the railway companies led to the creation of a dedicated unit within the army to support and protect the railways.

Free State Cabinet minutes from September noted that the activities of the IRA had forced about 1,200 railway employees to remain idle. It was suggested that their services might be utilised for police or military work in connection with maintaining railway services, and the matter was referred to the Commander-in-Chief.⁶⁷ On 20 September 1922, Mulcahy told Dalton to enrol a number of these unemployed workers in the army to repair and guard the lines, adding that he would arrange with the quartermaster general to send rifles 'for the immediate arming of some of these men.'⁶⁸ This force of railwaymen was formed into a specialised army unit commanded by a major general. It was to be known as the Railway Preservation, Maintenance and Repair Corps – or simply the Railway Protection Corps.⁶⁹

Members of the new corps were predominantly rail workers and navvies, and they were paid at very favourable rates. The Railway Protection Corps was deployed throughout the state, and in Cork was controlled from headquarters at Wellington Barracks in order to cover the important points along the Dublin-to-Cork line.⁷⁰ The corps soon became an imperative part of, and enabler within, the growing National Army.⁷¹ A report from January 1923 states that 'the closing down of the railways out of Cork to the west and north of the area is responsible for a very serious economic position' and highlights the importance of the initial works undertaken by the Railway Protection Corps:

> The people are almost entirely dependent on road transport, and if even goods trains could be run, the position would not be quite so bad. The Railway Maintenance Corps have begun work on the smaller lines out of Cork … but in the immediate future, there seems very little hope that the people will be facilitated in this matter.⁷²

The National Army magazine *An t-Óglách* published articles on the corps in the spring of 1923. One from 2 April refers to its 'worthwhile jobs of bridge repairing and maintaining the railway service', while another from 21 April described the protection work in more detail:

> The tactics utilised by the Railway Protection, Repair and Maintenance Corps to protect the railway network was varied. The Corps established blockhouses at all important bridges, signal cabins and stations. Use

THE RESTORATION OF ESSENTIAL SERVICES

was also made of improvised armoured trains, consisting of Lancia cars attached to the roofs of railway carriages; later in the war, swivel turrets were used [on the trains] to enable the machine-gunners to fire in all directions.

The Railway Protection Corps grew exponentially in both size and capabilities. By 1 April 1923, it had a strength of 165 officers plus 3,789 other ranks.[73] By this time it had become one of the most effective and important units in the army. A mid-April army report noted the remarkable progress: 'The improved rail and line (telephonic and telegraphic) communications is perhaps one of the best indications of the changed situation ... The Railway Protection and Maintenance Corps are engaged on the work of repair on the few closed sections.'[74]

An after-action report on National Army operations in West Cork and South Kerry gives the following examples of the efficiency that had been achieved by the end of April:

Sunday 29 April 1923
On this day the Railway Corps started operations from Headford Junction and proceeded along the line towards Kenmare ... The line ... was badly damaged and progress was very slow ... At some points along the line the train with troops and supplies was moved along by lifting rails behind the train and placing them in front. The Railway Corps, however, succeeded in establishing all posts and reached Kenmare on Sunday night.

...

For the past week our troops have swarmed all over the area, penetrated into the most remote places, trickled here, there, and everywhere, roads have been opened to motor traffic (some of which were closed since the War against the English), bridges down for years have been rebuilt. At first the people were interested spectators in all this week but by degrees they began to take a hand and could be seen towards the end of the week helping at the building of bridges and assisting our troops in every way ... Of course there are still sections of the people suspicious and irresponsive but the constructive work done under their eyes is helping more than anything else to overcome their fears and suspicions.

...

Every important road in Cork and Kerry has been opened in a way which will allow the people to travel between villages and towns.[75]

The work undoubtedly played a major part in restoring not only infrastructure but also the credibility of the Free State government within this region. The participation of local people in the repair of essential infrastructure undermined IRA efforts to provoke disorder and drive a wedge between the population and the government.

The corps won much praise in the Dáil, where Labour TD William Davin declared that the units had saved the country millions of pounds.[76] The formation of the Railway Protection Corps certainly repaired and protected the railway system and saved the Irish population from undue hardship. It also helped save the government's authority among that population.

THE SALVAGE PROTECTION CORPS

The Railway Protection Corps was not the only specialist National Army unit involved in restoring essential services. The Salvage Protection Corps was a precursor to the Army Engineer Corps. It overcame formidable difficulties to help stabilise the Irish Free State in the face of the IRA onslaught against essential services.[77]

As the civil war was drawing to an end, the Commander-in-Chief mentioned that National Army soldiers should be used for construction work before they were demobbed.[78] The Salvage Protection Corps prepared schemes for new work and vetted projects initiated by commands that were now subdivided into districts serviced by an engineer officer with technical staff and essential stores.[79]

An example of the kind of work undertaken by the Salvage Protection Corps can be seen in the restoration of Carrig Viaduct, located four miles from Mallow in North Cork. IRA forces had destroyed this important piece of regional railway and transport infrastructure on 30 August 1922.[80] Nearly a year later, on 21 August 1923, the consulting engineers J.F. Crawley and Partners reported to the Ministry of Defence that reconstruction had been completed. Throughout this process, which continued for some months after the end of the war, a military guard of one officer and 18 men had been placed on the viaduct to protect it and the ongoing engineering works despite financial restraints.[81]

The 13 September 1923 meeting of the Cork County Council reflects the difficulty of funding the arduous process of reconstruction:

> A long discussion took place on the damaged and dangerous bridges which were many and widespread throughout the county … The Council had no money to do the work, the overdraft was £100,000, the Government were delaying the payment of grants and would not allow the Council to retain the motor tax collected in the county.[82]

Nevertheless, financial support for the work slowly started to flow to the local authorities. On 28 February 1924, Cork County Council 'welcomed the notification of a grant of £100,000 from the Department of Local Government for the improvement of Trunk Roads.'[83] Along with National Army support these funds helped county officials rebuild essential infrastructure in the months and years after the withdrawal of IRA forces. The Carrig Viaduct was a symbolically significant element of this plan.

RESTORING MUNSTER'S INFRASTRUCTURE

Army reports in the spring of 1923 observed that rail and line destruction had decreased and the main road routes in all command areas were 'trafficable, and in most commands, in good condition.'[84] Army engineers had overcome many difficulties with 'any slight interruptions being remedied in a few hours.'[85]

Lieutenant Mullane, an officer based in Cork, noted that efforts to repair sometimes included forced civilian labour: 'Left Macroom with a party of 25 men. When I got to Carriganimma, which was the objective, I commandeered about 20 [local] men and got them to repair the bridge which was broken.'[86] Troops from the National Army, 59th Infantry Battalion, based in the vicinity of Blarney, also regularly conducted infrastructure protection patrols and 'captured two prominent Irregulars … [who admitted to] blowing up bridges, robbing of mails and robbing of St. Ann's Post Office.'[87] By removing IRA saboteurs and activists from the battlefield, the Free State helped prevent the destruction of more essential infrastructure. A weekly command situation report from 15 March 1923 notes that there had been only '6 Attacks on Commercial Transport [and] 1 Bridge wrecked.'[88]

The National Army understood the positive effect its works were having on the population, detailing that 'a quiet optimism is general'. Restoration of train services 'has awakened business in country towns. Food supplies and civilian transport are adequate.'[89] By May 1923, all roads in the command area were available for transportation apart from a portion of south-western Cork, and all rail services were restored except for the problematic Mallow–Waterford and Cork–Macroom lines.[90]

Army intelligence reports from 1924 continued to reflect the importance the Free State placed on the restoration of essential infrastructure: 'Government grants for road improvement are very welcome at the present time, and will help to some extent.'[91]

CARROTS, NOT STICKS

The IRA policy of making government impossible translated into wholesale destruction during the civil war; it used up scarce resources and delayed development. It also lost the support of the Irish population – and ultimately the war. As the Free State government protected and repaired essential infrastructure, especially in Munster and Cork, it slowly gained the upper hand in the battle for public support. Principally the Free State government understood the psychological effect of restoring and protecting essential services. It allowed trade to resume, helped to restore normal life, and improved living standards. Moreover, entities such as the Railway and Salvage Protection corps brought freedom of movement for both the military and civilians. As key roads, railways, and communication lines were resuscitated, so too was the economy. The process swung public opinion behind the government and marginalised the IRA.

11

SUPPORTING GOVERNANCE

> Simply eight young men in the City Hall, standing amidst the ruins of one administration, with the foundations of another not yet laid, and with wild men screaming through the keyholes.
>
> Minister for Justice Kevin O'Higgins, Irish Free State, Address to the Irish Society at Oxford University, 31 October 1924

With poverty comes instability. Poor economic conditions lead to unemployment, disenfranchisement, discontent, and subversion. Conversely, with improved governance, economic management, and living conditions come an enhanced standard of living, less corruption, and stronger popular support. Military tasks executed to support governance and the financial sector are essential to sustainable economic and infrastructure development, and help a government to restore stability.[1]

The Free State understood that a functioning government must be financially viable, uphold a common set of rules, and operate in a stable environment both nationally and locally. Government policies were connected with, and directly affected, regional activity, especially in Munster and Cork, and governance was pushed down to the local level in order to stabilise the new Irish state.

GOOD GOVERNANCE

> The government is simply a Committee with a mandate to make certain conditions prevail, to make life and property safe, and to vindicate the legal rights of their fellow citizens.
>
> Kevin O'Higgins, memorandum, 11 January 1923

US Army Doctrine FM 3-07 defines governance as the state's ability to serve its citizens through the rules, processes, and behaviour by which interests are articulated, resources are managed, and power is exercised in a society. This includes the representative, participatory decision-making processes typically guaranteed under inclusive and constitutional authority.

Good governance, according to Jacqueline Hazelton, must provide political, economic, and social reforms that meet the needs of the population and gain its support, and it must make sure that these reforms reduce the grievances fuelling the insurgency.[2] Effective, legitimate governance is transparent, accountable, and incorporates public participation; the activities of good governance are among the most important in ensuring lasting stability.[3] In the Ireland of 1922, Minister Kevin O'Higgins argued, 'nothing could be more disastrous than the virtual isolation of the government. A responsible government meant one that had to answer to the people.'[4]

Military support essentially sets the enabling conditions for governance by providing the requisite security. In other words, it empowers national and local governments to perform their elected duties during and in the aftermath of conflict: restoring public administration, the economy, infrastructure, and public services. While military support, so necessary at the start of a crisis, also fosters longer-term efforts to establish a functional, effective political system, it cannot take precedence over civil governance. Separation of powers is essential to a functioning and stable state.

The Free State government and army found themselves in conflict over the independence of state institutions and the division of civil and military powers. That this dispute was settled in favour of civil institutions was crucial to the democratic development of the new Irish state, but that outcome was by no means certain at the outset of the civil war.[5] The governing political party of the Irish Free State during this period believed that the people's loyalty depended on its ability to satisfy the needs and hopes of its supporters.[6] But the governing party must respond to the needs of the entire population, throughout the whole country.

A DANGEROUS ALTERNATIVE

> The Government has made it fully clear that its desire is to secure obedience of proper authority. When an expression of such obedience comes from the Irregular leaders, I take it that there will no longer be any necessity for armed conflict. When the Irregulars—leaders and men—see fit to obey the wishes of the people, as expressed through their elected representatives, ... there will be no longer need for hostilities.
>
> Michael Collins to Michael O Cuill,
People's Rights Association, Cork, 4 August 1922

With the signing of the Treaty, most people on both sides of the divide had hoped that the Free State government could be trusted to provide political and economic stability and protect the rights of property owners. They feared the alternative: that if the IRA were to gain the upper hand the country would be plunged into renewed war with little prospect of a functioning civil administration.[7] As the British government apparatus in Ireland began to be dismantled, it left an obvious and dangerous vacuum in civil governance and security. This ungoverned space was initially filled at the local level by Irish Republican forces, especially in the western and southern regions.[8]

W.T. Cosgrave, the President of the Executive Council of the Irish Free State, realised the urgent need to replace their dominance with governance operations:

> It is my intention to implement this Treaty as sanctioned by vote of the Dáil and the electorate in so far as it was free to express an opinion; to enact the Constitution not yet framed; to assert the authority and supremacy of the parliament; to support and assist the National Army in asserting the people's rights; to ask parliament, if necessary, for such powers as may be deemed essential for the purpose of restoring order.[9]

Restoring public order is a key provision of effective governance operations, because it establishes the rule of law and satisfies the needs of the entire country, regardless of political affiliation.[10]

Chaos and crisis thrive in a security vacuum, especially if the government is unable to fill the contested space and faces adversaries determined to do so. The Free State had to fill the ungoverned areas – and quickly – with 'governance operations—those political and military activities undertaken by military forces to establish and institutionalize a desired political order during and following the combat phase of war.'[11] As one of the state's first functioning organisations, the National Army was initially the only entity available to respond to this challenge.

The independence movement had spawned a rebel counter-state to undermine the British civil administration throughout Ireland during the War of Independence.[12] As previously mentioned, for six weeks at the start of the new conflict, it seemed the anti-Treatyites would do the same, offering something like a Republican government apparatus, based in Cork. In the spring and early summer of 1922, the IRA established the Munster Republic as a direct and dangerous alternative to the predominantly Dublin-based Irish Free State government.[13] Michael Collins and his colleagues worried that the south-western province would form a breakaway region within the new state.[14] Lord Midleton had previously warned of just such a possibility, telling King George V, 'the hasty withdrawal of British troops, against which your Majesty's Government were repeatedly warned, has left the South of Ireland without any force to preserve order and even if individuals were made amenable, there are no courts sitting effectively to deal with them.'[15]

The Munster Republic was not a functioning economic entity, however, and Charles Townsend suggests that the IRA had no intention of replicating the earlier Republican civil administration. For many, the Munster Republic remained primarily symbolic.[16] It was essentially a military government, with Liam Lynch as military governor.

Had the IRA managed to establish an actual shadow government in Cork, it would undoubtedly have increased its credibility and legitimacy. But this did not materialise, and criticism of Lynch's reluctance to consider social and economic issues spread throughout the Republican movement.[17] He was not a strategic politician, and he was increasingly preoccupied by the military sphere. In early September 1922, Lynch himself confirmed as much to his deputy commander, Liam Deasy:

> I know of no alternative policy to the present one of fighting we could adopt.... At present it is a waste of time to be thinking too much about policy; we should strike our hardest for some time, and this would make the question of policy easier to settle.'[18]

Peader O'Donnell, a member of the IRA executive in 1922, sums up its failings: it was 'a very pathetic executive, an absolutely bankrupt executive. All it did was oppose the Treaty. It had no policy of its own.'[19] Without a coherent alternative to the Free State, the IRA was at a marked disadvantage.

BUILDING DEMOCRACY

> The people here want no compromise with the Irregulars ... Civil administration urgent everywhere in the south. The people are splendid.
>
> Michael Collins, undated diary entry

The people may be splendid, but a population does not actively support any form of government without being convinced that it has the means, ability, stamina, and will to win and to govern.[20] The IRA's failed attempts to form an alternative government are a case in point. Republican efforts in Munster did not gain public traction because the population lacked confidence in them. The businesses and population of Cork were also very dissatisfied with IRA attempts to collect taxes to fund the war effort.[21]

In contrast, by August 1922, the Free State government had begun building up the army, establishing a civil service, and developing government departments.[22] It was, in essence propelled from being the administrator of revolutionary Sinn Féin's proto-state to a collection of ministers responsible for a well-equipped and functioning modern government with a full range of departments.[23] Good governance was evolving, but the transition was not all smooth. Lord Midleton gave voice to public frustration early on, declaring that the Free State government had only 'a vague war policy but absolutely no civil policy; they would not concentrate on 'constructive projects' being too preoccupied with propaganda.'[24] Gavin Foster disagrees, suggesting that the new Irish government was functioning despite initial problems, a remarkable achievement considering that its leaders found themselves assuming control of a formal state apparatus for the first time in Irish history.[25]

At the start of the civil war, most government departments – including 'the mainstay of other state departments, namely Local Government and Agriculture, but especially Home Affairs [Justice]' – relied on the National Army for support.[26] Minister Kevin O'Higgins explained that military help was initially required in all these departments because no police force or system of justice was operating.[27]

Bill Kissane reflects on Irish democratic aspirations and military involvement in governance at the time, wondering whether perhaps 'Irish society was still not quite ready for democracy.' Did the task of democratic state building in reality conceal authoritarian actions in its 'ruthless imposition of centralized authority?'[28] Charles Townsend likewise contends that Collins became, in effect, a kind of generalissimo, combining military and political supremacy and relying on his personal ascendancy. He suggests that Collins might have done more before his death to equip the nascent Free State with what it needed most, a symbolic political objective to match and neutralise the invocation of the Republic as the symbol of independence.[29]

Notwithstanding that debate, it became the National Army's responsibility to create the right conditions to spread government authority throughout the country via state ministries and allow it to rebuild the economy, re-establish law and order, and implement a functioning civil administration.[30] To reinforce both the authority of the Free State and its democratic credentials, a meeting of the Dáil was convened on 5 September 1922, a fortnight after the assassination of Michael Collins. This was a strategically important decision. Mr A. Belton, a leading Southern Unionist, told Lord Midleton in early October 1922 that 'I really believe that the assembling of the Dáil and the progress already made with the constitution has done more to damage the Republican forces than any action taken by the Free State Army.'[31]

Liam de Róiste emphasises that Liam Lynch needed to unite the people behind the IRA and against the Free State if he was to create a viable political alternative.[32] But as already stated, Lynch and the IRA had difficulties in this regard. National Army reports observed that the IRA was operating with 'lack of resources and unified control, and almost complete ineffectiveness from a military standpoint, [and as a result] their policy of militant action is slowly changing to one of sheer destructiveness and obstruction of the civil government.'[33] Without a commitment to sound governing and economic principles, the Munster Republic and the other IRA attempts to offer a shadow government were ultimately doomed to fail.

In contrast, the vast majority of National government officials worked to construct a viable new state. Governance became a primary function and duty, despite pressing security concerns in the initial phases of the civil war. Senior civil servants withdrew to protected administrative centres in Dublin's City Hall, Dublin Castle, and government buildings in

Merrion Street, which took on the appearance of ministerial bunkers. From this green zone, the Free State provided coherent leadership, especially in comparison to the IRA.[34]

Later on, as Dublin became more secure, the government adopted an increasingly collaborative approach. On 11 January 1923, each minister of the Cabinet, or Executive Council, submitted a memorandum of his personal opinions on military, economic, and political developments. These opinions were pooled at a centralised strategic level and certain 'lines of policy were provisionally agreed on by the various Departments within the Free State Government, to be further reviewed.'[35] The Free State was beginning to demonstrate an inclusive and democratic approach to governance.

PROVIDING LOCAL GOVERNMENT

In 1922, Irish local authorities delivered only rudimentary services that dated from the nineteenth century: public roads, highways, streets, and footpaths; relief of the poor and care of the sick; and some public housing.[36] As the Free State was finding its feet, advice arrived from all corners of society. Father Peter Coffey, a professor of philosophy at Maynooth University, advocated a practical scheme whereby the government could 'utilise the nation's credit to raise money for public work schemes such as housing. The returns, interest-free, would then be reinvested in more public schemes.'[37] Cosgrave replied to Coffey that he 'need not refer to the fact that your scheme would require some detailed criticism. If I might say so without offence, it is the scheme of an amateur.'[38] Though he was undoubtedly being discourteous, Cosgrave was guided primarily by his civil servants, who were inherited from the previous administration and had British experience.[39]

During this transitional period, Free State civil servants endorsed a policy of proceeding along 'conservative well-established lines; for one thing we cannot afford to frighten English finance.'[40] Thus the initial

Free State economic and governance policy was born in part from caution and in part from fear of upsetting British sensibilities, not from what was best for the population.

Yet inheriting civil servants from the former British administration had many advantages, and their distance from the revolutionary state-building process ensured stability and continuity.[41] The over 21,000 of them who opted to transfer to the Irish Free State were fully trained, professional, theoretically apolitical and, by 1922, predominantly Irish born.[42] Ireland had been bequeathed a complete central and local government apparatus.[43] This was a significant boost to the nascent state, guaranteeing trained administrators who were removed from the complex ideological strains and loyalties of a Sinn Féin movement at war with itself for supremacy in Southern Ireland.[44]

Once again, a British legacy provoked complex feelings. According to government documentation there was a 'distinct uneasiness throughout the whole country because of the fear that vital Irish interests are in the hands of those men whose allegiance does not lie in Ireland.'[45] Anti-Treaty elements, perhaps predictably, pounced on this as damning evidence of fundamental continuities between the new regime and its colonial predecessor.[46] Those who had served in Sinn Féin's shadow Dáil administration during the War of Independence but had supported the Treaty were now also disenfranchised. For the most part, they were immediately locked out of the new administration by the nearly direct transfer of all civil servants from the British to the Irish administration.[47]

Martin Maguire agrees that the stability and continuity associated with the transition of the civil service had its bumps and knots, and offers an example of how reconciliation was difficult but necessary. The Sinn Féin Dáil Department of Local Government had been one of the successes of the revolutionary shadow administration, and had effected radical changes in local administration by the time the Treaty was signed. But considering that the IRA had burned down the Customs House, which had previously housed the British Local Government offices, tensions were obviously carried forward after the Truce between the pro-

Treaty Sinn Féin and British administrators who were now meant to work together. As a result, the new joint working environment became fractious and the two sides became distinctly unfriendly towards one another.[48] Despite tensions and suspicions, however, the inherited civil service did reconcile, ensuring that the same tasks of administration and governance continued to be performed with the same general organisation and procedure as before the war.[49]

GOVERNANCE TAKES HOLD

For the IRA, funding its insurgency took precedence over establishing a functioning, viable government. For that reason, control of Cork as a commercial centre was important to the survival of the Munster Republic.[50] By the end of July 1922, prior to the National Army taking control, the government and economy of Cork were in hiatus. Construction projects were postponed for fear that street fighting would make them pointless; fuel shortages threatened to shut the Ford factory; rising unemployment was matched only by rising taxes levied by the IRA. According to Liam de Róiste, the occupiers didn't care: 'While they rob the revenues, they take no responsibilities for administration.' Their main purpose was 'to demonstrate that the Free State will not and cannot function' and, he asserted, 'no feeling for the poor, for the weak, the indigent, moves them.'[51]

Entering Cork City in early August 1922, General Dalton quickly distinguished the intention of the National Army from that of the IRA. It was to restore normal life as quickly as possible.[52] Following his lead, the Cork Commercial Committee was established as a provisional municipal government, formed from the Cork Chamber of Commerce, Cork Employers' Federation, and Cork Farmers' Union.[53] On occasion, the military had to fill gaps in civilian positions of leadership and Dalton in effect assumed the temporary role of de facto civil governor of Cork City.[54] This demonstrated the realistic approach of the new government, as he was even authorised by the Minister for Home Affairs to issue passports to people leaving Cork for the United States.[55]

But Dalton realised not only that his role was temporary but that he needed professional assistance to administer Cork efficiently. Even before seizing the city, he asked for a representative from each government department to be sent south.[56] Consequently, on 14 August 1922, when the chartered Free State ship *Alexandra* steamed back into Cork with additional stores for the troops, various officials were on board to assist with relief, reconstruction, and the development of a civil administration.[57] A National Army situation report indicates that 'a representative of each of the following Departments has been sent to take up duty at Cork: Home Affairs, Industry and Commerce, Local Government.'[58] In prioritising these important departments, the Free State government demonstrated its commitment to provide vital services to the population of Cork and support the stability of the region.

Liam de Róiste described an interesting conundrum in his diary. By destabilising law, order, and governance in Cork, he suggested that some IRA leaders harboured the hope that the British would be forced to return and rectify the situation in favour of their commercial interests. The IRA then hoped 'the whole country would unite again against the English, as it was united in 1920.' After all, 'to construct, govern, build up, with the dead weight of public opinion against them [the IRA] is an impossibility.'[59] However, through a mixture of force and cajolement, the Free State elite in Cork managed instead to rectify the situation with National government support. They turned the economic situation around and even managed to reconcile many of the IRA to democratic government after the war was over.[60]

Tom Garvin notes that because the existence of an authoritative state is usually regarded as a precondition for the development of democracy, 1922 could actually be regarded as the birth of Irish democracy.[61] Bill Kissane agrees, asserting that after the war, the establishment of a viable party system, the consolidation of democracy more generally, and the elite's ability to project an Irish identity in international affairs can all be interpreted as the fruits of an uncommonly able revolutionary elite.[62]

From early on, the Free State leadership understood the significance of Cork as an important centre of governance, institutions, and public services for the South. Cork had a powerful chamber of commerce, and it was easier for its citizens and those in other established Munster centres to take the reins of order and exert civil authority than it was in smaller, more volatile communities.[63] Cork had a tradition as an influential business centre and the administrative capital of Munster. It had a commercial and military port, as well local authority to provide a centre of gravity from which to project Free State power into the remaining areas of southern Ireland.

As such, the local governance and administration of Cork was a turning point in Irish political development, enabling the Free State government to exert its authority over Irish society and weaken the shaky foundations of the Munster Republic. It also determined the basis on which subsequent governments would lay claim to popular legitimacy.[64] In post–civil war Ireland, normality was returning to daily life. The expansion of, and reliance on, local government could take enormous credit.

12

SUPPORTING THE ECONOMY

> Along with placating the interests of supporters and the overall population, the Free State government recognised the need to manage the economy efficiently and secure the stability of the State.
>
> Cumnann na nGaedheal, Minute Book, 10 October 1924

By 1922, the boom years following the First World War – when Britain's European war effort meant higher agricultural prices and wages in Ireland – had given way to a sharp recession with high unemployment, wage cuts, and the return of mass emigration.[1] What's more, the Free State had been shorn of the industrial wealth of Ulster and had no viable alternative to the established, if unequal, Anglo–Irish economic relationship.[2] It was completely economically reliant on the larger partner: 92 per cent of Ireland's exports went to Britain, and 78 per cent of its imports came from there.[3]

If that was not bad enough for the nascent Irish government, the civil war was an enormous economic burden for a newly independent dominion to sustain, with 30 per cent of all national expenditure devoted to defence in 1923 and 1924.[4] The Irish Free State government had to raise a large army, establish a civil service, and restore financial stability.[5] It was also desperately short of money. At the same time, the infant government had to reassure sceptical British and Anglo-Irish observers in the country's main commercial markets of its adult attitude.[6] Britain was, after all, its primary economic and military guarantor. Ultimately, the Irish government needed to be in economic control at both the national and local levels in order to finance the war, placate outside interests and stabilise the economy.

FREE STATE FISCAL POLICY

The Free State government's financial policy was underpinned by an understanding that the state was required to enable all elements of society – from individuals and local governments to the national assembly – to participate actively in economic life. A robust banking system and a stock exchange were among the first orders of the day to serve the interests of the Irish economy and sever links with British capital.[7] The skewed loyalties of the banking elite and a lack of financial expertise at all levels within Irish society made that a difficult proposition. The Free State government wanted the Bank of Ireland to act as its financial agent and to accommodate an initial £1 million line of credit, but the bank was slow to respond.[8] Then, over 1–2 May 1922, the IRA raided 26 banks, causing losses of £156,392. It finally dawned on the Bank of Ireland: the Free State government was all that stood between the country and fiscal chaos. It loosened the purse strings accordingly.[9]

Nevertheless, the continued economic obduracy and incoherence of banks operating in Ireland forced the government to take corrective fiscal measures. Supplies of silver had dried up because of hoarding, banks withdrew cashier cheques and currency from circulation, and the Munster and Leinster Bank found itself unable to produce an annual balance sheet.[10] It was essential to keep the banks operational, head off cash hoarding, and prevent a run on the banks. Under the heading 'Closing of Banks in Cork', the Cabinet minutes from 7 July 1922 reflect this necessity stating that 'it was arranged the acting Chairman should discuss this matter with the governor of the Bank of Ireland at an interview on the following day.'[11]

The need for a sound banking sector headed by a central bank was especially pressing to permit economic expansion to flow into regions of so-called maximum opportunity: parts of the country with the highest potential capacity to benefit. Cork was a prime candidate strategically, geographically, and economically. But maximum opportunity depends as much on the political considerations of security and economic growth as on questions of profit. Even if a region seems to have substantial economic opportunity, it cannot be absorbed into an expanding economy unless it is stable.[12] Thus the government would have to provide regional security in Cork and Munster in order to enable economic stimulus.

STIMULATING THE MUNSTER ECONOMY

From the start, Cosgrave labelled the struggle a war 'upon the economic life of the Irish people.'[13] The civil war brought particular hardship to some regions and under IRA stewardship the Port of Cork was losing £1,700 a week in shipping revenue. In mid-July 1922, John Borgonovo tells us, the 'Lee Boot factory closed, while the *Cork Constitution* shut its doors rather than submit to IRA censorship.'[14] Commerce was further damaged as outside suppliers refused to send goods to the Republican strongholds in Munster, including Cork. Shopkeepers who tried to shut up shop were ordered by the IRA to carry on trading – even without stock. Like most military governments, Cork Republicans found that there were strict limits to their capacity to stimulate the economy.[15]

It became obvious to the National government that Cork City – and along with it Waterford, Limerick, Tralee, and Clonmel, which dominated the approaches to the provincial capital – must be secured in order to spread the economic influence of the Free State. These cities had ports, and through these ports flowed the commerce of several counties. Roads penetrating the anti-Treaty positions also radiated from the ports, and the livelihood of many people behind anti-Treaty lines depended on the Free State securing these commercial centres and their transportation networks. Once secured the pro-Treatyites had the opportunity to build up troop numbers, increase supplies, and base logistics depots in these Munster urban centres in preparation for the final assaults on Cork and the remainder of the Munster Republic.[16]

This became a very influential strategy for the Free State on local populations because the National Army war machine was expensive, but with it came security and economic prosperity. Some people who lived beyond its security influence were envious of those living within this protective bubble.[17] As Jacqueline Hazelton remarks, civilians who feel safe in government-controlled areas, or who yearn for the goods and services that a government can provide, will be supportive and often divulge useful information.[18]

IRA ECONOMIC PRIORITIES IN CORK

Munster, and especially County Cork, had been one of the worst-affected regions in Ireland economically, having been badly disrupted by the War of Independence. Hundreds of workers downed tools for three weeks in late January 1922, shutting the Munster railway network, closing the port of Cork, and crippling trade.[19] Already in recession, the Munster economy slipped into a depression following the IRA seizing control. Newspaper correspondents reported that business was at a standstill, or worse, that 'enterprise is dead.'[20]

Regrettably for the local population, the IRA was not so much interested in stimulating the economy as it was in taking from it what it could. Liam de Róiste noted that commandeering was prevalent in Cork city, though he suggested that many accounts of it were 'without foundation, and numbers biased.'[21] Nonetheless, IRA commandeering was a reality and the practice was active throughout the Republican regions of Munster, causing one exasperated doctor in Tipperary to exclaim, 'As bad as the 'Black and Tans' were they never interfered with the cars of doctors.'[22]

In Cork city it got so bad that the mayor had to establish a committee to mitigate the losses caused by commandeering. As matters got worse, Frank Daly, an elected representative for the city, went to Mallow to see IRA Chief Liam Lynch, and got an assurance that, as far as possible, business would not be interfered with. Whether it was Daly's communications with Lynch or a general understanding that started to develop in the IRA, an official notice appeared in the *Cork Examiner* in this regard, as de Róiste noted in his diary: 'O.C. Cork No. 1 Brigade orders persons having motor vehicles to get permits. Also, it is announced that goods "Commandeered" will be commandeered on orders signed by Sean Mac Swiney, the impressions being conveyed that they will be paid for, though this is not explicit.'[23] Any payments for such goods remain unconfirmed, and Michael Hopkinson believes that commandeering continued throughout the civil war as a necessary means of IRA survival.[24]

To make matters even worse for the beleaguered population in Cork, the IRA also imposed taxes on the citizens, banks, factories, and retail establishments, and appropriated the customs and excise revenue that was still being generated in Cork Harbour. According to its own calculations, city residents owed £1,250,000 in uncollected tax revenue – a remarkable figure – and the leadership estimated that a third of that could be recovered in order to fund IRA activities.[25] Supplies considered to be essential to the Republican war effort were also taken from local shops by way of requisition.

By doing this indiscriminately, the IRA more or less ignored the social fabric of Cork and the needs of the population in favour of their Republican cause. On 18 July 1922, de Róiste's diary entry records that IRA activists were taking Cork customs proceeds. Two days later, he noted that they had got more than £50,000 of customs revenue over the previous fortnight and were making arrangements to capture income tax proceeds. The *Irish Independent* reported on 7 August that the IRA was seeking additional funds from the local economy within the Munster Republic and occupied Cork by issuing the following message to local businesses, much to their annoyance: 'Irish Republican Army Cork No. 1

Brigade: It appears that Income Tax amounting to £— is payable by your firm for the financial year 1921–22.' The demand came as a bombshell, especially to the directors of the local breweries, distilleries, bacon-curing factories, and other large firms. The Cork Incorporated Chamber of Commerce and Shipping and the Cork Employers Federation Ltd held a joint meeting to discuss their opposition.[26]

Social class, standing, and associated resentments were very prevalent in Cork. Most of the city's clergy and merchant class supported the Treaty and opposed the IRA, which had a low social status in the city, as personified in the leadership triumvirate of 1st Southern Division. Liam Deasy was a junior clerk, Florence O'Donoghue was a draper's shop assistant, and Liam Lynch a hardware shop assistant. The merchant princes of Cork resented what they saw as high-handed IRA Republican officers rising above their place.[27]

The business elites of the city also considered the Republicans to be socialists and anti-commerce. They watched uneasily as Irish Transport Group Workers Union leaders urged their members to 'arise to action', promising that 'all privileges of wealth and birth shall be abolished.'[28] Minister Kevin O'Higgins also employed scare tactics on the subject, issuing dire warnings about 'Bolsheviks' and insisting that 'red flag elements' were exploiting the crisis.[29]

The communist-socialist IRA threat, exaggerated by some politicians for politician gain was nonetheless real. Liam Mellows, who was captured in the Four Courts, was certainly a socialist supporter. Writing from prison on 29 August 1922 before his execution, he advocated the nationalisation of the banks and industry within a fairly full-blooded socialist republic in which industry would be controlled by the state for the benefit of workers and farmers.[30] His socialist visions were never implemented.

The merchants of Cork stood firm against the Republican military government, pledging to pay tax only to the Free State. All the firms in the city agreed to take the drastic step of halting industrial and trading operations and discharging all hands if the IRA decided to punish any business. Crucially, the vehicle manufacturer Ford, based in Cork and with a weekly wage bill of £10,000, supported this move.[31] Cork city businesses that threw their weight behind the decision would later provide a strong foundation for Free State economic policies. Pro-Treaty supporters built up a powerful economic coalition in Cork that offered very potent opposition to IRA governance.[32] They also helped to damage the IRA's reputation, mooting that its presence was bad for the economy. Therefore, it was not surprising that under these conditions of crisis, it didn't take long for Cork banks to run short of ready money. Their head offices ordered them to close down as part of a Free State economic attack on the Republican-controlled South.[33] Commercial and economic life in Cork was paralysed as pro-Treaty supporters refused to co-operate with IRA, or co-operated as little as possible.[34] The *Irish Times* reported that with its main railway paralysed and roads seriously damaged, Cork would be entirely isolated if not for its port facilities.[35]

Prior to the arrival of Dalton and the National Army, the mayor and merchants of Cork had held a meeting to determine the city's immediate economic requirements and establish a committee to ensure food supplies.[36]

Fortunately, upon the arrival of Free State forces into Cork, the landscape changed. Shortly after his arrival General Dalton received deputations from all representative bodies in Cork city, covering almost every branch of life.[37] He interviewed all the major manufacturers in the city and instructed them to get their factories working as quickly as possible.[38] As described in previous chapters, the National Army provided the requisite security and immediately set about restoring essential services and the Cork transportation network. Traders were influenced to re-open and re-trade with active encouragement and security as part of the government's overall efforts to restore the financial and economic institutions in the entire state. These incentivisations worked and National Army reports from the end of the civil war support this assertion. By placing certain government contracts in Cork and the remainder of Munster the Free State had weaponised the economy, having an excellent effect on commerce in the region.[39]

LIMITING ILLICIT FINANCIAL ACTIVITIES

Preventing commandeering, targeting illicit activities, and rebuilding the economy proved decisive in gaining popular support for the Free State government and army. The restoration of normality and economic stability to the lives of the people in Munster would be a difficult proposition, especially at the start of the civil war because the Free State had no police force, and the collection of rates and taxes was hampered by the disorderly conditions prevailing in most counties. The IRA was still taking income tax in Cork as late as the first week of August 1922.[40] But once secured, the Free State authorities in Cork tried to seize these funds and actively target the IRA economic machinery in the county, as the London *Times* explained on 23 August:

> From the start, the IRA were at a disadvantage in the fiscal side of the civil war. The National government gained the upper hand when a temporary injunction of the Supreme Court of the United States was granted which restrained the Irregular IRA leaders from drawing upon funds collected in that country for the Republican cause. This struck directly at the most sensitive part of their organisation.

Because corruption can hinder efforts to establish governance and promote economic recovery, military forces should initially create mechanisms to curtail it across government institutions.[41]

The Free State understood this implicitly and this was vital because the IRA had received a substantial amount of revenue from commandeering and the illegal collection of customs and excise duties. This funding was illicitly lodged in the National Land Bank, of which Robert

Barton was a director.⁴² Barton was a Sinn Féin politician and supporter of the anti-Treaty IRA. In order to secure the funds, de Róiste wrote on 20 July 1922, the IRA notified the bank that they had appointed new Honorary Treasurers of the fund. Previous to this, Barry Egan was one of the Honorary Treasurers: now the two gentlemen named by the IRA [writing obscured in the diary] replaced Egan and his services had been dispensed with! According to de Róiste, the IRA objective was to get access again to the funds in order to utilise the money for anti-Treaty activities, 'Irregular Forces', and their dependents.

In essence, the IRA was trying to control the banking system in Cork, or at least parts of it. Initially the Cork banks tried to take matters into their own hands by 'cancelling their [IRA] notes ... The Irregulars are running short of cash because of this, notes not being available for exchange of large cheques.' Although the prospect for a genuine banking system in Cork City was 'as black as it can be' de Róiste wrote, 'there is an attempt which is almost pathetic, to go on as usual.'⁴³

In order to immediately remedy the situation, Dalton and his officers saw the local bank managers collectively and ordered them to re-open. The meetings helped to pave the way for fiscal support that was supplied by the Free State government to the beleaguered banking sector. Decisive actions like this along with fiscal stimulation measures by the Free State, helped to end the economic blockade of the region and put the economy back on a more even keel.⁴⁴ Michael Collins joined Dalton in Cork in mid-August 1922, and the two of them actively engaged local employers and financial institutions in an effort to regenerate the economy and limit illicit economic activity. Together they revisited several local banks as part of the mission to recover funds by tracking down lodgements made by Republicans during their occupation of Cork.

Most of the IRA money had come from excise duties that had been collected and salted away.⁴⁵ This early form of money laundering was prevalent among Republican forces. Although de Róiste proposed a somewhat lower figure, it is likely that by early August 1922, the IRA had collected an estimated £100,000 in customs revenue and other illicit activities and hidden it in accounts held by sympathisers.[46]

Having served as the Sinn Féin and Free State finance minister, Collins realised the significance not only of the money laundering but also of co-operating with the banking sector. In a notebook entry dated 21 August 1922, he outlined possible meetings with members of the banking community, including a Mr Crosbie and Mr Pelly of the Hibernian Bank. Collins noted his intention to contact the banks to 'ask for a brief statement in general position.'[47]

In Meda Ryan's opinion, the purpose of the Cork bank visits was to allow Collins the opportunity to seize the IRA assets, having asked bank directors to identify suspicious accounts.[48] Although the banks were initially reluctant to supply the required information to Free State government authorities, Dalton threatened to close them if they did not comply. As a result, some £90,000 that had gone to the IRA was eventually recovered.[49]

The Free State then set about enacting a policy of not recognising transactions previously conducted with the IRA by commercial interests. Collins remarked in his notebook on 21 August on the urgent necessity to 'collect back rent even though it may have already been paid to the Irregulars.' Any business that conducted trade with the IRA, illicit or otherwise, would be financially sanctioned. In another entry on the same day, Collins emphasised the importance of the economic element of the war:

> The bank position here is slightly obscure. It will require a full investigation, there must be an examination of the customs and excise position—all moneys paid in and out must come under this. We shall require three first class independent men … Unfortunately Brennan has gone to London.

He was referring to a Mr Joseph Brennan, a senior civil servant with the Ministry of Finance. Brennan had previously served in Dublin Castle under British rule and was now working for the new Irish Government.⁵⁰ As one of the primary enforcers of anti-corruption measures for the Free State, he was eventually dispatched to Cork.

The use of skilled accounting practitioners such as Brennan demonstrates the priority the government gave to countering the IRA's financial activities and facilitating a functioning, transparent economy. Collins authorised Brennan to deal with the situation in Cork arising out of the Republican expropriation of bank funds and seizure of government revenue.⁵¹

SQUEEZING IRA FUNDING

By early September 1922, Liam Lynch reported that banks under Free State orders to refuse to release funds to the IRA were putting the organisation in dire straits.⁵² The IRA, Lynch admitted, 'needed the funds badly.'⁵³ At the beginning of October, Lynch asked his colleague, Ernie O'Malley, to attempt to withdraw the money by other methods.⁵⁴ He told O'Malley to meet Barton, the director of the National Land Bank, to urge him to advance the money privately to the IRA. Lynch argued that it was 'doubtful if the Provisional Government can prove the money was collected as [illegal] revenue.'⁵⁵

The Free State policies were having an effect, bringing the IRA close to bankruptcy. But the latter's grasp on power, financial and otherwise, continued even in exile in rural Munster. Letters dated 25–26 October, 31 October, and 1–2 November, captured by the National Army revealed the resolve of IRA fighters to live off the livelihoods of local people and businesses.⁵⁶ The Free State needed to protect communities from both physical and economic attack.

Preventing IRA attacks on businesses, chasing the money, and limiting illicit activity proved to be an undoubtedly successful strategy for the Free State government and army, as it seriously degraded the capabilities of the IRA war machine. Without sufficient funding, the IRA found it increasingly difficult to finance its insurgency, forcing it to attack the population it hoped to represent and isolating the volunteers from local communities and businesses.

UNEMPLOYMENT IN REPUBLICAN CORK

Economic regeneration begins with stimulus packages, government contracts, and the reopening of local factories and industries. The implementation of employment programs reinforces efforts to establish security and civil order by providing meaningful employment and compensation for an actively engaged labour force.[57]

The unemployment picture in Ireland at the beginning of the civil war was stark. Minister Kevin O'Higgins remarked that in the spring of 1922, the economic life of the country was ebbing away.[58] He relayed his concerns to the Dáil: 130,000 unemployed at a time when there was little jurisdiction.[59] As early as 3 March, the Free State started to act, agreeing to make money available to county councils that had submitted approved unemployment relief schemes.[60] On 8 March, Cosgrave persuaded Cabinet to agree to transfer £275,000 to various county councils for unemployment relief.[61] This was well timed because on 13 March 1922, up to 50,000 people attended a protest in Cork against economic hardship and unemployment.[62] Realising the inflammatory nature of such gatherings, Michael Collins promised jobs and funding, declaring in a visit to the city, 'There is no mistaking the attitude of Cork' before granting an extra £250,000 in reconstruction aid and £112,000 in housing assistance.[63]

However, matters got worse for Cork and after Collins' visit, the IRA consolidated its occupation of the county. In response, the National Army implemented an economic blockade of the South – with a profoundly serious impact on unemployment. Workers and office staffs were dismissed; production and distribution came to a standstill.[64] The situation in Cork particularly deteriorated as the blockade took effect.

De Róiste described the scale of the problem: 'There are 12,000 registered at the Unemployment Bureaux; and ... 4/5,000 more not receiving unemployment benefits now; and estimating two dependents as an average for each unemployed persons, it may be estimated that there are some 50,000 persons on the starvation line in Cork City and County.' He detailed the 'absolute want in respectable homes' and suggested that 'paralysis of business is growing gradually, as the unrest prevails and communications are interrupted.'[65]

The *Irish Independent* supported his estimates, adding on 2 August that 'people live from hand to mouth, from day to day ... not knowing what the morrow may bring.' The *Irish Times* put unemployment somewhat lower – approaching 8,000 – but this still constituted over 30 per cent of the male working population of the county.[66] Whatever the precise numbers, by the summer of 1922, unemployment in Cork had reached a potential boiling point. Destabilising labour agitation occurred throughout the first half of the year. Moreover, amid rampant unemployment, employers stirred up industrial strife by attempting to reduce wages further.[67]

But the IRA missed an opportunity to exploit this instability and dissatisfaction to their advantage. As poverty grew during the Free State blockade of Cork, the anti-Treaty IRA forces made little effort to solve the unemployment crisis. Instead of co-operating with local industries to stimulate the economy, the IRA did the opposite. Its engineers attempted to commandeer pig iron for the construction of mines and grenades. Edward Grace, the American manager of the Ford factory, told the Republicans that if they seized anything, he would shutter the plant and throw 2,000 staff out of work.[68] The IRA desisted.

ALLEVIATING UNEMPLOYMENT

Once it took control in August 1922, the National Army quickly set about trying to alleviate the unemployment crisis in Cork. The *Cork Examiner* on 14 August issued a notice: '*TO THE MERCHANTS,*

EMPLOYERS AND CITIZENS OF CORK: All those who have been appealed for financial or other aid to help the starving people will please notify the Secretary at once at Connolly Hall.' The following day, the *Cork Examiner* reported on a well-attended meeting on the Grand Parade of the city, intended to take practical steps to deal with the distress in the city and district and 'to devise the ways and means by which the greatest industrial danger that has ever threatened the country may be promptly averted.'[69]

The initial stimulus and government contracts handed out by the National Army did a lot to alleviate unemployment. The *Cork Examiner* reported on 16 August that it was 'most gratifying to be in a position to state that, notwithstanding the gloomy outlook for the country generally, the conditions locally are receiving immediate attention.' An article in the same paper the next day reported that a conference had been held between members of the Cork Reconstruction Committee and representatives of the Free State government with a view to taking steps to secure the relief of unemployment in the city. As reported by a National Army intelligence officer, the key to ongoing violence was to get people working: 'A man, on seeing some lorries with armed men pass by, said to his companion, 'if they were hungry as we are, they would not have much stomach for fight'.'[70]

IMPLEMENTING A RELIEF SCHEME

In mid-August the Cork Unemployed Central Committee made the following declaration to the citizens of Cork:

> As unemployment benefits have been stopped for some time past owing to unsettled conditions, the above committee are in a position to announce that these benefits will be almost immediately restored; that Fords and other works and industries will be encouraged by the army authorities; that all classes of pensions will be paid as usual, as soon as the essential communications can be restored. In the way of a temporary relief to meet the present distress £200 will be immediately handed to

the St. Vincent de Paul Society to relieve very acute cases, pending representations being made for relief on a large scale, in view of conditions in Cork.[71]

As time went on, the Free State unemployment policy became more effective. On 28 August 1922, the *Cork Examiner* reported that 'the scheme for the relief of unemployment ... took a practical turn yesterday, when about 80 men were employed restoring the surface of the North Main Street.' At the same time, the paper reported daily on the role of the IRA in adding to the army of unemployed. Trade was being held up, railway traffic dislocated, the highways made impassable, telegraph lines cut, and other means adopted to ruin trade, on which employment depended.[72] The *Irish Times* noted the observation of the Cork Workers' Council that high unemployment in the city was directly related to the activities of armed men.

By 5 October 1922, the government took another step, announcing an amnesty for all those who handed in their weapons by 15 October.[73] By offering an alternative and motivating those who practised violence to desist, the Free State government hoped to set the right conditions to improve security, stimulate the economy, and decrease unemployment.

REPORTING ON THE ECONOMIC PICTURE

As Free State government economic and employment policies started to take effect, National Army reports began to record the improvements. Reporting itself had improved by the start of 1923, as had the professionalism, comprehensive nature, and administration of the force. An early April 1923 report stated that the number of unemployed in Cork City had been reduced by another hundred, to 4,687, a level that compared well with any period even before 1914.[74] By mid-April, the number had dropped to 4,587, a result the report ascribes to the 'excellent effect' of government contracts.[75] Towards the end of the month, unemployment for Cork City and surrounding districts was down to 4,426 (of whom only 2,864 were men). The corresponding report indicates that 'the industry is in a fairly good condition … [such that] the restoration of ordinary conditions will restore employment to normal.'[76] As the war entered May 1923, the weekly army report showed yet more improvement: unemployment at 4,348 for Cork City and district.[77]

Considering that unemployment had stood between 8,000 and 12,000 before the war, the Free State had made remarkable progress, as the newspapers attested.[78] Nonetheless, unemployment in the county was still acute at the end of the war, and the problem was being accentuated by the demobilisation of soldiers and release of prisoners. An army report noted that the issue must be met with action: 'It is desirable that every effort be made during the coming months to promote reconstruction works and set up and encourage industries.'[79]

Despite the obstacles, government schemes to encourage industry, restore services, and deal with unemployment did begin to make an imprint on the Cork economy, especially after the war. On 21 August 1923, the Free State placed advertisements in the *Cork Examiner* claiming it had paid unemployment benefits to a weekly average of 30,000 workers in Cork since October 1922, that 12,000 workers had been placed in employment, and that 80 industrial disputes had been settled. These figures were important in influencing the local population to support the government – even if they may have been exaggerated, or calculated differently from those in the National Army reports; 30,000 workers were unemployed across southern Ireland (not just Cork) by the close of the civil war.[80]

The economic situation in Cork remained a focus of Free State attention after the conflict ended. In November 1923, the fortnightly review from Command HQ in Cork declared that 'the success of the National Loan had a very salutary and steadying effect on the opinions of the civil population, and was responsible for an increase in confidence in the Government and its administration.'[81] A National Army Intelligence Report in February 1924 looked to a rosier future:

> With the coming of spring and a settled country a great boost in commercial and agricultural life is looked forward to ... Fairs and markets are presently being conducted in the old style ... Business in small towns is improving and when the Government schemes for employment are put into effect a general 'buck-up' in all business is confidently anticipated.[82]

Of course, emigration was still an economic way of life in Free State Ireland and the March 1924 intelligence report noted that 'hundreds of able-bodied young men are anxiously awaiting the summer months in order to cross to America for work ... [and] the quota at the moment is filled.'[83] Irish economic necessity was such that emigration helped reduce unemployment, but it also inadvertently kept the dreams of a Republic alive on both sides of the Atlantic.

POLITICS, AFTER ALL

Capacity building is a vital cog in a counterinsurgency campaign. It rebuilds the economic capabilities of a country by bringing stability to its regions. During and following the civil war, Free State programmes and policies to improve the economy, prevent illicit activity and reduce unemployment underlay the capacity-building effort. In comparison, the IRA provided little but the hollow aspirations of the Munster Republic, an alternative that was ultimately weakened by the lack of functioning administration and an inability to break the Free State's coherent strategy.

Money and the economy are at the heart of war. To be defeated, especially in a counterinsurgency, an opponent must be attacked on all fronts, including economic ones. The Free State successfully isolated the IRA financially by blocking its outside support and curbing its illicit economic activity. It also prevented the Republican cause from capitalising on the appeal of communism and the discontent caused by unemployment, immediately implementing measures to alleviate the economic suffering. The growing numbers of unemployed, combined with IRA indifference to their plight, significantly damaged public perceptions of the organisation while raising broader concerns about the stability of the state. With an urgent imperative to restore stability, the government focused on consolidating power and making reconstruction efforts, while practising a fiscal conservativism that was based on the knowledge it would have to pay its way without outside help.[84]

Nevertheless, the Free State priority of creating strong state institutions came at the expense of political considerations.[85] Its leadership wrongly believed that the continuation and maintenance of peace, stability, and good governance, along with a balanced budget, would be sufficient to retain majority electoral support.[86] This demonstrated a lack of political savvy, especially in believing that the government must continue a policy of austerity long after the civil war had ended. The belt tightening alienated a considerable body of public opinion, and in the long term aided Éamon de Valera's return to power less than 10 years after losing the civil war.[87] The political naïveté of the Free State government – rather than its positive achievements in subduing the military challenge to the new state's existence – was to shape its destiny in the following years.[88]

CONCLUSION

> Our man-power is proving too weak. The enemy are too well established and . . . any further weakness on our side caused by further arrests or executions of our best men will leave us simply a wasted shadow of what was once a glorious little Army of Independence.
>
> O'Donovan to Lynch, 27 January 1923

WHY DID THE FREE STATE WIN THE IRISH CIVIL WAR?

Fundamentally, the Free State won the Irish Civil War because they turned tactical victories into strategic successes. They did this during the Clear and Hold phases when the National Army capitalised on the initial victories by holding key terrain and reinforcing the initial conventional triumphs. Later on as the war progressed they built upon their momentum by rebuilding Irish society, thus engendering support for the government from the population.

By May 1923, National Army reports pointed to the undeniable. In almost every command area, the IRA was "absolutely broken or else hampered in such a way as to render it almost impossible for them to carry out any major operation. The large numbers of arrests and captures of dumps during the week is evidence of the effective manner in which the troops are clearing the parts of the country that yet call for attention."[1]

Impelled by the many setbacks, the anti-Treaty Republican Cabinet met the Army Council on May 13th and 14th to discuss the options. From a military point of view, the Republican effort was beyond hope. With IRA peace proposals rejected, however, the two sides were unable to agree on terms for the cessation of hostilities. The state slipped into an uneasy peace.[2] Eventually Frank Aiken, who had replaced Liam Lynch as IRA Chief of Staff, suspended any offensives, and on 24 May 1923, he ordered the IRA to dump arms.[3] A decade of conflict and turmoil had come to an end.

By the end of the civil war, the government reported over 800 National Army deaths.[4] No accurate tally of total civilian and IRA deaths exists, though some estimates run into the several thousands.[5] I would put the overall figure of deaths as a result of the civil war at about 2,000.

In order to achieve this victory during a brutal campaign, the leadership of the National Army developed a strategy which inherently allowed for the synchronisation of military and civilian activities during the Irish Civil War. It facilitated flexibility, compellence, and collaboration that allowed initial tactical victories to be converted into overall success. In short, the Free State government utilised a doctrine that had not yet been written to prosecute a successful campaign against the anti-Treaty IRA.

COMBINING GOOD GOVERNANCE AND COMPELLENCE

Hazelton argues that what succeeds most in counterinsurgency is "uglier, costlier in lives, more remote from moral and ethical considerations, and far less ambitious than what western countries are attempting in trying to build and reform the political systems in so-called weak states and ungoverned spaces."[6] I agree, particularly with respect to ungoverned spaces, where there has to be a sharper edge. Realistic actions are called for, especially during the initial clear, or clearance, and conventional phase of a counterinsurgency campaign. Counterinsurgency success can be defined as the "marginalization of the insurgents to the point at which they are destroyed, co-opted, or reduced to irrelevance in numbers and capability."[7] Colin Gray remarks that government forces need to be steadfast in their conduct because half-hearted repression executed by self-doubting persons does not work, though Frank Ledwidge issues a caveat by noting that such force must be applied within a coherent and solid strategic framework, against the backdrop of a firmly understood end-state.[8] Clear–Hold–Build is such a framework.

The clearance of insurgents from key locations and holding of key terrain are vital, but these operations should be informed by useable intelligence provided by a population living in safe spaces. As Berman and his colleagues point out, when civilians can safely share information, dramatic results can be achieved.[9] Targeted kinetic operations are made possible and collateral damage avoided. From these secure environments—these governed spaces—and from better living conditions, the ReBuild principle then takes priority. Thus, success should be defined not only as the marginalisation of insurgents but also as the creation of a safe, secure environment.

In other words, kinetic actions, or compellence, must coincide and co-exist with good governance, ideally on a reducing scale.[10] Once the necessity to target the insurgent with kinetic actions subsides, a "better good" can be developed to prevent insurgency from restarting. The ability to rebuild is what makes a counterinsurgency campaign sustainable, flexible, and effective. The "build back better" after initial clear and hold operations counters the prolonged warfare of the insurgent and helps to achieve strategic successes.

Nevertheless, a better good still needs a constant edge, as advocated by Hazelton, Gray, and Ledwidge, if it is to be sustainable, protected, and accepted. Berman et al. convincingly argue that the main task of the military is to provide local security and the crucial space for follow-on developments and governance efforts. Winning hearts and minds over the long term demands a complementary process to convince the population that supporting the government is a more attractive option than supporting the insurgency.[11] As mentioned, Berman et al. refer to this issue of converting initial tactical successes into political settlement as the "gap" in current doctrine. The priority is to fill the ungoverned spaces, preventing a vacuum in which insurgency can flourish. And as Nadia Schadlow explains, this can be achieved by a concurrent combination of good governance and kinetic operations.

GOOD GOVERNANCE AND COMPELLENCE – A FREE STATE PERSPECTIVE

The Free State government instinctively understood that good governance fills the vacuum created by ungoverned spaces, and it therefore ensured that the primary tasks involved in governing would be performed throughout the fighting, following the same general organisation and procedures as before the civil war.[12] In January 1923, Free State Minister of Justice Kevin O'Higgins issued a memorandum that declared a powerful truth: "The government is simply a Committee with a mandate to make certain conditions prevail, to make life and property safe, and to vindicate the legal rights of their fellow citizens."[13]

Good governance needs a democratic framework, with opposing political parties. Through a mixture of force and cajoling, the Free State managed to defeat the IRA. Even more remarkable is that its leadership later reconciled the Republicans to democratic government.[14]

A counterinsurgency, however, requires compellence alongside good governance, a proposition that Free State actions reflected during the hold and clearance phases of the war. As democratic institutions were being established, the National Army was fighting a substantial conventional campaign for survival. In the Battle of Kilmallock, for example, its forces consisted of some 2,000 troops supported by armoured cars and artillery advancing on a wide front.[15] Intense fighting on a large scale at Kilmallock and in other battles across Munster meant that nearly two-thirds of civil war deaths occurred during the conventional fighting and clearance phases of the first three months.[16]

National newspapers consistently reported on the National Army's effective use of artillery in battles ensuing in Waterford, Tipperary, and Limerick, remarking on "the deadly accuracy of the Irish gunners" which proved to be decisive and "compelled the irregulars to vacate their best positions."[17] Compellence and harassment were certainly envisioned by former British gunnery officer Lieutenant Colonel Patrick Paul, who conducted an effective artillery barrage on IRA defenders in Waterford City.[18] Major General Emmet Dalton's harassment policy in Cork, conducted during the hold phase, was also highly kinetic, reducing the numbers of IRA fighters and keeping them on the move.[19]

Mobile light infantry forces with light armoured vehicles make the best counterinsurgency soldiers. The National Army policy of living within the population it wanted to protect was supported and supplemented by mobile columns. As the National Army moved out into the more remote parts of Cork, its counter columns brought the fight to the enemy, rounding up anti-Treaty fighters in their safe areas, seizing arms, and inflicting casualties.[20] The columns reduced the flow of resources to the insurgency and broke the IRA fighters' will and capability to fight on.[21] As the war continued, additional mobility—especially armoured mobility provided by the British government—brought flexibility to the Free State forces.

Mobility and freedom of movement allowed the army to keep its lines of communication open and the IRA on the back foot. This undoubtedly contributed to the domination of key terrain and the suppression of IRA activities.[22]

Free State bombardment, harassment, pasting, and compellence operations corresponded with the concept that force must be applied within a coherent and solid strategic framework, against the background of a clear and realistic political context and a firmly understood end state.²³ The kinetic force applied by the National Army throughout the fighting coincided and co-existed with ongoing good governance efforts at the national and local levels. This complementary process may have been ad hoc at first but ultimately, when properly co-ordinated, it led to the defeat of the IRA by summer 1923.

UNDERMINING THE CAUSES OF INSURGENCY

Insurgencies are political events possessing an underlying cause. One of their principal goals is to isolate the population from the established power and its security forces, and to restrict the freedom of movement of the counterinsurgent forces. They use violence to achieve strategic goals, because it is on the political and strategic level, not the tactical, that insurgencies are won or lost.²⁴ A common cause prolongs a conflict and acts as a unifying call to arms, providing the political and financial capital to sustain the insurgency and undermining the legitimacy of the government. When the cause is combined with police and administrative weaknesses in the counterinsurgent camp, a not-too-hostile geographic environment, and outside support, the conditions for a successful insurgency are established. As Galula elaborates, the cause must also last, if not for the duration of the revolutionary war, at least until the insurgent movement is well on its feet. This differentiates a strategic cause from a tactical one.²⁵ Strategic causes normally result in strategic successes for the insurgent. Similarly, local causes lead to local successes.

A key factor in strategic success for the counterinsurgent forces is thus to deprive the insurgent of a unifying cause, as Ledwidge emphasises.²⁶ Whatever that cause is, the population will divide into an active minority who support it, an active minority who oppose it, and a neutral majority.²⁷ The neutral population can be won over by good governance in all its aspects: education, democratic transparency, restoration of services, and the security provided by close co-operation of the police and the army.²⁸ In other words, by building back better the essential services and infrastructure of a country, and even more so after years of conflict and neglect. The uncommitted majority is thus a key target in counterinsurgency operations, especially information operations.

Clearly, at the heart of any counterinsurgency campaign lies one fundamental requirement, as Michael Crawshaw affirms: to encourage the perception that the government offers a better deal.[29] Since Mao Zedong proclaimed that it was the insurgent fish that swam in the sea of the local population and gained support and protection from them, counterinsurgency theory has had as its guiding principle the idea that the population has to be won over.[30]

UNDERMINING THE INSURGENT CAUSE - A FREE STATE PERSPECTIVE

The IRA left a trail of destruction through Cork and the larger region, and caused the inhabitants much hardship by commandeering supplies for its own survival and siphoning off revenues wherever it could. The Free State reacted by repairing, restoring, and protecting essential infrastructure and offering better services to the population. In the process, it was able to win over the neutral majority of the population and erode the IRA cause.[31]

The Free State also used the Church and the press as vital information operations tools. The Church came out very strongly against the IRA in Cork, alleging that young minds were being poisoned by its false principles. Although the disapprobation had a serious effect on IRA volunteers, the social ostracism engendered by both Church and state had a deeper effect on their partners and parents.[32] As well as religious condemnation, the Republican narrative came in for a pasting in the press. As the National Army gradually gained control across the country, mainstream newspapers reached those who had previously been fed solely on Republican ideology. The papers reported favourably on Free State actions while challenging IRA activities, further damaging the insurgent cause.

CONCLUSION

Additionally, the Free State bolstered its presence, posture, and profile through parades and shows of force. They paid off. The general survey for the period ending 17 October 1923 noted that civilians "are at last beginning to realise that the soldiers of the National Army are the friends and protectors of the people rather than the representatives of military tyranny as they were formerly led to believe".[33] The survey also noted that "from all parts come very favourable reports as to the attitude of the people generally towards our troops."[34] The favour of the people in Cork was the prize for the National Army. Ultimately, the key terrain in the insurgency in Munster was not a physical space but the political loyalty of the people who inhabit that space.[35]

USING LOCAL AND SPECIALISED FORCES

Information is a key enabler in counterinsurgency warfare. How to obtain information and how to act on it are essential issues in a successful campaign. Using many examples, Berman et al. outline the benefits of obtaining information and using local forces in counterinsurgency operations—and notably in sweep and search operations. They cite evidence that the number of insurgent attacks drops when local forces are deployed, rather than outside forces.[36] Additionally, their data reveal that when local forces were supported by specialised intelligence forces who helped plan and prepare raids and sweeps, more than three times the number of rebels were apprehended and over 50 percent more rebel firearms recovered. These substantial gains occurred because "locally recruited and employed units had preferential access to information since they were operating in areas where they lived and among populations they knew intimately."[37]

Drawing on extensive research and practical experience Joseph Felter, a former US deputy assistant secretary of defence, outlines the advantages of using local forces to obtain information from the civilian population, explaining how to use it in breaking down insurgent networks. Felter asserts that this form of collaboration between local troops and specialised units facilitates better small-unit leadership with the capacity to accurately assess and respond to changing local conditions, high-quality training with a focus on tactical readiness, and doctrine and command-and-control measures that permit rapid adaption and innovation along with flexible responses and tactics.[38]

The organisation of an insurgent network is crucial to its effectiveness, and American theorist John Arquilla advocates an understanding of how networks fight as a central counterinsurgency concept.[39] As Samuel Huntington argues, "numbers, weapons, and strategy all count in war, but major deficiencies in any one of those may still be counterbalanced by superior cohesion and discipline."[40] Integrated and cohesive insurgent organisations are characterised by leadership, unity, and discipline at the centre and high levels of local compliance on the ground. These groups are not necessarily widely popular or even ultimately victorious, but their organisational cohesion makes them effective militarily, resilient in the face of pressure from counterinsurgent forces, and politically relevant.[41] Douglas Porch agrees with Huntington on this point, stating, "Successful insurgencies evolve resiliency through ideological commitment that rises above clan or tribe and the organizational capacity and popular stamina to engage in protracted war."[42]

Insurgent networks are often driven by local issues and alliances, making them particularly vulnerable to local forces because these forces understand the specific cause of insurrection in a particular area and know what is required on the ground. Supported by specialised units, local forces also understand how the insurgent networks recruit, operate, and sustain themselves, and where they operate. Additionally, local forces have a close understanding of the social networks, family relationships, and local culture ingrained within the insurgent network. Thus, using local forces enables key information to be gathered on insurgent networks and facilitates coherent actions at the tactical level.

The performance in combat of insurgent networks has often led to the assumption that the rebels are highly dedicated to an ideological cause, but as Davd Grossman points out, numerous studies conclude that men in combat are usually motivated by group pressures, regard for their comrades, respect for their leaders, concern for their own reputation with both, and an urge to contribute to the success of the group—in other words, by highly particular alliances and concerns.[43] Grossman also observes that training processes are usually rooted in network dynamics. Indeed, IRA companies were very often founded on such networks. Cork veterans recollect that the Treaty itself and Republican ideology were rarely discussed within their ranks. Politics took second place at times, and most veterans couched the reasons for their choice of sides in the civil war in the same general terms as their reasons for joining the IRA in the War of Independence.[44]

USING LOCAL AND SPECIALISED FORCES- A FREE STATE PERSPECTIVE

Locally recruited forces have preferential access to information since they are operating in areas where they have lived and among populations they know.[45] When local forces are supported by specialised forces, the results are significantly enhanced.[46] In Waterford, for example, Lieutenant Colonel Patrick Paul—a native son and also the commander of an East Waterford IRA Unit during the War of Independence—proved a remarkable force multiplier for the Free State because both his local knowledge and his expertise enabled the National Army to hold, compel, and exert tremendous pressure on the IRA.[47] Paul also urged the recruitment of local men like himself who had served in the British Army in order to fill the knowledge and experience vacuum.[48] Similarly, Major General Emmet Dalton realised the benefit of local troops, observing that about 100 of his newly recruited soldiers were local and had previous military experience.[49][50]

Along with local troops who could provide local knowledge and intelligence, the National Army had the ability to mass forces, sometimes using over 2,000 local and specialised troops to cover more than a thousand square kilometres of difficult terrain.⁵¹ Local soldiers were especially needed to hold the terrain after clearance operations, and for that reason, extra rifles were often taken on operations. Each contingent would rapidly expand its strength after the initial fighting by recruiting and arming local volunteers who were pro-Treaty IRA members or ex-British Army veterans.⁵² The additional recruitment also permitted the National Army to establish bases throughout County Cork.⁵³ This may explain why the army presence in Cork was less oppressive than in other counties and why, after the war, there was very little resurgence of support for the IRA.

Specialised troops were organised to support the garrisons: the Intelligence Corps, the Railway Protection Corps, and counter columns. The columns comprised experienced soldiers who would link up with local soldiers in search operations. As local forces manned the outer cordons, the counter columns normally operated in the interior to search for IRA flying columns.⁵⁴ This arrangement became a very effective tactic in harassing and tiring out the IRA. National Army intelligence officers would also typically attend the searches and sweeps to report on infrastructure damage and other IRA activities. Even after the fighting, continued intelligence reports reflected the importance placed by the Free State on the restoration of essential infrastructure.⁵⁵

Specialised troops also came in the form of the Special Infantry Corps (SIC), which consisted of roughly 4,000 men stationed semi-permanently in strategic locations across the country.⁵⁶ As a whole, they acted as an additional gendarmerie security force to support local soldiers and the local Civic Guard in exerting civil control.⁵⁷

Insurgent networks tend to be driven by local issues and alliances, and that makes them particularly vulnerable to the use of local forces. Local soldiers are familiar with the particular cause of an insurrection in a particular area and know what is required on the ground. When they are supported by specialised units, they are more effective than other troops in finding out how the insurgent networks recruit, train, operate, and sustain themselves and where they operate.

CONCLUSION

Peter Hart observes that the most important bonds holding the IRA volunteers together during the civil war were those of family and neighbourhood.[58] By the end of war, most IRA networks, families, and vulnerabilities—including the devastating effect of Catholic censure—were known to Free State personnel.[59] As a result, Republicans ultimately believed that the IRA would "not have a man left owing to the great number of arrests and casualties" stemming from information supplied by civilians to local National Army troops.[60]

BEING AN ADAPTIVE LEARNING ORGANISATION

John Nagl emphasises the need to build what he refers to as "adaptive learning organizations" to succeed in counterinsurgency campaigns.[61] Once the particular elements of a campaign have been decided, they must not be set in stone. Common sense, flexibility, and learning are key tenets to effectively counter an insurgency, which is why US Army Field Manual 3-24 notes that an emphasis on learning and adaptation makes it possible to maintain an advantage over insurgents. Adaptive learning can facilitate the co-existence of compellence and good governance, and support a plan to sustain operations effectively.

Conventional military forces have historically struggled to adapt and defeat insurgencies, and as Nagl notes, those that succeeded did so because they were adaptive learning organisations.[62] Adaptive military forces use their wartime experience to "react positively to the unexpected, adjusting their methods of operation rapidly to the circumstances actually prevailing."[63] Victory is gained through a tempo of adaptation that the opponent cannot match. As Nagl explains, "Learning is also demonstrated in . . . the structure of military organizations, in the creation of new organizations to deal with new or changed situations, and in the myriad other institutional responses to change."[64] Adaptive organisations can react and change in order to rectify setbacks and exploit opportunities. A military force must also be flexible enough to make the transition from the kinetic actions associated with conventional or clearance operations to the non-kinetic actions associated with a hold or build campaign—to move effectively and efficiently between kinetic combat and humanitarian peacekeeping/stabilisation operations. These operations can occur concurrently, depending on the area of deployment.[65] Flexibility, doctrine, local knowledge, and a military education allow a military force to enact transitions within a complex environment. Being an adaptive learning organisation, in sum, is a key combat multiplier, giving the counterinsurgent force a marked advantage.

In counterinsurgency operations, a liberal dose of humility is also essential if we are to learn from the experience of others.[66] Previous conflicts offer lessons, but history in this case does not repeat itself. However prepared, trained, and indoctrinated a counterinsurgent force may be, reality will always differ from theory. Mistakes are bound to happen, but it would be inexcusable not to document and learn from them.[67] Counterinsurgency doctrine, like all doctrine, should be used as overarching guidance and constantly updated by lessons learned.

BEING AN ADAPTIVE LEARNING ORGANISATION- A FREE STATE PERSPECTIVE

A successful counterinsurgency force is built on an adaptive learning organisation that can react quickly to unexpected circumstances, adjust its methods of operation accordingly, and thereby facilitate compellence and good governance at the same time.[68] The ability to learn and adapt is demonstrated in the structure of a military organisation, and in its willingness to develop new organisations to deal with changing situations.[69]

The National Army leadership quickly realised that veterans would be a vital cog in the combat effectiveness and training expertise of a growing army. After the IRA fight in the autumn months of 1922, when the Free State started to lose the momentum, National Army Chief of Staff Richard Mulcahy suggested to his fellow general, Seán Mac Mahon, that despite their widespread unpopularity former British Army officers should be enlisted onto a technical committee so that "their ideas would . . . provide a base line against which we would compare what we're actually doing ourselves." [70] As a result of the findings of the technical committee, the infantry forces were battle-grouped and counter columns were formed. Training establishments were established for key combat support capabilities, including an artillery and armour school.[71]

The formation of the Railway Protection Corps also proved how flexible and adaptable the Free State government was. Cabinet papers from September 1922 proposed that 1,200 railway employees who were idle might be usefully engaged in police or military work to help maintain rail services.[72] These workers were quickly recruited by the National Army into specialised units, proving an enormous success in the restoration and protection of essential services.

Flexibility, doctrine, and a military education allow a military force to make transitions in a complex environment. As General Michael Costello said at an army inquiry after the civil war, every officer admitted that the army had made extraordinary improvement between December 1922 and April 1923, much of it as a result of a re-organisation and restructuring that occurred in January.[73] Mulcahy had a clear strategic vision of the type of organisation he wanted to achieve, namely a permanent and centrally controlled Defence Force that would take its orders from the Free State government.[74] Within the organisation of the National Army, the creation of district or regional commands made it possible—at least in principle—for the Free State to develop a strategic plan of action that offered a vital advantage over its IRA adversaries.[75]

The newly adopted leadership format, the streamlining of command and control, and the breakdown of territory for these units allowed battle groups to operate and co-operate in a very cohesive and effective manner. It also gave the infantry units the elasticity and flexibility that Mulcahy had advocated as early as August 1922.[76] By deploying and reinforcing their forces throughout the country, the army increased its mobility, harassed the IRA, and learned from mistakes. As a learning organisation, the

Free State reconstituted the army and brought the fight back to the IRA with improved tactics and strategy.

A strategic plan enables strategic success, when one side operates with a rhythm of adaptation that is beyond the other side's ability to achieve or sustain.[77] Learning and adaptation allow military forces to regain the initiative and swing the momentum back in their favour.

FOSTERING THE POPULATION'S TRUST

Protracted warfare should be the goal of insurgent organisations because time is a vulnerable resource. Trinquier explains, "The goal of the guerrilla, during what can be a long period of time, is not so much to obtain local successes as to prolong the campaign . . . It is to create a climate of insecurity, compel the forces of order to retire into their most easily defensible areas."[78] This must be resisted.

Countering the drawn-out violence of an insurgency involves emphasising intelligence, focusing on the needs and security of the population, establishing and expanding secure areas, avoiding a concentration of military forces in large bases for protection, engaging the populace rather than overemphasising killing or capturing the enemy.[79] When forces are scattered across the population—living among its members—they need not be told how to win support. They realise instinctively that their own safety depends on good relations with local people.[80] Security cannot be provided from large, isolated bases or during daylight hours only. Troops must live among and protect the population until it is able to protect itself with minimal outside support.[81] Civilians who feel sufficiently safe in government-held areas or who want government-supplied services and commerce will provide tactical information that can be used to target insurgents, their leaders, and their supplies, but they will do so only if their security is assured.[82]

Living within the local area allows forces to build a mutual trust that helps to ensure security on both sides and separates the population from both the insurgents and the underlying causes of conflict.[83] This indirect approach to defeating an insurgency is achieved by removing the support that insurgents must have in order to challenge the government. In the long term, it is usually more effective than a direct approach.[84]

Counterinsurgency operations must maintain the unconditional support of the populace at any price.[85] The counterinsurgent force should adopt a presence, posture, and profile that reassures and protects the local population. Thus, winning the population is a major battlefield of revolutionary war.[86] Counterinsurgent forces should not commute to work; instead, embedded within the local population they become intelligence collectors and analysts—and the keys to overall victory. They are the holders and builders.[87]

FOSTERING TRUST WITH THE POPULATION- A FREE STATE PERSPECTIVE

The goal of the insurgent is to create a climate of insecurity and compel the forces of order to retire into their most easily defensible areas.[88] But security cannot be provided from large, isolated bases or only during daylight hours. It must be all-encompassing. Troops must live among and protect the population until it is able to protect itself.[89] The provision of a safe environment makes it easier to deliver services to citizens and for citizens to share crucial information.[90] Community inhabitants will identify the insurgents in their midst only if they can be certain that they will survive the experience.[91]

The National Army bases established across the towns and villages of County Cork proved highly successful both in garnering information to subdue the IRA and in fostering good relations with the local people.[92] By the end of the war, most army reports referred to the steadily improving relationship between the army and the people, especially in Cork.[93]

Additionally, the Civic Guard was extensively deployed to unoccupied police stations throughout the country, sometimes without the assistance of experienced police personnel or even manuals.[94] The government realised the dangers but insisted on putting the unarmed guards out into communities in hostile areas: "You may be murdered, your barracks burned, your uniform taken off you, but you must carry on and bring peace to the people."[95] Thus embedded in the local communities, Civic Guard became a noticeable security presence and a vital building block of the new Irish Free State.[96]

The Civic Guard also had preferential access to information since its members were operating in areas they knew intimately.[97] Dramatic results were achieved through this strategy of making information sharing safer for civilians. Free State intelligence and after-action reviews claimed that by 1923, IRA supporters left fighting were for the most part "men who have been led astray and who really did not know what they were doing. They simply followed certain leaders."[98]

The people who matter are the ones on the margins.[99] They constitute the target audience for information sharing and information operations. Providing all-round security separates the population from the insurgents and the underlying causes of the conflict. This indirect approach to defeating an insurgency is usually more effective than a direct one over the long term.[100] As the war concluded, even the most stridently Republican population areas became more favourable towards the National Army.

THE ALL IMPORTANT BRIDGING OF THE GAP!

The difference between what it takes to win a village and what it takes to win a war strategically matters greatly, yet it is little understood and scarcely acknowledged in policy debates. How does winning the village help in the greater scheme of things? Simply put, quelling violence locally can create opportunities for larger political bargains that do not exist when insurgency is strong. Mainly local victories can reduce violence to a level society can tolerate. Additionally, they may open up political

CONCLUSION

opportunities to settle underlying issues contributing to the conflict—again, opportunities that don't exist when the fighting is raging.[101] Finally, local victories fill the ungoverned spaces, facilitating political and military activities to establish a desired political order during and following the combat phase of war.[102]

But local victories must be underpinned by a recognisable improvement to the environment. A counterinsurgency plan has to include realistic expectations, sustainability, and rebuilding. The government doesn't need to win over the broad mass of the population. The people who matter are the ones on the margins, the neutral majority who want peace and security.[103] They are the target audience for a better good—for the ReBuild.

In order to achieve this, counterinsurgent forces should not commute to work. Forces embedded with and living among local communities become intelligence collectors and analysts. *They are the holders and builders*, the keys to ultimate victory.[104] By fostering trust and recruiting locally, the Free State weakened support for the IRA, enhanced its own standing, and improved its ability to obtain useable information. As it untangled IRA support networks and undermined their cause, restored essential infrastructure, rebuilt the economy, and provided better governance, the Free State bridged the gap between local victories and overall strategic success.

This was the difference between winning the villages of Cork and Munster tactically and winning a counterinsurgency war strategically. Although the National Army made mistakes throughout the campaign, by being adaptive and flexible—by being a learning organisation—it was able to take the kinetic fight to the IRA, harassing their fighters and overwhelming their safe havens.

How fully the hearts and minds of the Munster and Cork populations were won cannot be measured, but by the end of the fighting, Free State reports did record positive attitudes towards the National Army. The neutral majority was ultimately won over when essential services and infrastructure were rebuilt after years of conflict and neglect. At the heart of any counterinsurgency campaign lies a fundamental requirement: undermine the insurgent cause by offering a more attractive alternative. By 1923, after 10 years of turmoil, most people in Ireland had formed the perception that the Free State government offered a better deal than the IRA.[105]

BIBLIOGRAPHY

ARCHIVAL COLLECTIONS

Cambridge University Archives Department, UK
    Churchill Archives
Collins Barracks Museum, Cork
    Notebook belonging Michael Collins
Cork City and County Archives
    Liam de Róiste Diaries
    Cork Corporation Law and Finance Committee, Meeting Minutes (Corporation Law and Finance)
Cork County Library
    Minutes of the Cork County Council Meetings
Military Archives Ireland, Dublin
    Bureau of Military History Witness Statements and Documents
    Civil War Captured Documents
    Civil War Intelligence Reports
    Civil War Papers Cork
    Cork Brigade Activity Reports
    Department of Defence (DoD) Papers
    Michael Collins Papers
    Military Service Pensions Collection – IRA Nominal Rolls
National Archives Ireland, Dublin

Department of Finance Papers
Department of Taoiseach Papers
National Library of Ireland, Dublin
  Emmet Dalton Papers
  Ephemera Collection
  Erskine Childers Papers
  Joseph McGarrity Papers
  Dáil Éireann
    Debates
    Executive Council Minutes
Parliamentary Archives, Westminster, UK
  Lloyd George Papers
University College Dublin Archives
  Frank Aiken Papers
  Ernest Blythe Papers
  Éamon De Valera Papers
  Desmond FitzGerald Papers
  Seán MacEoin Papers
  Eoin MacNeill Papers
  Con Moloney Papers
  Ernie O'Malley Papers
  Richard Mulcahy Papers
  Moss Twomey Papers
Villanova University, Pennsylvania, US
  Joseph McGarrity Papers

NEWSPAPERS AND MAGAZINES

An t-Oglach
Connacht Tribune
Cork Constitution
Cork Examiner

Freeman's Journal
Irish Independent
Irish Times
Kilkenny People
Limerick Chronicle
New York Times
Poblacht na hEireann
The Times (London)

OTHER PRIMARY SOURCES

Allen, Gregory. *The Garda Síochána: Policing Independent Ireland, 1922–1982*. Dublin: Gill and Macmillan, 1999.

Australian Defence Force. Australian Defence Doctrine Publication (ADDP) Operation Series 3.13. Information Activities Edition 3. Canberra: Defence Publishing Service, 2013.

Boyd, G.M. Dublin District Weekly Intelligence Summary. October 1922. DT/3/S1784, University College Dublin Archives.

Brennan Commission. *Commission of Inquiry into the Civil Service 1932–35*. Dublin: Stationery Office, 1936.

North Atlantic Treaty Organization (NATO). Troop Contributions. http://www.nato.int/cps/en/natohq/topics_50316.htm. Updated 11 April 2023.

United Kingdom. *Hansard*. House of Commons (HC). Debates. Army. 1923. Vol. 151-167.

—. Army Reservists, Southern Ireland. 1922. Vols. 151 and 154.

—. Free State Army. 1922. Vols. 153 and 156.

—. Munitions and Stores. 1923. Vol. 166.

United States, Department of the Army. *Field Manual 3-0: Operations*, 2001.

—. *Field Manual 3-0: Operations*, 2017.

—. *Field Manual 3-07: Stability Operations*, 2008.

—. *Field Manual 3-24: Counterinsurgency*, 2006.

—. *Field Manual 3-24.2: Tactics in Counterinsurgency*, 2009.

—. *Field Manual FM 5-102: Countermobility,* 2004.
—. *U.S. Army Readiness Guidance,* 2016.
US Government Interagency Counterinsurgency Initiative. *U.S. Government Counterinsurgency Guide.* Washington, DC: US Government Printing Office, 2009.

BOOKS AND ARTICLES

Bacevich, A.J. *The New American Militarism: How Americans Are Seduced by War.* Oxford: Oxford University Press, 2005.

Berman, Eli, Jospeh H. Felter, and Jacob N. Shapiro. *Small Wars, Big Data: The Information Revolution in Modern Conflict,* Princeton, NJ: Princeton University Press, 2018.

Borgonovo, John. *The Battle for Cork: July–August 1922.* Cork: Mercier Press, 2011.

Boyce, David George. *Englishmen and Irish Troubles: British Public Opinion and the Making of Irish Policy 1918–1922.* Cambridge, MA: MIT Press, 1972.

Boyne, Sean. *Emmet Dalton: British Soldier, Irish General, Film Pioneer.* Dublin: Merrion Press, 2015.

Brady, Conor. *Guardians of the Peace: The Early Years of the Irish Police Force.* Dublin: Gill and Macmillan, 1974.

British Army. *Design for Operations: The British Military Doctrine.* London: Her Majesty's Stationery Office, 1989.

Brown, Malcolm, ed. *T.E. Lawrence in War and Peace: An Anthology of the Military Writings of Lawrence of Arabia.* London: Greenhill Books, 2005.

Cain P.J. and Hopkins A.G. *British Imperialism: Crisis and Deconstruction 1914–1990.* London: Longman, 1993.

Callwell, C.E. *Small Wars: Their Principle and Practice.* 3rd ed., 1906. Reprint, Lincoln: University of Nebraska Press, 1996.

Churchill, Winston. *The Aftermath.* London: Thornton, 1929.

Corcoran, Donal. *Freedom to Achieve Freedom: The Irish Free State 1922–1932.* Dublin: Gill and Macmillan, 2013.

Cottrell, Peter. *The Irish Civil War, 1922–1923.* Oxford: Osprey Publishing, 2008.

Cronin, Mike, and John M. Regan, eds. *Ireland: The Politics of Independence, 1922–49*. London: Palgrave Macmillan, 2000.

Crowley, John, Donal Ó Drisceoil, and Michael Murphy, eds. *Atlas of the Irish Revolution*. Cork: Cork University Press, 2017.

Deasy, Liam. *Brother against Brother*. Cork: Mercier Press, 1982.

Dolan, Anne. *Commemorating the Irish Civil War: History and Memory, 1923–2000*. Cambridge: Cambridge University Press, 2003.

Dooney, Seán. *The Irish Civil Service*. Dublin: Mount Salus Press, 1976.

Doyle, Tom. *The Summer Campaign in Kerry*. Cork: Mercier Press, 2010.

Duggan, John P. *A History of the Irish Army*. Dublin: Gill and Macmillan, 1991.

Dwyer, T. Ryle, *"I Signed My Death Warrant": Michael Collins and the Treaty*. Cork: Mercier Press, 2006.

——. *Tans, Terror and Troubles: Kerry's Real Fighting Story, 1913–23*. Cork: Mercier Press, 2001.

Ewart, Wilfrid. *A Journey in Ireland*. London: Putnam, 1922.

Fanning, Ronan. "Britain's Legacy: Government and Administration". In *Irish Studies*, vol. 5: *Ireland and Britain since 1922*, edited by P.J. Drudy, 46–64. Cambridge: Cambridge University Press, 1986.

Farrell, Theo, and Terry Terriff. *The Sources of Military Change: Culture, Politics, Technology*. Boulder, CO: Lynne Rienner Publishers, 2002.

Felter, Joseph. "Sources of Military Effectiveness in Counterinsurgency: Evidence from the Philippines." In *The Sword's Other Edge: Trade-offs in the Pursuit of Military Effectiveness*, edited by Daniel Reiter Cambridge: Cambridge University Press, 2017.

Ferriter, Diarmaid. *Between Two Hells: The Irish Civil War*. London: Profile Books, 2021.

Fitzpatrick, D. "Militarism in Ireland, 1900–1922". In *A Military History of Ireland*, edited by Thomas Bartlett and Keith Jeffery, Cambridge: Cambridge University Press.

Foster, Gavin Maxwell. *The Irish Civil War and Society: Politics, Class, and Conflict*. London: Palgrave Macmillan, 2015.

Galula, David. *Counterinsurgency Warfare: Theory and Practice*. Westport, CT: Praeger Security International, 1964.

Garvin, Tom. *1922: The Birth of Irish Democracy*. Dublin: Gill and Macmillan, 1996.

Gentile, Gian. *Wrong Turn: America's Deadly Embrace of Counterinsurgency*. New York: The New Press, 2013.

Gray, Colin. *Another Bloody Century: Future Warfare*. London: Phoenix Press, 2005.

Grossman, Dave. *On Killing: The Psychological Cost of Learning to Kill in War and Society*. Boston: Little, Brown and Company, 1995.

Harrington, Michael. *The Munster Republic: The Civil War in North Cork*. Cork: Mercier Press, 2009.

Harrington, Niall C. *Kerry Landing, August 1922: An Episode of the Civil War*. Dublin: Anvil Books, 1992.

Hart, Peter. *The I.R.A. and Its Enemies: Violence and Community in Cork, 1916–1923*. Oxford: Clarendon Press, 1998.

—. *The I.R.A. at War, 1916–1923*. Oxford: Oxford University Press, 2003.

Harvey, Dan, and Gerry White. *The Barracks: A History of Victoria/Collins Barracks*. Cork: Mercier Press, 1997.

Hazelton, Jacqueline L. *Bullets Not Ballots: Success in Counterinsurgency Warfare*. Ithaca, NY: Cornell University Press, 2021.

Hopkinson, Michael. "The Civil War: The Opening Phase". In *Atlas of the Irish Revolution*, edited by John Crowley, Donal Ó Drisceoil, and Michael Murphy, Cork: Cork University Press, 2017.

—. *Green against Green: The Irish Civil War*. Dublin: Gill and Macmillan, 2004.

Hosmer, Stephen T., and Sibylle O. Crane. *Counterinsurgency: A Symposium, April 16–20, 1962*. Santa Monica, CA: RAND Corporation, 1963.

Huntington, Samuel P. *Political Order in Changing Societies*. New Haven, CT: Yale University Press, 1968.

Jones, Thomas. *Whitehall Diary*. Vol. 3, *Ireland 1918–25*, edited by Keith Middleton. Oxford: Oxford University Press, 1971.

Kaldor, Mary. *New and Old Wars: Organised Violence in a Global Era*. Redwood City, CA: Stanford University Press, 1999.

Kalyvas, Stathis N. *The Logic of Violence in Civil War*. Cambridge: Cambridge University Press, 2006.

—. *"New" and "Old" Civil Wars: A Valid Distinction*. Cambridge: Cambridge University Press, 2001.

Kautt, William H. *Ambushes and Armour: The Irish Rebellion, 1919–1921*. Dublin: Irish Academic Press, 2010.

—. *Arming the Irish Revolution: Gunrunning and Arms Smuggling, 1911–1922*. Lawrence: University Press of Kansas, 2021.

Kennedy, Padraic. *Key Appointments and the Transition of the Irish Volunteers, the Irish Republican Army and the National Army (1913–23)*. Dublin: Irish Defence Forces, 2016.

Kilcullen, David. "Twenty-Eight Articles: Fundamentals of Company-Level Counterinsurgency". *Miitary Review* 86, no. 3 (May–June 2006): 103–8.

Kissane, Bill. *The Politics of the Irish Civil War*. Oxford: Oxford University Press, 2005.

—. "The Politics of the Treaty Split and the Civil War". In *Atlas of the Irish Revolution*, edited by John Crowley, Donal Ó Drisceoil, and Michael Murphy. Cork: Cork University Press, 2017.

Kitson, Frank. *Low Intensity Operations: Subversions, Insurgency and Peacekeeping*. London: Faber, 1971.

Kraft, Herman Joseph S. "The Philippines: The Weak State and the Global War on Terror". *Kasarinlan: Philippine Journal of Third World Studies* 18, nos. 1–2 (2003): 133–52.

Lawlor, Sheila. *Britain and Ireland, 1914–1923*. Dublin: Gill and Macmillan, 1983.

Ledwidge, Frank. *Losing Small Wars: British Military Failures in the 9/11 Wars*. London and New Haven, CT: Yale University Press, 2017.

Lee, J.J. *Ireland 1912–85: Politics and Society*. Cambridge: Cambridge University Press, 1989.

Leonard, J. "Facing the Finger of Scorn: Veteran's Memories of Ireland after the Great War". In *War and Memory in the Twentieth Century*, edited by Martin Evans and Ken Lunn. Oxford: Berg Publishers, 1997.

Long, Patrick. "The Army of the Irish Free State, 1922–1924." MA thesis, University College Dublin, 1983.

—. "Organization and Development of the Pro-Treaty Forces, 1922–1924." *The Irish Sword: Journal of the Military History Society of Ireland* (Winter 1997).

Luttwark, Edward. "Dead End: Counterinsurgency Warfare as Military Malpractice." *Harper's Magazine* (February 2007).

Lyons, F.S.L. *Ireland since the Famine*. London: Weidenfeld and Nicholson, 1971.

Macardle, Dorothy. *The Irish Republic: A Documented Chronicle of the Anglo-Irish Conflict and the Partitioning of Ireland, with a Detailed Account of the Period 1916–1923*. London: Corgi Books, 1968.

Maguire, Martin. *The Civil Service and the Revolution in Ireland, 1912–38, 'Shaking the Blood-stained Hand of Mr Collins*. Manchester: Manchester University Press, 2010.

Mahon, Tom. *The Ballycotton Job: An Incredible True Story of IRA Pirates*. Cork: Mercier Press, 2022.

Marlowe, A. "Forgotten Founder: The French Colonel Who Wrote the Book(s) on Counterinsurgency." *Weekly Standard* 15, no. 5 (19 October 2009).

Marnane, Denis G. *The Civil War in County Tipperary*. Tipperary: Ara Press, 2021.

Martin, Micheál. *Freedom to Choose: Cork and Party Politics in Ireland, 1918–1932* Cork: The Collins Press, 2009.

McCance, Captain S. *History of the Royal Munster Fusiliers, 1861 to 1922*. Uckfield, UK: Naval and Military Press, 2017.

McCarthy, Brian. *The Civic Guard Mutiny*. Cork: Mercier Press, 2012.

McCarthy, Pat. *The Irish Revolution, 1912–23: Waterford*. Dublin: Four Courts Press, 2015.

McColgan, John. *British Policy and the Irish Administration, 1920–22*. London: George Allen and Unwin, 1983.

McGinty, Tom. *The Irish Navy*. Kerry: The Kerryman, 1995.

McNamee, L. "The Cavalry Corps." *An Cosantóir* 36, no. 1 (January 1976).

McNiffe, Liam. *A History of the Garda Siochana: A Social History of the Force 1922–52, with an Overview of the Years 1952–97*. Dublin: Wolfhound Press, 1997.

Murphy, William. "Imprisonments during the Civil War". In *Atlas of the Irish Revolution*, edited by John Crowley, Donal Ó Drisceoil, and Michael Murphy, Cork: Cork University Press, 2017.

Murray, Patrick. *Oracles of God: The Roman Catholic Church and Irish Politics, 1922–1937*. Dublin: University College Dublin Press, 2000.

Nagl, John A. *Knife Fights: A Memoir of Modern War in Theory and Practice*. New York: Penguin Press, 2014.

—. *Learning to Eat Soup with a Knife: Counterinsurgency Lessons from Malaya and Vietnam*. Chicago: University of Chicago Press, 2005.

Neeson, Eoin. *The Civil War in Ireland*. Cork: Mercier Press, 1966.

O'Callaghan, John. *The Battle for Kilmallock*. Cork: Mercier Press, 2011.

O Caoimh, Padraig. *Richard Mulcahy: From the Politics of War to the Politics of Peace, 1913–1924*. Newbridge: Irish Academic Press, 2019.

Ó Conchubhair, Brian, ed. *Dublin's Fighting Story, 1916–1921: Told by the Men Who Made It*. Cork: Mercier Press, 2009.

O'Donoghue, Florence. *No Other Law: The Story of Liam Lynch and the Irish Republican Army, 1916–1923*. Dublin: Irish Press, 1954.

Ó Drisceoil, Donal. "Irish Newspapers, the Treaty and the Civil War". In *Atlas of the Irish Revolution*, edited by John Crowley, Donal Ó Drisceoil, and Michael Murphy, Cork: Cork University Press, 2017.

—. "The Military Service (1916–1923) Pensions Collection: The Brigade Activity Reports". In *Atlas of the Irish Revolution*, edited by John Crowley, Donal Ó Drisceoil, and Michael Murphy, Cork: Cork University Press, 2017.

Ó Gadhra, Nollaig. *Civil War in Connacht, 1922–23*. Cork: Mercier Press, 1999.

O'Halpin, Eunan. *Defending Ireland: The Irish State and Its Enemies since 1922*. Oxford: Oxford University Press, 1999.

O'Malley, Ernie. *The Men Will Talk to Me: The West Cork Interviews*, edited by Andy Bielenberg, John Borgonovo, and Pádraig Óg Ó Ruairc. Cork: Mercier Press, 2015.

—. *The Singing Flame: A Memoir of the Civil War, 1922–24*. 1936. Reprint, Cork: Mercier Press, 2012.

—. *"No Surrender Here!" The Civil War Papers of Ernie O'Malley, 1922–24*, edited by Cormac O'Malley and Anne Dolan. Dublin: Lilliput Press, 2007.

O'Neill, Thomas P., and the Earl of Longford. *Eamonn De Valera*. Dublin: Gill and Macmillan, 1970.

O'Sullivan, Donal J. *District Inspector John A. Kearney: The R.I.C. Man Who Befriended Roger Casement*. Victoria, BC: Trafford, 2005.

Power, Joseph. *Clare and the Civil War*. Dublin: Eastwood Books, 2020.

Porch, Douglas. *Counterinsurgency: Exposing the Myths of the New Way of War*. New York: Cambridge University Press, 2013.

Prager, Jeffrey. *Building Democracy in Ireland: Political Order and Cultural Integration in a Newly Independent Nation*. Cambridge: Cambridge University Press, 1986.

Radin, Andrew. *Institution Building in Weak States: The Primacy of Local Politics.* Washington, DC: Georgetown University Press, 2020.

Regan, J.M. "The Politics of Utopia: Party Organisation, Executive Autonomy and the New Administration". In *Ireland: The Politics of Independence, 1922–49*, edited by Mike Cronin and John M. Regan, (London, 2000).

—. *Myth and the Irish State.* Dublin: Irish Academic Press, 2013.

Riccio, Ralph A. *The Irish Artillery Corps since 1922.* Petersfield: Mushroom Model Publications, 2012.

Schadlow, Nadia. *War and the Art of Governance: Consolidating Combat Success into Political Victory.* Washington, DC: Georgetown University Press, 2017.

Sheehan, William. *A Hard Local War: The British Army and the Guerrilla War in Cork 1919–1921.* Stroud: The History Press, 2017.

Staniland, Paul. *Networks of Rebellion: Explaining Insurgent Cohesion and Collapse.* Ithaca, NY: Cornell University Press, 2014.

—. "States, Insurgents and Wartime Political Orders." *Perspectives in Politics* 10, no. 2 (June 2012): 243–54.

Strachan, Hew. *The Politics of the British Army.* Oxford: Clarendon Press, 1997.

Street, Cecil J.C. *Ireland in 1921.* London: Philip Allan, 1922.

Taylor, Paul. *Heroes or Traitors? Experiences of Southern Irish Soldiers Returning from the Great War, 1919–1939.* Liverpool: Liverpool University Press, 2015.

Thompson, Sir Robert. *Defeating Communist Insurgency: Experiences from Malaya and Vietnam.* London: Chatto and Windus, 1972.

Townshend, Charles. *The Republic: The Fight for Irish Independence, 1918–1923.* London: Penguin Books, 2014.

Trinquier, Roger. *Modern Warfare: A French View of Counterinsurgency.* 1964. Reprint, Westport CT: Praeger Security International, 2006.

Valiulis, Maryann Gialanella. *Portrait of a Revolutionary: General Richard Mulcahy and the Founding of the Irish Free State.* Lexington: University Press of Kentucky, 1992.

—. *Almost a Rebellion: The Irish Army Mutiny of 1924.* Cambridge: Cambridge University Press 1992.

van Creveld, Martin. *The Changing Face of War: Lessons of Combat, from the Marne to Iraq,* New York: Presidio Press/Ballantine Books, 2006.

von Clausewitz, Carl. *On War*. 1832. Reprint, Princeton, NJ: Princeton University Press, 1989.

Walsh, Paul V. "The Irish Civil War 1922–1923: A Military Study of the Conventional Phase, 28 June–11 August, 1922." Paper delivered to New York Military Affairs Symposium, New York, 11 December 1998. http://bobrowen.com/nymas/irishcivilwar.html.

White, Gerry. "Free State vs. Republic: The Opposing Armed Forces in the Civil War." In *Atlas of the Irish Revolution*, edited by John Crowley, Donal Ó Drisceoil, and Michael Murphy, Cork: Cork University Press, 2017.

Younger, Calton. *Ireland's Civil War*. New York: Taplinger Publishers, 1968.

NOTES

Preface

1. Patrick Prendergast's Application for Service (1917–1921) Medal identifies Maurice Horgan, Michael Spillane and Patrick Allmon as the IRA Unit Commanders for Patrick during this period. This document also outlines the Company (A), Battalion (4th), Brigade (2nd Kerry) and Division (First Southern) that Prendergast enlisted in on 4 August 1919.
2. John Borgonovo, *The Battle for Cork: July–August 1922* (Cork: Mercier Press 2011), 120.

Introduction

1. Thomas Jones, *Whitehall Diary*, vol. 3, *Ireland 1918–25*, ed. Keith Middleton (Oxford: Oxford University Press, 1971), 48.
2. Ernie O'Malley, *The Singing Flame: A Memoir of the Civil War, 1922–24* (1936; reprinted Cork: Mercier Press, 2012), 23.
3. William H. Kautt, *Arming the Irish Revolution: Gunrunning and Arms Smuggling, 1911–1922* (Lawrence: University Press of Kansas, 2021), 208.
4. For the conditions of the Treaty and the Republican response, see John McColgan, *British Policy and the Irish Administration 1920–22* (London: George Allen and Unwin, 1983), 90; John Borgonovo, *The Battle for Cork: July–August 1922* (Cork: Mercier Press, 2011), 23.
5. Eoin Neeson, *The Civil War in Ireland* (Cork: Mercier Press, 1966), 39.
6. T. Ryle Dwyer, *"I Signed My Death Warrant": Michael Collins and the Treaty* (Cork: Mercier Press, 2006), 207.
7. Bill Kissane, "The Politics of the Treaty Split and the Civil War"*, in Atlas of the Irish Revolution*, ed. John Crowley, Donal Ó Drisceoil, and Michael Murphy (Cork: Cork University Press, 2017), 652.
8. O'Malley, *The Singing Flame*, 58.

9. De Róiste Diaries, 19 October 1922, Cork City and County Archives, U271/A/46.
10. Kissane, "The Politics of the Treaty Split", 652.
11. O'Malley, *The Singing Flame*, 61.
12. Dorothy Macardle, *The Irish Republic: A Documented Chronicle of the Anglo-Irish Conflict and the Partitioning of Ireland, with a Detailed Account of the Period 1916–1923* (London: Corgi, 1968), 617.
13. *Cork Examiner*, 7, 9, 10, 12 December 1921,
14. *Cork Constitution*, 31 December 1921 and 31 January 1922.
15. O'Malley, *The Singing Flame*, 63.
16. Kissane, "The Politics of the Treaty Split", 652–53.
17. Eunan O'Halpin, *Defending Ireland: The Irish State and Its Enemies since 1922* (Oxford: Oxford University Press, 1999), 2.
18. The National Army can also be referred to as the Free State Army, but for continuity and simplicity, I refer to the Free State forces fighting to support the Treaty as the National Army throughout.
19. Unsigned notes (possibly by Collins), University College Dublin Archives (UCDA), Richard Mulcahy Papers P7a/145.
20. O'Malley, *The Singing Flame*, 65.
21. Ibid., 73.
22. Maryann Gialanella Valiulis, *Portrait of a Revolutionary: General Richard Mulcahy and the Founding of the Irish Free State* (Lexington: University Press of Kentucky), 100.
23. Churchill to Lloyd George, letter, 19 April 1922, Parliamentary Archives, Westminster, UK, PAW, Lloyd George Papers LG/F/10/2/68.
24. Cope to Churchill, letter, 16 April 1922, PAW, LG/F/10/2/68.
25. General Macready to Churchill, letter, 16 April 1922, PAW, LG/F/10/2/67(b).
26. Peter Hart, *The I.R.A. at War, 1916–1923* (Oxford: Oxford University Press, 2003), 194–222.
27. Charles Townsend, *The Republic: The Fight for Irish Independence, 1918–1923* (London: Penguin Books, 2014), 404.
28. Borgonovo, *The Battle for Cork*, 45.
29. O'Malley, *The Singing Flame*, 112.
30. Lloyd George to Collins, letter, 22 June 1922, PAW, LG/F/10/6/4.
31. Townsend, *The Republic*, 405, 408.
32. Keith Jeffrey, "Sir Nevil Macready" in *Dictionary of Irish Biography* (DIB), 9 vols., ed. James McGuire and James Quinn (Cambridge: Cambridge University Press, 2009), 6:181–82.
33. Diarmaid Ferriter, *Between Two Hells: The Irish Civil War* (London: Profile Books 2021), 44.
34. Bill Kissane, *The Politics of the Irish Civil War* (Oxford: Oxford University Press, 2005), 74.
35. O'Malley, *The Singing Flame*, 137.
36. Sean Boyne, *Emmet Dalton: British Soldier, Irish General, Film Pioneer* (Dublin: Merrion Press, 2015), 141, who also cites Aaron R.B. Linderman, *Lessons Learnt by SOE from the Irish War of Independence*, 5, on these details.
37. Ferriter, *Between Two Hells*, 46.
38. For example, Denis G. Marnane, *The Civil War in County Tipperary* (Tipperary: Ara Press, 2021); Pat McCarthy, *The Irish Revolution, 1912–*

23: Waterford (Dublin: Four Courts Press, 2015); Tom Doyle, *The Summer Campaign in Kerry* (Cork: Mercier Press, 2010); Joseph Power, *Clare and the Civil War* (Dublin: Eastwood Books, 2020); T. Ryle Dwyer, *Tans, Terror and Troubles: Kerry's Real Fighting Story, 1913–23* (Cork: Mercier Press, 2001).

39 Power, *Clare and the Civil War*, 55.

40 Tom Mahon, *The Ballycotton Job: An Incredible True Story of IRA Pirates* (Cork: Mercier Press, 2022), 112.

41 Peter Hart, *The I.R.A. and Its Enemies: Violence and Community in Cork, 1916–1923* (Oxford: Clarendon Press, 1999), 113.

42 Dáil Éireann, Executive Council Minutes vol. 21, 16 November 1927; Andy Bielenberg, Cork Civil War Fatality Register, 1919–23, University College Cork, https://www.ucc.ie/en/theirishrevolution/collections/cork-fatality-register; and the National Army Report on Strength and Posts, 1 April 1923, National Archives of Ireland, NAI, D/T S3361.

43 Cited in Townsend, *The Republic*, 428.

44 Dwyer, *Tans, Terror and Troubles*, 366.

45 Hopkinson, *Green against Green*, 239.

46 David Galula, *Counterinsurgency Warfare: Theory and Practice* (Westport, CT: Praeger Security International, 1964), 2.

47 C.E. Callwell, *Small Wars: Their Principle and Practice*, 3rd ed. (1906; reprint, Omaha, NB: University of Nebraska Press, 1996), 21.

48 The private papers of Winston Churchill, Michael Collins, W.T. Cosgrave, Tom Ennis, David Lloyd George, Con Moloney, Richard Mulcahy, Ernie O'Malley, and Liam de Róiste were particularly helpful in this regard.

49 Anne Dolan, *Commemorating the Irish Civil War: History and Memory, 1923–2000* (Cambridge: Cambridge University Press, 2003), 200.

50 F.S.L. Lyons, *Ireland since the Famine* (London: Weidenfeld and Nicholson, 1971), 460.

51 Hopkinson, *Green against Green*, 272.

Chapter 1

1 David Galula, *Counterinsurgency Warfare: Theory and Practice* (Westport, CT: Praeger Security International, 1964).

2 Douglas Porch, *Counterinsurgency: Exposing the Myths of the New Way of War* (New York: Cambridge University Press, 2013), 179.

3 The US Army published *Field Manual 3-24: Counterinsurgency* (FM 3-24) in December 2006 and *Field Manual 3-07: Stability Operations* (FM 3-07) in October 2008. FM 3-24 was supplemented in April 2009 with *Field Manual 3-24.2: Tactics in Counterinsurgency* (FM 3-24.2).

4 FM 3-24.2, 3–17.

5 FM 3-24, 5–18; FM 3-07.

6 John A. Nagl, *Knife Fights: A Memoir of Modern War in Theory and Practice* (New York: Penguin Press, 2014), 134.

7 US Army, *Field Manual 3-24: Counterinsurgency*, 2006.

8 Ann Marlowe, "Forgotten Founder: The French Colonel Who Wrote the Book(s) on Counterinsurgency,"

Weekly Standard 15, no. 5 (19 October 2009), cited by Gian Gentile, in *Wrong Turn: America's Deadly Embrace of Counterinsurgency* (New York: The New Press, 2013), 26, asserts that Galula's *Counterinsurgency Warfare* and essays on the French experience in Algeria were instrumental in the writing of FM 3-24.

9   Roger Trinquier, *Modern Warfare: A French View of Counterinsurgency* (1964; reprint, Westport CT: Praeger Security International, 2006).

10   Edward Luttwark, "Dead End: Counterinsurgency Warfare as Military Malpractice," *Harper's Magazine*, February 2007.

11   Gian Gentile, "Time for the Deconstruction of FM 3-24," *Joint Force Quarterly*, 58 (July 2010).

Chapter 2

1   See John P. Duggan, *A History of the Irish Army* (Dublin: Gill and MacMillan, 1991), 121; Maryann Gialanella Valiulis, *Almost a Rebellion: The Irish Army Mutiny of 1924* (Cambridge: Cambridge University Press 1992), 23–24; Tom Garvin, *1922: The Birth of Irish Democracy*, 2nd ed. (Dublin: Gill and Macmillan, 1996), 122–23.

2   US Army, STAND-TO! – US Army Readiness Guidance, May 2016.

3   D.G. Boyce, *Englishmen and the Irish Troubles: British Public Opinion and the Making of Irish Policy 1918–22* (Cambridge, MA, MIT Press, 1972), 99.

4   Douglas Porch, *Counterinsurgency: Exposing the Myths of the New Way of War* (New York: Cambridge University Press, 2013), 118.

5   Hew Strachan, *The Politics of the British Army* (Oxford: Clarendon Press, 1997). 165–66.

6   John McColgan, *British Policy and the Irish Administration, 1920–22* (London: George Allen and Unwin, 1983), 90.

7   Lloyd George to Collins, 23 June 1922, Parliamentary Archives, Westminster, UK, PAW, Lloyd George Papers LG/F/10/6/4.

8   Indirect manning and training was conducted by British Army veterans of Irish descent who populated the new National Army, giving it the requisite leadership and experience. The British did not have direct control over this process, but organisations like the British Legion certainly supported the endeavour.

9   Diarmaid Ferriter makes this point in *Between Two Hells: The Irish Civil War* (London: Profile Books, 2021), 48, drawing from Colonial Office, note, 20 July 1922, National Archives, Colonial Office 739/6, Irish Free State 1922, vol. 6.

10   John Nagl, *Knife Fights: A Memoir of Modern War in Theory and Practice* (New York: Penguin Press, 2014), 177.

11   Churchill to Under Secretary Cope, April 1922, PAW, LG/F/10/2/67d.

12   Porch, *Counterinsurgency*, 114.

13   US Army, *FM 3-24.2: Tactics in Counterinsurgency*, 2009.

14   Winston Churchill, *The Aftermath* (London: Thornton, 1929), 297.

15   Theo Farrell and Terry Terriff, *The Sources of Military Change, Culture, Politics, Technology* (London: Lynne Rienner Publishers, 2002), 76.

16 National Army Organisational Charts, 1922, NAI, D/T S3361.
17 Ferriter, *Between Two Hells*, 46.
18 Dáil Éireann, Quartermaster-General Files, NAI, D/E 6/8/2.
19 Patrick Long, "The Army of the Irish Free State, 1922–1924", MA thesis (University College Dublin, 1983), 5.
20 Valiulis, *Almost a Rebellion*, 22–24.
21 Eoin Neeson, *The Civil War in Ireland* (Cork: Mercier Press 1966), 51.
22 John M. Regan, *Myth and the Irish State* (Dublin: Irish Academic Press, 2013), 126–29.
23 Ernie O'Malley, *The Singing Flame: A Memoir of the Civil War, 1922–24* (1936; reprinted, Cork: Mercier Press 2012), 48.
24 Valiulis, *Almost a Rebellion*, 24.
25 Florence O'Donoghue, *No Other Law: The Story of Liam Lynch and the Irish Republican Army, 1916–1923* (Dublin: Irish Press, 1954), 199.
26 Executive Council, minutes, 22, 27, 30 March 9, 17 April 1923, cited in Michael Hopkinson, *Green against Green: The Irish Civil War* (Dublin: Gill and Macmillan, 2004), 227.
27 General Mulcahy, Statement to the Army Inquiry Committee, 29 April 1924, Military Archives Ireland MAI, IE/MA/03021.
28 O'Halpin, *Defending Ireland*, 16.
29 Eunan O'Halpin, *Defending Ireland: The Irish State and Its Enemies since 1922* (Oxford: Oxford University Press, 1999), 16.
30 Bryan Cooper, Dáil Éireann, Vol. 21, 16 November 1927, cited in Paul Taylor, *Heroes or Traitors? Experiences of Southern Irish Soldiers Returning from the Great War, 1919–1939* (Liverpool: Liverpool University Press, 2015), 15.
31 For population data, see *Ibid.*; Lavery Report, National Archives Ireland (NAI), PIN 15/758; and Taylor, *Heroes or Traitors?* 12–13.
32 Taylor, *Heroes or Traitors?* 12.
33 Ferriter, *Between Two Hells*, 101.
34 John Borgonovo, *The Battle for Cork: July–August 1922* (Cork: Mercier Press, 2011), 63; De Róiste Diaries, 4 July 1922, Cork City and County Archives, U271/A/145.
35 Peter Hart, *The I.R.A. and Its Enemies: Violence and Community in Cork, 1916–1923* (Oxford: Clarendon Press, 1999), 312.
36 Jane Leonard, "Facing the Finger of Scorn: Veterans' Memories of Ireland after the Great War", in *War and Memory in the Twentieth Century*, ed. Geoff Eley (Oxford: Berg, 1997), 218.
37 Padraic Kennedy, *Key Appointments and the Transition of the Irish Volunteers, the Irish Republican Army and the National Army (1913–23)* (Dublin: Irish Defence Forces, 2016), 34.
38 O'Halpin, *Defending Ireland*, 15.
39 *Ibid.*, 42. The term *Trucer*, or *Trucileer*, refers to an individual who joined the IRA after the truce with the British in 1921.
40 John Borgonovo, "Army without Borders: The Irish Republican Army 1920–21", in *Atlas of the Irish Revolution*, ed. John Crowley, Donal Ó Drisceoil, and Michael Murphy (Cork: Cork University Press, 2017), 390.
41 Hopkinson, *Green against Green*, 187.

42 Mac Mahon to Army Inquiry Committee, 6 May 1924, University College Dublin Archives (UCDA), Richard Mulcahy Papers, P7/C/14.
43 Hopkinson, *Green against Green*, 136–37.
44 William Sheehan, "The British Army in Ireland", in *Atlas of the Irish Revolution*, 365–66.
45 Ferriter, *Between Two Hells, The Irish Civil War*, 32.
46 *Freeman's Journal*, 8 July 1922.
47 Maryann Gialanella Valiulis, *Portrait of a Revolutionary: General Richard Mulcahy and the Founding of the Irish Free State* (Lexington: University Press of Kentucky, 1992), 102.
48 Patrick Long, "Organization and Development of the pro-Treaty Forces, 1922–1924", *Irish Sword* 20 (82): 311; Michael Hopkinson, "The Civil War: The Opening Phase", in *Atlas of the Irish Revolution*, ed. Crowley, Ó Drisceoil, and Murphy, 679.
49 O'Malley, *The Singing Flame*, 182.
50 Valiulis, *Portrait of a Revolutionary*, 102.
51 Ibid., 103, 114.
52 Charles Townsend, *The Republic: The Fight for Irish Independence, 1918–1923* (London: Penguin Books, 2014), 421–22.
53 Long, "Organisation and Development of the pro-Treaty Forces", 311.
54 Estimates of Army, Quarter Master General's Department, GHQ, 29 November 1922, UCDA, Richard Mulcahy Papers, P7B/318.
55 Army Estimates, Dáil Éireann, Debates, 1 June 1923, 1450–62.
56 Hopkinson, *Green against Green*, 273.
57 Farrell and Terriff, *The Sources of Military Change*, 76.
58 Army Inquiry, Verbatim Report of Evidence Given by Mr. Kevin O'Higgins, Minister for Home Affairs, 22 April 1924, UCDA, Richard Mulcahy Papers, P7/C/23.
59 Valiulis, *Almost a Rebellion*, 111.

Chapter 3

1 Roger Trinquier, *Modern Warfare: A French View of Counterinsurgency* (1964; reprint, Westport CT: Praeger Security International, 2006), 85. See also Theo Farrell, "The Model Army: Military Imitation and the Enfeeblement of the Army in Post-Revolutionary Ireland 1922–42", *Irish Studies in International Affairs* 8 (1997): 111–28.
2 Emmet Dalton, interview with Cathal O'Shannon, *Emmet Dalton Remembers*, RTÉ, March 1978, cited in Sean Boyne, *Emmet Dalton* (Dublin: Merrion Press, 2015), 177.
3 Colonel Michael Costello, Report to Chairman Army Enquiry Committee, 22 April 1924, Military Archives Ireland (MAI), MJC/5, PC 586, 10, 12.
4 Mulcahy to Collins, Memorandum, University College Dublin Archives, UCDA, Richard Mulcahy Papers, P7/C/35.
5 Lt Col P.J. Paul, P/File, Military Archives Ireland, MAI, Bureau of Military History, BMH WS 0877.
6 Dalton to Commander-in-Chief, Cork Report, 13 September 1922, MAI, IE/MA/CW/OPS/4/1.
7 Colonel Moore, British Army, to Chief of Staff IRA, letter, 12 January 1922, UCDA, Richard Mulcahy Papers, P7A/56.

8   Michael Collins to Chief of Staff, letter, 12 December 1921, UCDA, Richard Mulcahy Papers, P7/B/153.
9   William H. Kautt, *Arming the Irish Revolution: Gunrunning and Arms Smuggling, 1911–1922* (Lawrence: University Press of Kansas, 2021), 151.
10 Trinquier, *Modern Warfare*, 85.
11 Ex British Servicemen in Commands and Services, 1923, Military Archives Ireland, cited in Padraic Kennedy, *Key Appointments and the Transition of the Irish Volunteers, the Irish Republican Army and the National Army (1913–23)* (Dublin: Irish Defence Forces, 2016); Garrett Fitzgerald, "Reflections on the Foundation of the Irish Free State", speech given in UCC, April 2003.
12 Emmet Dalton, interview with Cathal O'Shannon; Desart to Midleton, 20 and 22 October 1922, National Archives, Public Records Office 30/67/51, cited in Diarmaid Ferriter, *Between Two Hells: The Irish Civil War* (London: Profile Books, 2021), 64.
13 Maryann Gialanella Valiulis, *Almost a Rebellion: The Irish Army Mutiny of 1924* (Cambridge: Cambridge University Press 1992), 24, 95.
14 *Ibid.*, 24.
15 Mulcahy to Collins, memorandum, 1 July 1922, quoted by Mulcahy to AIC, para. 14, 29 April 1924, UCDA, Richard Mulcahy Papers, P7/C/10.
16 Mulcahy to Mac Eoin, letter, 14 August 1922, UCDA, Seán MacEoin Papers, P151/161/5.
17 Patrick Long, "The Army of the Irish Free State, 1922–1924", MA thesis (University College Dublin, 1983), 26–27.
18 Draft Copy of Roll of Deceased Personnel – Irish Civil War, provided to the author by Military Archives Ireland, 24 January 2022.
19 Michael Hopkinson, *Green against Green: The Irish Civil War* (Dublin: Gill and Macmillan, 2004), 138.
20 Long, "The Army of the Irish Free State, 1922–1924", 26–27.
21 David Fitzpatrick, "Militarism in Ireland 1900–1922", in *A Military History of Ireland*, ed. Thomas Bartlett and Keith Jeffery (Cambridge: Cambridge University Press, 1996), 400.
22 Theo Farrell and Terry Terriff, *The Sources of Military Change: Culture, Politics, Technology* (Boulder, CO: Lynne Rienner Publishers, 2002), 76.
23 MacManus to A/G, 18 September 1922, and memo by him, UCDA, Ernie O'Malley Papers, P17a/215.
24 Donal Corcoran, *Freedom to Achieve Freedom: The Irish Free State 1922–1932* (Dublin: Gill and Macmillan, 2013), 88.
25 GHQ, Volunteer Training Manual, IRA, 1921, UCDA, Richard Mulcahy Papers, P7a/22.
26 *Ibid.*
27 Search of all *An t-Óglách* issues dated 1921–23 contained in the Collins Barracks Museum, Cork.
28 Under Secretary Cope to Churchill, telegram, 17 April 1923, Parliamentary Archives, Westminster, UK, PAW, Lloyd George Papers LG/F/10/2/67I.
29 M.E.A. to Churchill, letter, 02 September 1922, Churchill Archives,

Cambridge University (CAC), CHAR 22/14, CAC.
30 John P. Duggan, *A History of the Irish Army* (Dublin: Gill and MacMillan, 1991), 109.
31 Liam McNamee, "The Cavalry Corps", *An Cosantoir*, January 1976.
32 Long, "The Army of the Irish Free State, 1922–1924", 46–47.
33 Duggan, *A History of the Irish Army*, 106.
34 Correspondence between Cope and Curtis, 8 September 1922, PAW, LG/F/10/3/48.
35 De Róiste Diaries, 26 August 1922, Cork City and County Archives, U271/A/146.
36 GOC SW Command Memo, UCDA, Richard Mulcahy Papers, P7/B/40.
37 O'Higgins to Executive Council, n.d., National Archives Ireland, NAI, D/T S6696.
38 Charles Townsend, *The Republic: The Fight for Irish Independence, 1918–1923* (London: Penguin, 2014), 422.
39 Dalton to Commander-in-Chief, Cork Report, 13 September 1922.
40 G.M. Boyd, Dublin District Weekly Intelligence Summary, October 1922, NAI, D/T 3/S1784, p. 57.
41 Dalton to Commander-in-Chief, Cork Report, 13 September 1922.
42 De Róiste Diaries, 13 November 1922, Cork City and County Archives, U271/A/147.
43 Desart to Midleton, 20 and 22 October 1922,
44 Duggan, *A History of the Irish Army*, 116.
45 Tom Garvin, *1922: The Birth of Irish Democracy* (Dublin: Gill and Macmillan, 1996), 125.
46 Cork Command, Fortnightly Report, 16 November 1922, MAI, IE/MA/S/12360.
47 Valiulis, *Almost a Rebellion*, 107.
48 Professor Hogan, testimony to the Army Inquiry Committee 1924, UCDA, Richard Mulcahy Papers, P7/C/21.
49 Lloyd George to Collins, letter, 22 June 1922, PAW, LG/F/10/6/4.
50 Churchill to Under Secretary Cope, telegram, 2 May 1922, CAC, CHAR 22/13.
51 Under Secretary Cope to Churchill, telegram, 17 April 1922, PAW, LG/F/10/2/67c.
52 Churchill to Under Secretary Cope, letter, April 1922, PAW, LG/F/10/2/67d.
53 Under Secretary Cope to Churchill, Telegram dated 17 April 1922, PAW, LG/F/10/2/67c.
54 M.E.A. to Churchill, letter, 2 September 1922, CAC, CHAR 22/14.
55 Commander-in-Chief of the Free-State to the President of the Free-State Cabinet, Arms and Equipment, letter, 2 February 1923, MAI, IE/MA/DoD/A/3389.
56 William H. Kautt, *Arming the Irish Revolution: Gunrunning and Arms Smuggling, 1911–1922* (Lawrence: University Press of Kansas, 2021), 150.
57 Ibid.
58 Ernie O'Malley, *The Men Will Talk to Me*, 30.
59 A. Solly-Flood (Military Advisor to NI Government) to Secretary Minister for Home Affairs, 22 July 1922, Public

Records Office, Northern Ireland, Home Affairs 32/1/247.
60 Bill Kissane, *The Politics of the Irish Civil War* (Oxford: Oxford University Press, 2005), 83.
61 Borgonovo, *The Battle for Cork*, 62.
62 Statement No. 7 & 8, List of Materials Taken over from the British from 31 January 1922 to 30 July 1922, NAI, D/T S3361.
63 Collins to Cosgrave, 5 August 1922, UCDA, Richard Mulcahy Papers, P7/B/29.
64 Conservative Government Secretary of State for the Colonies, the Duke of Devonshire, to the Governor General of Ireland Arms and Equipment, telegram, 8 December 1922, MAI, IE/MA/DoD/A/3389.
65 Donal MacCarron, *A View from Above: 200 Years of Aviation in Ireland* (Dublin: O'Brien Press, 2000), 57.
66 Long, "The Army of the Irish Free State, 1922–1924", 26–27; MacCarron, *A View from Above*, 57.
67 Duggan, *A History of the Irish Army*, 108.
68 Conservative Government Secretary of State for the Colonies, the Duke of Devonshire, to the Governor General of Ireland, Arms and Equipment, letter, 13 December 1922, MAI, IE/MA/DoD/A/3389.
69 Conservative Government Secretary of State for the Colonies, the Duke of Devonshire, to the Governor General of Ireland, Arms and Equipment, letter, 6th week of 1923, MAI, IE/MA/DoD/A/3389.
70 The Refund of Cost of Munitions, extract from *Financial Agreements made between British and Free State Governments in London*, 12 February 1923, MAI, IE/MA/DoD/A/3389.
71 Mr R.W. Scott, the Director of Equipment and Ordnance stores within the British War Office to the Secretary, High Commissioner for the Irish Free-State, Arms and Equipment, letter, 27 February 1923, MAI, IE/MA/DoD/A/3389.
72 Mr Ormsby Gore, Arms and Equipment, extract from the British House of Commons *Report*, vol. 166, no. 90, col. 618, MAI, IE/MA/DoD/A/3389.
73 Aireacht Airgid to a Mr. N.G. Loughnane in the Vice Regal Lodge Dublin, 14 February 1923, Arms and Equipment, MAI, IE/MA/DoD/A/3389.
74 The Office of the Commander-in-Chief – Free State Army to Mr. James McNeill, 2 March 1923, Arms and Equipment, MAI, IE/MA/DoD/A/3389.
75 Hopkinson, *Green against Green*, 273.
76 Handing over of Armoured Cars & Motor Cars by British HQ, MAI, IE/MA/DoD/A/7399.
77 Michael Hopkinson, "The Civil War: The Opening Phase", in *Atlas of the Irish Revolution,* ed. John Crowley, Donal Ó Drisceoil, and Michael Murphy (Cork: Cork University Press, 2017), 675.
78 John Borgonovo, "IRA Conventions", in *Atlas of the Irish Revolution*, ed. Crowley, Ó Drisceoil, and Murphy, 671.
79 Hart, *The I.R.A. and Its Enemies*, 113.
80 Ernie O'Malley, *The Singing Flame: A Memoir of the Civil War, 1922–24* (1936; reprinted, Cork: Mercier Press 2012), 84.

81. Fergus O'Farrell, *Cathal Brugha* (Dublin: University College Dublin Press, 2018), 85–88.
82. O'Malley, *The Singing Flame*, 69–71.
83. Kissane, *The Politics of the Irish Civil War*, 76.
84. Ibid.
85. GHQ to Minister of Defence, October 1921 and 19 December 1921, Statement of Munitions, UCDA, Ernie O'Malley Papers, cited in *Atlas of the Irish Revolution*, ed. Crowley, Ó Drisceoil, and Murphy, 390.
86. Ted O'Sullivan (West Cork IRA), interview by Ernie O'Malley, UCDA, Ernie O'Malley Papers, P17b/108, 1–27.
87. Hopkinson, "Civil War", 676.
88. Kautt, *Arming the Irish Revolution*, 151–52, 206.
89. Ibid., 153.
90. Eoin Neeson, *The Civil War in Ireland* (Cork: Mercier Press, 1981), 51. Other noteworthy raiding activities included one in Waterford at which the IRA raided a party of 40 British soldiers at the railway station and took their weapons, although Kautt, in *Arming the Irish Revolution*, 153, contends that these methods were unsustainable for the IRA.
91. Tom Mahon, *The Ballycotton Job: An Incredible True Story of IRA Pirates* (Cork: Mercier Press, 2022), 124.
92. Ibid., 154.
93. The Seizure of Upnor, 29 March 1922, A Coy, 4 Battalion, 1 Cork Brigade, Brigade Activity Reports, MAI, IE/MA/MSPC/A1-4.
94. Borgonovo, *The Battle for Cork*, 21; Mahon, *The Ballycotton Job*, 191–92, 218–19.
95. Borgonovo, *The Battle for Cork*, 21.
96. Department of Finance to the Department of Defence, letter, 21 November 1922, Arms and Equipment, MAI, IE/MA/DoD/A/3389.
97. Fitzgerald to Mulcahy, 2 December 1922, and Timothy Smiddy (Irish US Envoy) to Fitzgerald, 15 December 1922, UCDA, Desmond FitzGerald Papers, P80/338/3.
98. Hopkinson, *Green against Green*, 253.
99. Liam Lynch to Sean Moylan, letter, 6 February 1923, National Library of Ireland (NLI), Joseph McGarrity Papers, MS 17, 466/12/2.
100. Ernie O'Malley to Sean Lemass, 21 October 1922, and Ernie O'Malley to Liam Deasy, 9 October 1922, in *"No Surrender Here!" The Civil War Papers of Ernie O'Malley 1922–1924*, ed. Cormac O'Malley and Anne Dolan (Dublin: Lilliput Press, 2007), 148 and 165.
101. Duggan, *A History of the Irish Army*, 85.
102. Borgonovo, *The Battle for Cork*, 82.
103. Ibid.
104. Hopkinson, *Green against Green*, 127.
105. Duggan, *A History of the Irish Army*, 105.

Chapter 4

1. The Munster Republic was an attempt by the IRA to establish an independent entity in the southern province of Ireland during the early months of the civil war. Michael Harrington, *The Munster Republic* (Cork: Mercier Press, 2009).
2. *The Times* (London), 30 June 1922.

3. As Free State General Michael Costello told an enquiry after the civil war, every officer admitted that there had been an extraordinary improvement in the army between December 1922 and April 1923. Much of that was put down to a re-organisation that occurred in January 1923. (Costello at Army Enquiry), University College Dublin Archives [UCDA], Richard Mulcahy Papers, P7/C/25).

4. Niall C. Harrington, *Kerry Landing, August 1922: An Episode of the Civil War* (Dublin: Anvil Books, 1992), 14, 34; and Florence O'Donoghue, *No Other Law: The Story of Liam Lynch and the IRA, 1916–1923* (Dublin: Irish Press, 1954), 214.

5. John Borgonovo, *The Battle for Cork: July–August 1922* (Cork: Mercier Press, 2011), 21.

6. Inspector of Org. to O/C Org. 1st South Div., 7 September 1922, MAI, IE/A/0991/2; O/C 1st South Div., Report, 5 September 1922, MAI, IRA/2; and Pat O'Sullivan, UCDA, Ernie O'Malley Papers, P17b/111.

7. John O'Callaghan, "The Geography of the War of Independence: Munster", in *Atlas of the Irish Revolution,* ed. John Crowley, Donal Ó Drisceoil, and Michael Murphy (Cork: Cork University Press, 2017), 595.

8. John Borgonovo "Army without Borders: The Irish Republican Army 1920–21", in *Atlas of the Irish Revolution,* ed. Crowley, Ó Drisceoil, and Murphy, 395; Gavin Maxwell Foster, *The Irish Civil War and Society: Politics, Class, and Conflict* (London: Palgrave Macmillan, 2015), 26.

9. Gerry White, "Free State versus Republic: The Opposing Armed Forces in the Civil War", in *Atlas of the Irish Revolution,* ed. Crowley, Ó Drisceoil, and Murphy, 691.

10. Diarmaid Ferriter, *Between Two Hells: The Irish Civil War* (London: Profile Books, 2021), 77, 41.

11. Michael Hopkinson, "The Civil War: The Opening Phase", in *Atlas of the Irish Revolution,* ed. Crowley, Ó Drisceoil, and Murphy, 676.

12. John O'Callaghan, "The Geography of the War of Independence: Munster", in *Atlas of the Irish Revolution,* ed. John Crowley, Donal Ó Drisceoil, and Michael Murphy (Cork: Cork University Press, 2017), 558, compared to data from Military Service Pensions Collection – IRA Nominal Rolls, RO/1-611, https://www.militaryarchives.ie/en/collections/online-collections/military-service-pensions-collection-1916-1923/search-the-collection/organisation-and-membership/ira-membership-series.

13. Borgonovo, "Army without Borders: The Irish Republican Army 1920–21", 395.

14. Tom Mahon, *The Ballycotton Job: An Incredible True Story of IRA Pirates* (Cork: Mercier Press, 2022), 124.

15. De Róiste Diaries, 4–18 July 1922, Cork City and County Archives (CCCA), U271/A/45.

16. Maryann Gialanella Valiulis, *Portrait of a Revolutionary: General Richard Mulcahy and the Founding of the Irish Free State* (Lexington: University Press of Kentucky, 1992), 165.

17 Bill Kissane, *The Politics of the Irish Civil War* (Oxford: Oxford University Press, 2005), 78.
18 Charles Townsend, *The Republic: The Fight for Irish Independence, 1918–1923* (London: Penguin, 2014), 412.
19 O'Donoghue, *No Other Law*, 272.
20 Townsend, *The Republic*, 413.
21 Eoin Neeson, *The Civil War in Ireland* (Cork: Mercier Press, 1966), 107.
22 Jacqueline L. Hazelton, *Bullets Not Ballots: Success in Counterinsurgency Warfare* (Ithaca, NY: Cornell University Press, 2021), 2.
23 Townsend, *The Republic*, 421–22.
24 John P. Duggan, *A History of the Irish Army* (Dublin: Gill and MacMillan, 1991), 91.
25 Townsend, *The Republic*, 424.
26 *Ibid.*, 423.
27 The Outcome of Present Position, handwritten confidential memo, supposed to be by Barry Egan of Cork, n.d., UCDA, Frank Aiken Papers, P104/1244(2).
28 Kissane, *The Politics of the Irish Civil War*, 78.
29 De Róiste Diaries, 21 July 1922, CCCA, U271/A/45.
30 On IRA equipment strength, see Townsend, *The Republic*, 415.
31 Pat McCarthy, *The Irish Revolution, 1912–23: Waterford* (Dublin: Four Courts Press, 2015), 105.
32 Ralph A. Riccio, *Irish Coastal Landings 1922* (Petersfield, UK: Mushroom Model Publications, 2012), 17.
33 McCarthy, *The Irish Revolution, 1912–23*, 106.
34 Prout was born in County Tipperary and emigrated to the United States at an early age. In the First World War he enlisted in the US 69th National Guard Infantry Regiment, commonly known as "The Fighting 69th", and earned the rank of captain. Following the war he returned to Ireland and joined the IRA, becoming the training and intelligence officer of the Third Tipperary Brigade. With the outbreak of the civil war, he sided with the pro-Treaty forces.
35 Hopkinson, "The Civil War", 683; Borgonovo, *The Battle for Cork*, 65; McCarthy, *The Irish Revolution, 1912–23*, 106.
36 Riccio, *Irish Coastal Landings 1922*, 38.
37 Duggan, *A History of the Irish Army*, 89.
38 Riccio, *Irish Coastal Landings 1922*, 34; McCarthy, *The Irish Revolution, 1912–23*, 106.
39 Liam Deasy (West Cork IRA), interview by Ernie O'Malley, n.d., UCDA, Ernie O'Malley Papers, P17b/86, 6–24.
40 Townsend, *The Republic*, 416.
41 Ferriter, *Between Two Hells*, 50.
42 Duggan, *A History of the Irish Army*, 91.
43 *Ibid.*, 89–91.
44 Hopkinson, *Green against Green*, 155. The *Helga* was a former British gunboat that had been used to fire upon Dublin during 1916 Easter Rising, but had subsequently been given to the National Army by the British to assist them in the fight against the IRA.
45 Duggan, *A History of the Irish Army*, 89.
46 Townsend, *The Republic*, 416.
47 *Irish Independent*, 4 August 1922.

48 Harrington, *The Munster Republic*, 71.
49 Borgonovo, *The Battle for Cork*, 63.
50 Kissane, *The Politics of the Irish Civil War*, 78.
51 Cited in Ferriter, *Between Two Hells*, 53.
52 De Róiste Diaries, 21 July 1922, CCCA, U271/A/45. John Borgonovo reinforces de Róiste's assessment, noting that immediately after the attack on the Four Courts, the Cork City IRA formed two large flying columns totalling about 100 men and moved on Limerick (*The Battle for Cork*, 46). T. Ryle Dwyer notes that Kerry IRA men also headed for Limerick. See *Tans, Terror and Troubles: Kerry's Real Fighting Story 1913–23* (Cork: Mercier Press, 2001), 353.
53 Townsend, *The Republic*, 416.
54 *Irish Independent*, 22 July 1922.
55 Hopkinson, "The Civil War", 703.
56 *Limerick Chronicle*, 29 July 1922.
57 Calton Younger, *Ireland's Civil War* (New York: Taplinger Publishers, 1968), 393.
58 Duggan, *A History of the Irish Army*, 88.
59 Townsend, *The Republic*, 416.
60 Liam Deasy (West Cork IRA), interview by Ernie O'Malley.
61 Duggan, *A History of the Irish Army*, 88.
62 Hopkinson, "The Civil War", 681.
63 Eoin Neeson, *The Civil War in Ireland 1921–23* (Dublin: Poolbeg Press, 1989), 208
64 Duggan, *A History of the Irish Army*, 88.
65 John O'Callaghan, *The Battle for Kilmallock* (Cork: Mercier Press, 2011), 118.
66 *Irish Independent*, 5 August 1922.
67 T. Ryle Dwyer, *Tans, Terror and Troubles*, 354.
68 Younger, *Ireland's Civil War*, 396–97.
69 Riccio, *Irish Coastal Landings 1922*, 50.
70 Harrington, *Kerry Landing: August 1922*, 71.
71 Valiulis, *Portrait of a Revolutionary*, 103.
72 Duggan, *A History of the Irish Army*, 94.
73 *Irish Independent*, 5 August 1922.
74 Tom Doyle, *The Summer Campaign in Kerry*, cited in Borgonovo, *The Battle for Cork*, 77.
75 O'Donoghue, *No Other Law*, 266.
76 *Irish Independent*, 9 August 1922.
77 Dwyer, *Tans, Terror and Troubles*, 354.
78 McCarthy, *The Irish Revolution, 1912–23*, 109.
79 De Róiste Diaries, 21 July 1922, CCCA, U271/A/45.
80 Cabinet Meeting of the Provisional Government, minutes, 24 July 1922, National Archives Ireland, NAI, DT/1/1/1.
81 Borgonovo, *The Battle for Cork*, 129.
82 De Róiste Diaries, 21 July 1922.
83 Peader O'Donnell, 2 August 1984, and "Todd" Andrews, 3 August 1984, interviews cited by Padraig O Caoimh, *Richard Mulcahy: From the Politics of War to the Politics of Peace, 1913–1924* (Newbridge: Irish Academic Press, 2019), 130.

Chapter 5

1 Charles Townsend, *The Republic: The Fight for Irish Independence,*

2   Mulcahy to Commander-in-Chief, letter, 4 August 1922, University College Dublin Archives (UCDA), Richard Mulcahy Papers P7/B/143.
3   Peter Hart, *The I.R.A. and Its Enemies: Violence and Community in Cork, 1916–1923* (Oxford: Clarendon Press, 1999), 118.
4   Eoin Neeson, *The Civil War in Ireland* (Cork: Mercier Press, 1966), 144.
5   Ralph A. Riccio, *Irish Coastal Landings 1922* (Petersfield, UK: Mushroom Model Publications, 2012), 61.
6   Hart, *The I.R.A. and Its Enemies*, 118.
7   De Róiste Diaries, 25 July 1922, Cork City and County Archives (CCCA), U271/A/45.
8   Neeson, *The Civil War in Ireland*, 144.
9   John P. Duggan, *A History of the Irish Army* (Dublin: Gill and Macmillan, 1991), 94.
10 Emmet Dalton, interview with Padraig O Raghallaigh, *RTE Radio*, February–March 1977, cited in Sean Boyne, *Emmet Dalton: British Soldier, Irish General, Film Pioneer* (Dublin: Merrion Press, 2015), 180.
11 Report on the situation in Cork, 19 July 1922, UCDA, Richard Mulcahy Papers, P7/B/40.
12 De Róiste Diaries, 21 July 1922, CCCA, U271/A/45.
13 Neeson, *The Civil War in Ireland*, 152.
14 Riccio, *Irish Coastal Landings 1922*, 61; Boyne, *Emmet Dalton*, 178.
15 Taperecorded interview with Jim Byrne from Newtown Kildare, 1985, given to the author in October 2020 by Eamonn Mulvihill of Enfield, County Meath.
16 Maryann Gialanella Valiulis, *Portrait of a Revolutionary: General Richard Mulcahy and the Founding of the Irish Free State* (Lexington: University Press of Kentucky, 1992), 103.
17 Valiulis, *Portrait of a Revolutionary*, 103.
18 Michael Hopkinson, *Green against Green: The Irish Civil War* (Dublin: Gill and Macmillan, 2004), 163.
19 John Borgonovo, *The Battle for Cork: July–August 1922* (Cork: Mercier Press, 2011), 80.
20 Hybrid or proxy warfare occurs when a conventional force empowers a local militia to fight an adversary in order to enhance their combat power or effectiveness.
21 Casualty Form – Active Service, Lieut Dalton J.E, Attd 6th Leinsters – British Army, Dalton Papers, National Library, NLI, MS 46,687/3.
22 Captain S. McCance, *History of the Royal Munster Fusiliers, 1861 to 1922* (Uckfield: Naval and Military Press, 2017). 24; Aspinall Oglander, *Military Operations – Gallipoli*, vol. 1 (London: Imperial War Museum, 1928).,141. Chapter 3, section 41, 64–67, of Field Service Regulations 1909 outlines the general principles of co-operation between the Navy and the Army.
23 The Dalton Papers in the National Library contain examples of detailed handwritten operations orders produced by Dalton for combat operations and exercises by the 2nd Leinster Regiment during and after the First World War. For example, see Operation Orders – Emmet Dalton

NOTES

Papers, National Library of Ireland (NLI), MS 46,687/3.
24 Riccio, *Irish Coastal Landings 1922*, 60.
25 O'Malley in *Dublin's Fighting Story* (Tralee: Kerryman, 1947), 289.
26 Borgonovo, *The Battle for Cork*, 80.
27 *Ibid.*, 70.
28 Riccio, *Irish Coastal Landings 1922*, 27, 9.
29 File on Arvonia, Military Archives Ireland (MAI), IE/MA/DoD/A/5412–13.
30 Riccio, *Irish Coastal Landings 1922*, 14.
31 *Ibid.*, 15.
32 Borgonovo, *The Battle for Cork*, 53.
33 Riccio, *Irish Coastal Landings 1922*, 72; MOC [Micheál O Coileain], Air Services, 4 August 1922, UCDA, Richard Mulcahy Papers, P7/B/10.
34 MOC [Micheál O Coileain], Air Services, 4 August 1922.
35 Borgonovo, *The Battle for Cork*, 81.
36 *Ibid.*, 67.
37 Hart, *The I.R.A. and Its Enemies*, 118.
38 Boyne, *Emmet Dalton*, 181.
39 *Ibid.*
40 Valiulis, *Portrait of a Revolutionary*, 104.
41 Hopkinson, *Green against Green*, 163.
42 Riccio, *Irish Coastal Landings 1922*, 14.
43 Ibid, 75.
44 *Ibid.*
45 Major General J.E. Dalton to Chief of Staff National Army from on-board the Arvonia, letter, 7 August 1922, UCDA, Richard Mulcahy Papers, P7/B/66.
46 Liam Deasy (West Cork IRA), interview by Ernie O'Malley, UCDA, Ernie O'Malley Papers, P17b/86, 6–24.
47 Riccio, *Irish Coastal Landings 1922*, 15.
48 Borgonovo, *The Battle for Cork*, 79.
49 Riccio, *Irish Coastal Landings 1922*, 72.
50 *Ibid.*, 70.
51 Ted O'Sullivan (West Cork IRA), interview by Ernie O'Malley, UCDA, Ernie O'Malley Papers, P17b/108, 1–27.
52 *Ibid.*
53 Jim Byrne, interview, 1985.
54 Borgonovo, *The Battle for Cork*, 79; Report from Arvonia to GHQ Dublin (A/563), 13 August 1922, UCDA, Richard Mulcahy Papers, P7/B/70; *Irish Independent*, 12 August 1922
55 Valiulis, *Portrait of a Revolutionary*, 104.
56 Borgonovo, *The Battle for Cork*, 61–68.
57 *Ibid.*, 72–89.
58 Boyne, *Emmet Dalton*, 184.
59 Dalton to Commander-in-Chief, Cork Report, 11 September 1922, MAI, IE/MA/CW/OPS/2/4.
60 *Irish Times*, 15 August 1922.
61 Neeson, *The Civil War in Ireland*, 149.
62 Borgonovo, *The Battle for Cork*, 88.
63 Valiulis, *Portrait of a Revolutionary*, 105.
64 Riccio, *Irish Coastal Landings 1922*, 80.
65 Boyne, *Emmet Dalton*, 188.
66 Riccio, *Irish Coastal Landings 1922*, 80.
67 Boyne, *Emmet Dalton*, 181–82.
68 Borgonovo, *The Battle for Cork*, 79.
69 Dalton to Commander-in-Chief, Cork Report, 11 September 1922, MAI, IE/MA/CW/OPS/2/4.

70　Valiulis, *Portrait of a Revolutionary*, 104.
71　Neeson, *The Civil War in Ireland*, 151.
72　Hart, *The I.R.A. and Its Enemies*, 118.
73　Borgonovo, *The Battle for Cork*, 75.
74　Duggan, *A History of the Irish Army*, 96.
75　Hart, *The I.R.A. and Its Enemies*, 118.
76　Dalton to Commander-in-Chief, Cork Report, 11 September 1922, MAI, IE/MA/CW/OPS/2/4.
77　Hart, *The I.R.A. and Its Enemies*, 118.
78　Borgonovo, *The Battle for Cork*, 94–95.
79　Olga Pyne Clarke, *She Came of Decent People* (London, 1985), 55, cited in Hart, *The I.R.A. and Its Enemies*, 119.
80　Duggan, *A History of the Irish Army*, 96.
81　Tom Garvin, *1922: The Birth of Irish Democracy* (Dublin. Gill and Macmillan), 123.
82　Borgonovo, *The Battle for Cork*, 68.
83　Riccio, *Irish Coastal Landings 1922*, 87.
84　Borgonovo, *The Battle for Cork*, 119.
85　Riccio, *Irish Coastal Landings 1922*, 87.
86　John Dorney, *The Civil War in Dublin: The Fight for the Irish Capital 1922–1924* (Newbridge: Merrion Press, 2017), 124.
87　Orders from Southern Division Commander Liam Deasy, 12 August 1922, UCDA, Ernie O'Malley Papers P17a/87.
88　Dalton to Commander-in-Chief, Cork Report, 13 September 1922, MAI, IE/MA/CW/OPS/4/1; and Neeson, *The Civil War in Ireland*, 258.
89　Neeson, *The Civil War in Ireland*, 153.
90　Report from Arvonia to GHQ Dublin (A/563), 13 August 1922.
91　Borgonovo, *The Battle for Cork*, 121, drawing on *Irish Independent*, 12 August 1922; *Irish Times*, 14, 15 August 1922; *Freeman's Journal*, 14 August 1922; *Cork Examiner*, 19 August 1922.
92　Report on the Situation in Ireland, Week Ended 12 August 1922, CAB/24/138, Kew; Mick Leahy, OMN, cited in Borgonovo, *The Battle for Cork*, 121.
93　Dalton to Chief-of-Staff, letter, 12 August 1922, cited in Borgonovo, *The Battle for Cork*, 123.
94　Borgonovo, *The Battle for Cork*, 119–20.
95　Dalton to Commander-in-Chief, letter, 12 August 1922, UCDA, Richard Mulcahy Papers, P7B/20.
96　Boyne, *Emmet Dalton*, 211.
97　OC Eastern Command to Commander-in-Chief, 7 August 1922, UCDA, Richard Mulcahy Papers, P7B/16 ; *Irish Times*, 10 August 1922; *Freeman's Journal*, 15 August 1922.
98　Major General J.E. Dalton, Cork Command HQ, to Commander-in-Chief, letter, 12 August 1922, UCDA, Richard Mulcahy Papers, P/7/B/20.
99　Liam Deasy, *Brother against Brother* (Cork: Mercier Press, 1982), 83.
100　Cited in Hopkinson, *Green against Green*, 164.
101　Dalton to Commander-in-Chief, Cork Report, 11 September 1922, MAI, IE/MA/CW/OPS/2/4.
102　Peter Cottrell, *The Irish Civil War, 1922–1923* (Oxford: Osprey Publishing, 2008), 60–63; Sean Murray, OMN, *Dictionary of Irish Biography*, vol. 3, 7–9.

103 Report from the Office of the Adjutant General to the Minister for Defence, 12 August 1922, UCDA, Richard Mulcahy Papers, P7B/70.
104 Borgonovo, *The Battle for Cork*, 109; Andy Bielenberg, Cork Civil War Fatality Register, UCC, https://www.ucc.ie/en/theirishrevolution/collections/cork-fatality-register/register-index/#d.en.1399690.
105 Boyne, *Emmet Dalton*, 200.
106 Transport Order, 10 August 1922, UCDA, Richard Mulcahy Papers, P7/B/70.
107 Hopkinson, *Green against Green*, 164.
108 Boyne, *Emmet Dalton*, 200.
109 *Irish Independent*, 12 August 1922.
110 Riccio, *Irish Coastal Landings 1922*, 69.
111 Borgonovo, *The Battle for Cork*, 123.
112 Commander General Staff to Commander-in-Chief Limerick, 12 August 1922, UCDA, Richard Mulcahy Papers, P7/B/70.
113 Shelia Lawlor, *Britain and Ireland, 1914–1923* (Dublin: Gill and Macmillan, 1983), 210–11 and 267.
114 O'Duffy to Commander General Staff, 6 September 1922, UCDA, Mulcay Papers, P7/B/71.
115 Hopkinson, *Green against Green*, 150.
116 Lawlor, *Britain and Ireland*, 210–11 and 267.
117 Donal Corcoran, *Freedom to Achieve Freedom: The Irish Free State 1922–1932* (Dublin: Gill and Macmillan, 2013), 31.
118 Liam Deasy (West Cork IRA), interview by Ernie O'Malley, UCDA, Ernie O'Malley Papers, P17b/86, 6–24.
119 Hart, *The I.R.A. and Its Enemies*, 119.
120 Borgonovo, *The Battle for Cork*, 129.
121 Dalton to Commander-in-Chief, Cork Report, 11 September 1922, MAI, IE/MA/CW/OPS/2/4.
122 Emmet Dalton, interview with Cathal O'Shannon, *Emmet Dalton Remembers*, RTÉ, March 1978, cited in Sean Boyne, *Emmet Dalton* (Dublin: Merrion Press, 2015), 177.
123 Dalton to Commander-in-Chief Richard Mulcahy, letter, 13 September 1922, MAI, IE/MA/CW/OPS/4/1.
124 Michael Harrington, *The Munster Republic: The Civil War in North Cork* (Cork: Mercier Press, 2009), 131.
125 Dalton to Commander-in-Chief, letter, 12 August 1922, UCDA, Richard Mulcahy Papers, P/7/B/20.
126 Dan Harvey and Gerry White, *The Barracks: A History of Victoria/Collins Barracks* (Cork: Mercier Press, 1997), 258–60.
127 Boyne, *Emmet Dalton*, 200.
128 Dorney, *The Civil War in Dublin*, 124.
129 Townsend, *The Republic*, 428–29.
130 Free State Memorandum – Cork Command, 31 August 1922, UCDA, Richard Mulcahy Papers, P/7/B/270.
131 Tom McGinty, *The Irish Navy* (Kerry: The Kerryman, 1995), 99.
132 *Connacht Tribune*, 16 September 1922.
133 Boyne, *Emmet Dalton*, 209.
134 Hart, *The I.R.A. and Its Enemies*, 119.
135 O'Higgins at Army Enquiry, UCDA, Richard Mulcahy Papers, P7/C/33.
136 Commander General Staff to Major General Dalton, 14 August 1922, UCDA, Richard Mulcahy Papers, P7/B/70.

Chapter 6

1. David Galula, *Counterinsurgency Warfare: Theory and Practice* (Westport, CT: Praeger Security International, 1964), 85.
2. John A. Nagl, Foreword to Galula, *Counterinsurgency Warfare*, ix.
3. US Army, *Field Manual 3-24.2: Tactics in Counterinsurgency*, 2009), 3–21.
4. Charles Townsend, *The Republic: The Fight for Irish Independence, 1918–1923* (London: Penguin, 2014), 420
5. Michael Collins, interview, 28 April 1922, National Archives Ireland, Michael Collins: Statements and Speeches, NAI, D/T S10961.
6. Douglas Porch, *Counterinsurgency: Exposing the Myths of the New Way of War* (New York: Cambridge University Press, 2013), 114.
7. Eli Berman, Joseph H. Felter, and Jacob N. Shapiro, with Vestal McIntyre, *Small Wars, Big Data: The Information Revolution in Modern Conflict* (Princeton, NJ: Princeton University Press, 2018), 273.
8. FM 3-24.2, 3–21.
9. Ernie O'Malley, *The Singing Flame: A Memoir of the Civil War, 1922–24* (1936; reprint, Cork: Mercier Press, 2012), 187. O'Malley notes that the essential difference between the National Amy and the British Army was that the latter did not know the key members of the IRA.
10. Florence O'Donoghue, *No Other Law: The Story of Liam Lynch and the Irish Republican Army, 1916–1923* (Dublin: Irish Press, 1954), 266.
11. Townsend, *The Republic*, 417.
12. Casualty Form – Active Service, Lieut Dalton J.E, Attd 6th Leinsters – British Army. Emmet Dalton Papers, National Library of Ireland (NLI), MS 46,687/3.
13. Report from Commander-in-Chief to Acting Provisional Government, 5 August 1922, NAI, D/T S3361.
14. Dalton to Commander-in-Chief, Cork Report, 11 September 1922, Military Archives Ireland MAI, IE/MA/CW/OPS/2/4.
15. Round-ups were co-ordinated, intelligence-driven raids and sweeps on IRA strongholds that captured IRA suspects.
16. John Borgonovo, *The Battle for Cork* (Cork: Mercier Press, 2011), 124, 31.
17. Dan Harvey and Gerry White, *The Barracks: A History of Victoria/ Collins Barracks* (Cork: Mercier Press, 1997), 258–60.
18. Galula, *Counterinsurgency Warfare*, 61.
19. Dalton to Commander-in-Chief, Cork Report, 11 September 1922.
20. Sean Boyne, *Emmet Dalton: British Soldier, Irish General, Film Pioneer* (Dublin: Merrion Press, 2015), 245.
21. Dalton to Commander-in-Chief and other GHQ members, letter, No Date, University College Dublin Archives, UCDA, Richard Mulcahy Papers, P7/B/67.
22. Michael Hopkinson, *Green against Green: The Irish Civil War* (Dublin: Gill and Macmillan, 2004), 173.
23. Mulcahy to Mac Eoin, letter, 14 August 1922, UCDA, Mac Eoin Papers, P151/161/5.
24. Eoin Neeson, *The Civil War in Ireland* (Cork: Mercier Press, 1966), 98–121.

25 Dalton to Commander-in-Chief, Cork Report, 11 September 1922, MAI, IE/MA/CW/OPS/2/4.
26 National Army HQ to Dalton, cipher message, 19 September 1922, UCDA, Richard Mulcahy Papers, P7/B/66.
27 Bill Kissane, The Politics of the Irish Civil War (Oxford: Oxford University Press, 2005), 84.
28 Michael Harrington, *The Munster Republic: The Civil War in North Cork* (Cork: Mercier Press, 2009), 103.
29 Calton Younger, *Ireland's Civil War* (New York: Taplinger Publishers, 1968), 476.
30 Dalton to Commander-in-Chief, letter, 6 September 1922, UCDA, Richard Mulcahy Papers, P7/B/66.
31 FM 3-24.2, 3–20.
32 John A. Nagl, *Knife Fights: A Memoir of Modern War in Theory and Practice* (New York: Penguin Press, 2014), 117.
33 Dalton to Commander-in-Chief, Cork Report, 11 September 1922, MAI, IE/MA/CW/OPS/2/4.
34 Dalton letter to Commander-in-Chief, 05 October 1922, Mulcahy Papers, P7/B/66, UCDA.
35 Field Assesment, UCDA, Richard Mulcahy Papers, P7/B/93, cited in Harrington, The Munster Republic, 78.
36 Ted O'Sullivan (West Cork IRA), interview by Ernie O'Malley, UCDA, Ernie O'Malley Papers, P17b/108, 1–27.
37 Public Notice by IRA to Civilian Population, UCDA, Ernie O'Malley Papers, P17a/14.
38 De Róiste Diaries, 29 October 1922, Cork City and County Archives (CCCA), U271/A/46.
39 Ted O'Sullivan (West Cork IRA), interview by Ernie O'Malley.
40 De Róiste Diaries, 29 October 1922, CCCA, U271/A/47.
41 National Army Quarter Master General's Department Report, (no date) NAI, D/T S3361.
42 Dalton to Commander-in-Chief, letter, 18 November 1922, UCDA, Richard Mulcahy Papers, P7/B/67.
43 Shelia Lawlor, *Britain and Ireland, 1914–1923* (Dublin: Gill and Macmillan, 1983), 210–11 and 267.
44 National Army HQ to O'Duffy, letter, 31 August 1922, UCDA, Richard Mulcahy Papers, P7/B/70.
45 Russell to Commander-in-Chief, letter, 12 September 1922, UCDA, Richard Mulcahy Papers, P7/B/66.
46 Pro-Treaty South-Western Command Report, 8 September 1922, UCDA, Richard Mulcahy Papers, P7/B/113.
47 General criticisms of the state of the National Army detailing incompetency, lack of discipline, mutiny, cowardice and lack of hygiene', anonymous, n.p, Autumn [?] 1922: Mulcahy Papers, P7a/141.UCDA; cited by Padraig O Caoimh Richard Mulcahy From the Politics of War to the Politics of Peace, 1913-1924 (Newbridge, Irish Academic Press, 2019), p. 130.
48 General Seán Mac Mahon, Statement to the Army Inquiry Committee, 6 May 1924, MAI, IE/MA/AMTY/3/27.
49 Report on the Seizure of Upnor, 29 March 1922, A Coy, 4 Battalion, 1 Cork Brigade, Brigade Activity Reports, MAI, MA/MSPC/A1-4.

50 Borgonovo, *The Battle for Cork*, 64.
51 Townsend, *The Republic*, 420
52 Barry to Executive Council, 7 March 1923, UCDA, Éamon De Valera Papers, P150/1647.
53 Peter Hart, *The I.R.A. and Its Enemies: Violence and Community in Cork 1916–1923* (Oxford: Clarendon Press, 1999), 119.
54 De Róiste Diaries, 29 October 1922, CCCA, U271/A/46.
55 Tom Garvin, *1922: The Birth of Irish Democracy*, 164.
56 Free State Army, Statement No. 6, Prisoners in Custody on 31 July 1922, NAI, D/T S3361.
57 Dalton to Commander-in-Chief, Cork Report, 11 September 1922.
58 Neeson, *The Civil War in Ireland*, 157.
59 Maryann Gialanella Valiulis, *Portrait of a Revolutionary: General Richard Mulcahy and the Founding of the Irish Free State* (Lexington: University Press of Kentucky, 1992), 103.
60 Operation Order No. 9 from IRA Commander-in-Chief Liam Lynch, 19 August 1922, UCDA, Ernie O'Malley Papers P17a/87.
61 Ted O'Sullivan (West Cork IRA), interview by Ernie O'Malley, UCDA, Ernie O'Malley Papers, P17b/108, 1–27.
62 Garvin, *1922: The Birth of Irish Democracy*, 101–6.
63 Dalton to Commander-in-Chief, Cork Report, 11 September 1922. The casualty estimate is found in Dalton to Chief-of-Staff, letter, 2 September 1922, UCDA, Richard Mulcahy Papers, P7/B/70.
64 Neeson, *The Civil War in Ireland*, 168.
65 Ted O'Sullivan (West Cork IRA), interview by Ernie O'Malley.
66 Tom Mahon, *The Ballycotton Job: An Incredible True Story of IRA Pirates* (Cork: Mercier Press, 2022), 191–92.
67 Hopkinson, *Green against Green*, 173.
68 Harrington, *The Munster Republic*, 82.
69 A mass attack is an IRA attack numbering more than 200 fighters and is usually complex, involving support weapons.
70 Ted O'Sullivan (West Cork IRA), interview by Ernie O'Malley.
71 Andy Bielenberg, Cork Civil War Fatality Register, UCC, https://www.ucc.ie/en/theirishrevolution/collections/cork-fatality-register/register-index/#d.en.1399690.
72 Ted O'Sullivan (West Cork IRA), interview by Ernie O'Malley.
73 *Irish Independent*, 16 September 1922.
74 *Ibid*. The Cork Civil War Fatality Register confirms seven National Army fatalities in this attack, including Kehoe.
75 Hart, *The I.R.A. and Its Enemies*.
76 *Irish Times*, 28 October 1922.
77 Ted O'Sullivan (West Cork IRA), interview by Ernie O'Malley.
78 Dalton to Commander-in-Chief, letter, 18 November 1922, UCDA, Richard Mulcahy Papers, P7/B/67.
79 General Seán Mac Mahon, Statement to the Army Inquiry Committee, 6 May 1924, MAI, IE/MA/AMTY/3/27.
80 Valiulis, *Portrait of a Revolutionary*, 116.
81 Cabinet Meeting of the Provisional Government, minutes, 5 December 1922, NAI, D/T 1/1/1; Major General

E. Dalton Pension Records, MAI, IE/MA/MSPC/24SP13470.

82 Dalton to Commander-in-Chief, letter, 18 November 1922. Dalton is referring to the high jinks and trouble a bored soldier on outpost duty may get himself into if not properly supervised.

83 Report by Commandant General Galvin, O/C 1st Southern Division [National Army], MAI, IE/MA/CW/OPS/2/D.

84 *Cork Examiner,* 8 January 1923.

85 Harrington, *The Munster Republic,* 111.

86 Bielenberg, Cork Civil War Fatality Register.

87 Harrington, *The Munster Republic,* 111.

88 Townsend, *The Republic,* 420

89 De Róiste Diaries, 29 October 1922, CCCA, U271/A/46.

Chapter 7

1   US Army, *Field Manual 3-24: Counterinsurgency,* 2006.

2   David French, *The British Way in Counter-Insurgency, 1945–1967* (Oxford, University Press, 2011), 109.

3   John A. Nagl, *Knife Fights: A Memoir of Modern War in Theory and Practice* (New York, Penguin Press, 2014), 116.

4   John A. Nagl, *Learning to Eat Soup with a Knife: Counterinsurgency Lessons from Malaya and Vietnam* (Chicago: University of Chicago Press, 2005).

5   Mulcahy to Mac Mahon, 12 December 1922, University College Dublin Archives (UCDA), Richard Mulcahy Papers, P7/B/153.

6   Executive Council, minutes, 11 January 1923, National Archives Ireland NAI, D/T 1/2/1, C.1/28.

7   British Army, *Design for Operations: The British Military Doctrine* (London: Her Majesty's Stationery Office, 1989), vii.

8   Roger Trinquier, *Modern Warfare: A French View of Counterinsurgency* (1964; reprint, Westport CT: Praeger Security International, 2006), 72.

9   Ted O'Sullivan (West Cork IRA), interview by Ernie O'Malley, Ernie O'Malley Papers, UCDA, P17b/108, 1–27.

10 Public Notice by IRA to Civilian Population, UCDA, Ernie O'Malley Papers, P17a/14, S/12039.

11 National Army Report on Strength and Posts, 1 April 1923, NAI, D/T S3361.

12 Ibid.

13 Eoin Neeson, *The Civil War in Ireland* (Cork: Mercier Press, 1966), 163.

14 General Dalton to General Mulcahy, letter, 6 September 1922, UCDA, Richard Mulcahy Papers, P7/B/66; Michael Hopkinson, *Green against Green: The Irish Civil War* (Dublin: Gill and Macmillan, 2004), 173.

15 William H Kautt, *Ambushes and Armour: The Irish Rebellion 1919–1921* (Dublin and Portland: Irish Academic Press, 2010), 4.

16 US Army, *Field Manual - FM 5-102: Countermobility,* 2004.

17 Kautt, *Ambushes and Armour,* 4.

18 Sean Boyne, *Emmet Dalton: British Soldier, Irish General, Film Pioneer* (Dublin: Merrion Press, 2015), 246.

19 Trinquier, *Modern Warfare,* 67.

20 Boyne, *Emmet Dalton,* 246.

21 Jacqueline L. Hazelton, *Bullets Not Ballots: Success in Counterinsurgency Warfare* (Ithaca, NY: Cornell University Press, 2021), 5.
22 Mulcahy to Mac Eoin, 14 August 1922, UCDA, Seán MacEoin Papers, P151/161/5.
23 Major General Emmet Dalton to Commander-in-Chief, 18 November 1922, UCDA, Richard Mulcahy Papers, P7/B/67.
24 Statement Nos. 7 & 8, List of Materials Taken over from the British from 31st January 1922 to 30 July 1922, NAI, D/T S3361.
25 Ralph A. Riccio, *The Irish Artillery Corps since 1922* (Sandomierz, Poland: Mushroom Model Publications, 2012), 14 and 25.
26 Boyne, *Emmet Dalton*, 247.
27 *Ibid.*, 246
28 Major General Emmet Dalton to Commander-in-Chief, 18 November 1922.
29 Ted O'Sullivan (West Cork IRA), interview by Ernie O'Malley, UCDA, O'Malley Papers, P17b/108.
30 Ernie O'Malley, *The Men Will Talk to Me: The West Cork Interviews*, ed. Andy Bielenberg, John Borgonovo, and Pádraig Óg O Ruairc (Cork: Mercier Press, 2015), 138.
31 *Cork Examiner*, 29 November 1922.
32 Sean Lehane to Ernie O'Malley, 15 October 1922, in, *"No Surrender Here!" The Civil War Papers of Ernie O'Malley 1922–1924*, ed. Cormac O'Malley and Anne Dolan (Dublin: Lilliput Press, 2007), 282.
33 National Army Monthly Operational Report for December 1922 by General Lawlor on operations in the west, UCDA, Seán MacEoin Papers, P151/180.
34 US Army, *Field Manual 3-24.2: Tactics in Counterinsurgency*, 2009.
35 Eli Berman, Joseph H. Felter, and Jacob N. Shapiro, with Vestal McIntyre, *Small Wars, Big Data: The Information Revolution in Modern Conflict* (Princeton, NJ: Princeton University Press, 2018), 273.
36 National Army Report on the Military Situation, 31 March 1923, NAI, D/T S3361.
37 National Army Report on Operations carried out in the West Cork, and South Kerry areas, 29 April–5 May 1923, NAI, D/T S3361.
38 David Galula, *Counterinsurgency Warfare: Theory and Practice* (Westport, CT: Praeger Security International, 1964), 21.
39 *Ibid.*, 70.
40 Trinquier, *Modern Warfare*, 54.
41 Patrick Long, "The Army of the Irish Free State, 1922–1924", MA thesis (University College Dublin, 1983), 46–47.
42 Battle-grouping occurs when the combat arms are combined into one unit in order to maximize combat power, unity of effort, and command and control.
43 Army Organisation Report, September 1923, NAI, D/T S3361.
44 National Army Report on the Military Situation, 7 April 1923, NAI, D/T S3361.
45 National Army Report on Operations carried out in the West Cork, and South Kerry areas, 29 April–5 May 1923, NAI, D/T S3361.
46 Neeson, *The Civil War in Ireland*, 199.

47 Mulcahy to Mac Eoin, 14 August 1922, UCDA, Seán MacEoin Papers, P151/161/5.
48 Colonel Joseph Vincent Lawless (1896–1969), 9 December 1954, MAI, Bureau of Military History, Witness Statement No. 1,043. Lawless was a captain during the civil war and retired later as a colonel.
49 Cahir Davitt (1894–1986), 18 August 1958, Military Archives Ireland, MAI, Bureau of Military History, Witness Statement No. 1,751.
50 Costello at Army Inquiry, UCDA, Richard Mulcahy Papers, P7/C/25; Mulcahy to Brennan, letter, 8 February 1923, UCDA, Richard Mulcahy Papers P7/B/76.
51 National Army General Surveys of the Situation for Weeks Ending 31 March 1923, 7 April 1923, 15 April 1923, 21 April 1923, 28 April 1923, NAI, D/T S3361.
52 Deasy to Brigade O/Cs, 13 September 1922, UCDA, Ernie O'Malley Papers, P17a/88.
53 Charles Townsend, *The Republic: The Fight for Irish Independence, 1918–1923* (London: Penguin, 2014), 417.
54 Ted O'Sullivan (West Cork IRA), interview by Ernie O'Malley, UCDA, Ernie O'Malley Papers, P17b/108, 1–27.
55 DC/S to C/S, 6 March 1923, UCDA, Ernie O'Malley Papers, P17a/85.
56 Ernie O'Malley, *The Singing Flame: A Memoir of the Civil War, 1922–24* (1936; reprinted, Cork: Mercier Press 2012), 187.
57 1st Southern Division Meeting, 26 February 1923, UCDA, Richard Mulcahy Papers, P7/B/89.
58 Michael Harrington, *The Munster Republic: The Civil War in North Cork* (Cork: Mercier Press, 2009), 131.
59 Neeson, *The Civil War in Ireland*, 199.
60 Harrington, *The Munster Republic*, 114.
61 National Army Report on the Military Situation, 31 March 1923, NAI, D/T S3361.
62 Harrington, *The Munster Republic*, 126.
63 National Army Report on Operations Carried out in the West Cork and South Kerry areas, 29 April–5 May 1923, NAI, D/T S3361.
64 National Army Report on the Military Situation, 28 April 1923, NAI, D/T S3361.
65 Galula, *Counterinsurgency Warfare*, 77.
66 *Irish Times*, 11 April 1923. See also Hopkinson, *Green against Green*, 240.
67 Pa Murray, letter, 13 February 1923, UCDA, Richard Mulcahy Papers, P7/B/89.
68 Hopkinson, *Green against Green*, 240.
69 Neeson, *The Civil War in Ireland*, 286.
70 National Army Statistical Summary, 4 May 1923, NAI, D/T S3361.
71 National Army Report on the Military Situation, 5 May 1923, NAI, D/T S3361.
72 Hopkinson, *Green against Green*, 228.
73 *Ibid.*, 240.
74 Neeson, *The Civil War in Ireland*, 196.
75 Ted O'Sullivan (West Cork IRA), interview by Ernie O'Malley.
76 General Weekly Report No. 4 for the Week Ending 16 June 1923, NAI, D/T S3361.
77 Harrington, *The Munster Republic*, 143.

78 Peter Hart, *Mick: The Real Michael Collins* (London: Macmillan, 2005), 404; Harrington, *The Munster Republic*, 143.

79 Ernie O'Malley Notebooks, UCDA, P17B/108, cited in Michael Harrington, *The Munster Republic* (Dublin: Mercier Press 2009). 79.

80 Cabinet Meeting of the Provisional Government, minutes, 10 September 1922, NAI, D/TSCH 1/1/1.

81 Barry to Executive Council, 7 March 1923, UCDA, Éamon De Valera Papers, P150/1647.

82 National Army Report for Week Ending 21 April 1923, UCDA, Richard Mulcahy Papers, P7/B/139.

Chapter 8

1 Ministry of Home Affairs Report, April 1922, National Archives Ireland NAI, D/E 2/51.

2 US Army, *Field Manual 3-0*:2001.

3 Douglas Porch, *Counterinsurgency: Exposing the Myths of the New Way of War* (New York: Cambridge University Press, 2013), 192.

4 Evidence presented by Commissioner Michael Staines, Commission of Inquiry into the Civic Guard Mutiny, August 1922, NAI, D/J, H235/329.

5 Gregory Allen, *The Garda Síochána: Policing Independent Ireland, 1922–1982* (Dublin: Gill and Macmillan, 1999), 34.

6 Evidence presented by J.A. O'Connell, 14 July 1922, Commission of Inquiry, Minutes of Evidence, Book II, NAI, D/T S 9048.

7 Evidence presented by Commissioner Michael Staines, Commission of Inquiry, Minutes of Evidence, Book I, July 1922, NAI, DT, S 9048.

8 Evidence presented by Staines, July 1922, 'Commission of Inquiry, Minutes of Evidence, Book I', July 1922, D/T, S 9048, NAI, *Ibid*.

9 Diarmaid Ferriter, *Between Two Hells: The Irish Civil War* (London: Profile Books, 1921), 33.

10 Seán Liddy, "Smothered History", *An Síothadóir*, December 1962, 31.

11 *Ibid*.

12 Commission of Inquiry, "Facts, Charges and Counter-Charges", August 1922, NAI, D/T S9048, section 2, 17.

13 Brian McCarthy, *The Civic Guard Mutiny* (Cork: Mercier Press, 2012), 139, 186; Proceedings in the Commission of Inquiry into the Civic Guard, 13 July 1922, NAI, D/J 325/329, 16.

14 "Case for the Men", statement read by Guard J.A. O'Connell, 15 July 1922, Minutes of Evidence to Mutiny Inquiry, cited in McCarthy, *The Civic Guard Mutiny*, 88.

15 Commission of Inquiry, General Findings of the Commission, Part II, NAI D/T, S9048, 19.

16 Report of Commission of Inquiry into the Civic Guard: Findings of Commission, August 1922, University College Dublin Archives (UCDA), Ernest Blythe Papers, P24/69.

17 See Commander-in-Chief of the Free State to the President of the Free-State Cabinet, Arms and Equipment, letter, 2 February 1923, MAI, IE/MA/DoD/A/3389.

18 Ernest Blythe, BMH WS 939, cited in Brian McCarthy, Unpublished MA

thesis (University College Dublin, 1977), 1-7.
19 Kevin O'Shiel to Collins, 22 August 1922, TL, Commission of Inquiry, Recommendations for the Future of the Civic Guard', NAI, D/J H99/23.
20 James Donohue, "Depot Day at Kildare", *Garda Review*, July 1948, 617.
21 Charles Townsend, *The Republic: The Fight for Irish Independence, 1918–1923* (London: Penguin, 2014), 387.
22 Bill Kissane, *The Politics of the Irish Civil War* (Oxford: Oxford University Press, 2005), 166.
23 Galula, *Counterinsurgency Warfare*, 57.
24 Ferriter, *Between Two Hells*, 33.
25 McCarthy, Unpublished MA thesis, 1–7.
26 Fearghal McGarry, *Eoin O'Duffy: A Self Made Hero* (Oxford: University Press, 2005), 113.
27 Collins to Cosgrave, 5 August 1922, NAI, D/T, S3361.
28 Richard Mulcahy (Minister for Defence) to Kevin O'Higgins (Minister for Home Affairs), 3 September 1922, TLS, NAI, Civic Guard: General Distribution, 1922–26, D/J H99/29.
29 McCarthy, Unpublished MA thesis, 1–7.
30 *Irish Independent*, 13 June 1977.
31 Liam McNiffe, *A History of the Garda Síochána* (Dublin: Wolfhound Press, 1997), 28.
32 Monthly Confidential Report for the Civic Guard, Cork East Riding, January 1923, MAI, IE/MAI/A/8454.
33 Civic Guard Confidential Monthly Report for February, 14 March 1923, NAI, D/T S3361.
34 IRA, Proclamation – Civic Guard, 22 November 1922, MAI, Captured Documents, Lot No 110, cited in Gavin Maxwell Foster, *The Irish Civil War and Society: Politics, Class, and Conflict* (London, Palgrave Macmillan, 2015), 123.
35 General Order No. 10, 9 April 1923, MAI, Captured Documents, Lot No. 118; Foster, *The Irish Civil War and Society*, 123–24.
36 Foster, *The Irish Civil War and Society*, 124.
37 Ibid.
38 IRA General Order No. 12, Civilians Cooperating with Enemy, MAI, Captured Documents, Lot. No. 77. MAI, IE/MAI/CW/OPS/77.
39 Donal Corcoran, *Freedom to Achieve Freedom: The Irish Free State 1922–1932* (Dublin: Gill and Macmillan, 2013), 113.
40 Eunan O'Halpin, *Defending Ireland: The Irish State and Its Enemies since 1922* (Oxford: Oxford University Press, 1999), 9.
41 The General Survey for the Period Ending 17 October 1923, MAI, IE/MAI/CW/OPS/3/B.
42 Eli Berman, Joseph H. Felter, and Jacob N. Shapiro, with Vestal McIntyre, *Small Wars, Big Data: The Information Revolution in Modern Conflict* (Princeton, NJ: Princeton University Press, 2018), 321.
43 Hogan to Cosgrave, letter, 11 January 1923, UCDA, Richard Mulcahy Papers, P76/96(2).
44 Corcoran, *Freedom to Achieve Freedom*, 113.
45 Townsend, *The Republic*, 387.

46 Civic Guard Confidential Monthly Report for February, 14 March 1923, NAI, D/T S3361.
47 O'Halpin, *Defending Ireland*, 9.
48 Ibid., 40.
49 National Army Report on Operations Carried out in the West Cork, and South Kerry areas, 29 April–5 May 1923, NAI, D/T S3361.
50 O'Halpin, *Defending Ireland*, 9.
51 Cover memorandum RE: SIC scheme from Min for Home Affairs, 5 April 1923, NAI, D/T S582.
52 O'Halpin, *Defending Ireland*, 33.
53 Foster, *The Irish Civil War and Society*, 131.
54 O'Higgins to Cosgrave, 5 April 1923, NAI, D/T S582, cited in O'Halpin, *Defending Ireland*, 32–33.
55 Sean Boyne, *Emmet Dalton: British Soldier, Irish General, Film Pioneer* (Dublin: Merrion Press, 2015), 278; William Murphy, "Imprisonments during the Civil War", in *Atlas of the Irish Revolution*, ed. John Crowley, Donal Ó Drisceoil, and Michael Murphy (Cork: Cork University Press, 2017), 737. Ferriter, *Between Two Hells*, 75, puts the total at about 13,000, a figure that Foster, *The Irish Civil War and Society*, 146, agrees with.
56 Padraig O Caoimh, *Richard Mulcahy: From the Politics of War to the Politics of Peace, 1913–1924* (Newbridge: Irish Academic Press, 2019), 133.
57 Michael Hopkinson, *Green against Green: The Irish Civil War* (Dublin: Gill and Macmillan, 2004), 181.
58 Ernie O'Malley, *The Singing Flame: A Memoir of the Civil War, 1922–24* (1936; reprinted, Cork: Mercier Press 2012), 210.
59 Stathis N. Kalyvas, *"New" and "Old" Civil Wars, A Valid Distinction* (Cambridge: Cambridge University Press, 2001), 30.
60 Dáil Éireann, Debates, 27 September 1922, vol. 1, cols. 807–9.
61 Liam Lynch for Army Council to Ceann Comhairle, UCDA, Ernie O'Malley Papers, P17a/19.
62 Hopkinson, *Green against Green*, 190.
63 Townsend, *The Republic*, 437.
64 General Seán Mac Mahon, Statement to the Army Inquiry Committee, 6 May 1924, MAI, IE/MA/AMTY/3/27.
65 Townsend, *The Republic*, 443.
66 Ferriter, *Between Two Hells*, 94.
67 Cosgrave to General Sean MacEoin, January 1923, UCDA, Seán MacEoin Papers, P151/202.
68 Murphy to Mulcahy, December 1922, UCDA, Richard Mulcahy Papers, P7/B/72, 6–7, 8.
69 Foster, *The Irish Civil War and Society*, 157.
70 Jim Byrne, taperecorded interview, 1985, given to the author in October 2020 by Eamonn Mulvihill of Enfield Meath. Byrne was from Newtown Kildare and served with the National Army during the Civil War.
71 Kissane, *The Politics of the Irish Civil War*, 93.
72 Hopkinson, *Green against Green*, 239.
73 Boyne, *Emmet Dalton*, 278.
74 Emmet Dalton, interview with Cathal O'Shannon, *Emmet Dalton Remembers*, RTÉ television documentary, cited in Sean Boyne, *Emmet Dalton* (Dublin: Merrion Press, 2015), 177.
75 Bertie Scully, Ernie O'Malley Notebooks, UCDA, P17B/102.

Cited by Hopkinson, *The Civil War the Opening Phase; Atlas of the Irish Revolution*, 685.

76 P. Murray, letter, 13 February 1923, UCDA, Richard Mulcahy Papers, P7/B/89.

77 Michael Harrington, *The Munster Republic: The Civil War in North Cork* (Cork: Mercier Press, 2009), 115, 228–29.

78 Cosgrave, interview with Hannigan and Burke (of the neutral IRA), 27 February 1923, quoted in Sheila Lawlor, *Britain and Ireland, 1914–1923* (Dublin: Gill and Macmillan, 1983), 225 and 271.

79 *Irish Times*, 13 February 1923.

Chapter 9

1   John A. Nagl, Foreword to David Galula, *Counterinsurgency Warfare: Theory and Practice* (Westport, CT: Praeger Security International, 1964), vii.

2   Eoin Neeson, *The Civil War in Ireland* (Cork: Mercier Press, 1966), 169.

3   Barry to Executive Council, 7 March 1923, University College Dublin Archives UCDA, Éamon De Valera Papers, P150/1647.

4   Eli Berman, Joseph H. Felter, and Jacob N. Shapiro, with Vestal McIntyre, *Small Wars, Big Data: The Information Revolution in Modern Conflict* (Princeton, NJ: Princeton University Press, 2018), 9. See also pp. 54, 92.

5   Tim Hoyt, "Military Innovation in Ireland 1916–1923", *Defence Forces Review*, 16.

6   National Army Report on the Military Situation, 7 April 1923, National Archives Ireland NAI, D/T S3361.

7   Editorial, "The IRA and the People", *An t-Óglách*, 31 March 1922.

8   See Patrick Murray, *Oracles of God: The Roman Catholic Church and Irish Politics, 1922–1937* (Dublin: UCD Press, 2000), 90; Bill Kissane, *The Politics of the Irish Civil War* (Oxford: Oxford University Press, 2005), 129

9   Statement Issued by the Cardinal Primate and the Archbishops and Bishops of Ireland on the Present Condition of their Country, 26 April 1922, UCDA, Fitzgerald Papers P80/179.

10 De Róiste Diaries, 12 October 1922, Cork City and County Archives (CCCA), U271/A/46.

11 Murray, *Oracles of God*, 69.

12 *Cork Examiner*, 14 August 1922.

13 Neeson, *The Civil War in Ireland*, 154.

14 *Cork Examiner*, 25 September 1922.

15 *Irish Times*, 11 October 1922.

16 De Róiste Diaries, 12 October 1922.

17 *Irish Times*, 12 October 1922.

18 Catholic Bishops' Pastoral, 10 October 1922, cited in Michael Hopkinson, *Green against Green: The Irish Civil War* (Dublin: Gill and Macmillan, 2004), 182.

19 Hopkinson, *Green against Green*, 182.

20 Seán O'Faoláin, *Inishfallen: Fare Thee Well* (London, 1940), cited in Ferriter, *Between Two Hells*, 7.

21 De Róiste Diaries, 4–6 and 11 November 1922, 18 April 1923, CCCA, U271/A/48.

22 Florence O'Donoghue, *No Other Law: The Story of Liam Lynch and the Irish Republican Army, 1916–1923* (Dublin: Irish Press, 1954), 289.

23 Ernie O'Malley, *The Singing Flame: A Memoir of the Civil War, 1922–24* (1936;

24 reprinted, Cork: Mercier Press 2012), 221, 250.
25 Ferriter, *Between Two Hells*, 87.
26 De Róiste Diaries, 12 October 1922.
27 Austin Stack to Joseph McGarrity, letter, 18 October 1922, National Library of Ireland (NLI), MS 17, 489/8.
28 IRA Handbill, NLI, Erskine Childers Papers, MS 48, 086/5.
29 Hopkinson, *Green against Green*, 182.
30 O'Malley, *The Singing Flame*, 183.
31 See Galula, *Counterinsurgency Warfare*, 94; Roger Trinquier, *Modern Warfare: A French View of Counterinsurgency* (1964; reprint, Westport CT: Praeger Security International, 2006), 6.
32 Sean Gaynor, IRA 2nd Division Adjutant, Tipperary Report, 29 July 1922, UCDA, Moss Twomey Papers, cited in Brian Hanley, *The IRA: A Documentary History, 1916–2005* (Dublin: Gill and Macmillan, 2010), 45.
33 O'Malley, *The Singing Flame*, 305–6.
34 Frances Blake, *The Irish Civil War 1922–1923 and What It Still Means for the Irish People* (London: Information on Ireland, 1986), 36.
35 Commander-in-Chief in Portobello to Commander General Staff (CGS), 15 July 1922, UCDA, Richard Mulcahy Papers, P7/B/1.
36 Cabinet Meeting of Provisional Government, minutes, 28 June 1922, NAI, D/T G1/1.
37 Cabinet Meeting of the Provisional Government, minutes, 11 July 1922, NAI, D/T G 1/1/1.
38 Collins to FitzGerald, letter, 12 July 1922, NAI, DT, S595.
39 National Army Report on the Military Situation 21 April 1923, NAI, D/T S3361.
40 Galula, *Counterinsurgency Warfare*, 86.
41 National Army Report on the Military Situation 21 April 1923.
42 Cabinet Meeting of the Provisional Government, minutes, 18 July 1922, NAI, D/T G1/1/1.
43 Donal Ó Drisceoil, "Irish Newspapers, the Treaty and the Civil War", in *Atlas of the Irish Revolution*, ed. John Crowley, Donal Ó Drisceoil, and Michael Murphy (Cork: Cork University Press, 2017), 663.
44 "The Pen Is Mightier than the Sword", NLI, NIC 53.
45 Ernie O'Malley, *"No Surrender Here!" Civil War Papers of Ernie O'Malley, 1922–1924*, ed. Cormac O'Malley and Anne Dolan (Dublin: Lilliput Press 2007), 47, 51.
46 National Army Report on Operations Carried out in the West Cork, and South Kerry areas, 29 April–5 May 1923, NAI, DT S3361.
47 Edmund Downey, *Waterford News*, to W.T. Cosgrave, 19 August 1922, UCDA, Desmond FitzGerald Papers, P80/282.
48 *Irish Independent*, 12 August 1922; *Freeman's Journal*, 12 August 1922; *Cork Examiner*, 29 September 1922.
49 IRA Handbill, NLI, Erskine Childers Papers, MS 48,087/1.
50 IRA Handbill, NLI, Ephemera Collection, EPH B12.
51 IRA Newsletter, NLI, Erskine Childers Papers, MS 48,058/13.
52 IRA Handbill, NLI, Ephemera Collection, EPH B11.

52 Cabinet Meeting of the Provisional Government, minutes, 18 August 1922, NAI, D/T G1/3.
53 IRA Handbill, NLI, Ephemera Collection, EPH B11.
54 National Army Report on the Military Situation, NAI, 15 April 1923, D/T, S3361.
55 Sean Lehane to Ernie O'Malley, 19 September 1922, in *"No Surrender Here!"*, ed. O'Malley and Dolan, 200.
56 Cabinet Meeting of the Provisional Government, minutes, 18 July 1922, NAI, D/T G1/1/1.
57 Borgonovo, *The Battle for Cork*, 117.
58 See Frank Geary, "The Taking of Cork, July 1922", in *Great Irish Reportage: Ground-Breaking Irish Journalism, Eyewitness Accounts, and Dispatches since 1922*, ed. John Horgan (Dublin: 2013), 1–16; Sean Boyne, *Emmet Dalton: British Soldier, Irish General, Film Pioneer* (Dublin: Merrion Press, 2015), 202.
59 Boyne, *Emmet Dalton*, 174.
60 Dalton to Commander-in-Chief, Cork Report, 11 September 1922, Military Archives Ireland MAI, IE/MA/CW/OPS/2/4.
61 Lt. A. Barry, Publicity, Command Headquarters, Cork Report, Week Ending 13 Jan [1923], MAI, IE/MA/CW/OPS/04/13.
62 Hopkinson, *Green against Green*, 132.
63 Ibid.
64 Liam Deasy to Seamus O'Donovan, letter, 30 January 1923, NLI, O'Donovan Papers, MS 22,306.
65 Harry Boland to Luke Dillon, 27 July 1922, UCDA, Desmond FitzGerald Papers, cited in Gerry White, "Free State versus Republic; The Opposing Armed Forces in the Civil War", *Atlas of the Irish Revolution*, ed. Crowley, Ó Drisceoil, and Murphy, 704.
66 Collins to Cosgrave, letter, 25 July 1922, cited in Hopkinson, *Green against Green*, 140.
67 National Army Report on the Military Situation, 7 April 1923, NAI, D/T S3361.
68 National Army Report on the Military Situation, 5 May 1923, NAI, D/T S3361.
69 Ibid.
70 National Army Report on Operations Carried out in the West Cork, and South Kerry areas, 29 April–5 May 1923, NAI, D/T S3361.
71 Ibid.
72 National Army Report for Week Ending 15 April, NAI, D/T S331.
73 Michael Harrington, *The Munster Republic: The Civil War in North Cork* (Cork: Mercier Press, 2009), 131.
74 *Cork Examiner*, 9 February 1923.
75 Harrington, *The Munster Republic*, 118.
76 Frank Barrett to Lynch, 11 February 1923, UCDA, P69/39/18.
77 Bill Kissane, *The Politics of the Irish Civil War* (Oxford: Oxford University Press, 2005), 166.
78 Hopkinson, *Green against Green*, 182.
79 Trinquier, *Modern Warfare*, 24.

Chapter 10

1 Charles Townsend, *The Republic: The Fight for Irish Independence, 1918–1923* (London: Penguin, 2014), 430.
2 John P. Duggan, *A History of the Irish Army* (Dublin: Gill and MacMillan, 1991), 92.

3   Townsend, *The Republic*, 425.
4   US Army, *Field Manual 3-24.2: Tactics in Counterinsurgency*, 2009.
5   US Army, *Field Manual 3-07: Stability Operations*, 2008.
6   Eli Berman, Joseph H. Felter, and Jacob N. Shapiro, with Vestal McIntyre, *Small Wars, Big Data: The Information Revolution in Modern Conflict* (Princeton, NJ: Princeton University Press, 2018), 17.
7   FM 3-07.
8   Spring Rice to Knox, 28 September 1922, University College Dublin Archives (UCDA), Mary Spring Rice Diary, 235/30, cited in Diarmaid Ferriter, *Between Two Hells: The Irish Civil War* (London: Profile Books 2021), 67.
9   Con Moloney to Ernie O'Malley, memorandum, 28 September 1922, in *"No Surrender Here! The Civil War Papers of Ernie O'Malley, 1922–1924*, ed. Cormac O'Malley and Anne Dolan (Dublin: Lilliput Press, 2007), 235.
10 David Galula, *Counterinsurgency Warfare: Theory and Practice* (Westport, CT: Praeger Security International, 1964), 6.
11 John Borgonovo, *The Battle for Cork: July–August 1922* (Cork: Mercier Press, 2011), 88.
12 Maryann Gialanella Valiulis, *Portrait of a Revolutionary: General Richard Mulcahy and the Founding of the Irish Free State* (Lexington: University Press of Kentucky, 1992), 105–6.
13 Borgonovo, *The Battle for Cork*, 93, 89.
14 *Irish Independent*, 12 August 1922.
15 Borgonovo, *The Battle for Cork*, 95.
16 Frank Brewitt, diary providing an eyewitness account of the arrival of the National Army into Cork, cited in Valiulis, *Portrait of a Revolutionary*, 108.
17 Report from Pilot Commandant Russell, 13 August 1922, UCDA, Mulcahy Papers P7B/39.
18 *Cork Examiner*, 16 August 1922.
19 *Cork Examiner*, 2 September 1922.
20 Ibid.
21 *Cork Examiner*, 9 September 1922.
22 Borgonovo, *The Battle for Cork*, 126.
23 Railway Position Report No. 115, from the Ministry of Economic Affairs to Chief of Staff, Commander in Chief, Director of Intelligence and Ministry of Agriculture, 24 August 1922, UCDA, Richard Mulcahy Papers, P7B/23.
24 Ibid.
25 Ibid.
26 Railway Position Report No. 115, 25 August 1922.
27 Railway Position Report No. 115, 26 August 1922.
28 Ibid.
29 Railway Position Report No. 114, from Ministry of Economic Affairs to Chief of Staff, Commander in Chief, Director of Intelligence, Minister of Agriculture, 29 August 1922, UCDA, Richard Mulcahy Papers, P7B/23.
30 Railway Position Report No. 115, 30 August 1922.
31 Postmaster General Office Report, 2 September 1922, UCDA, Richard Mulcahy Papers, P7B/108.
32 Michael Hopkinson, *Green against Green: The Irish Civil War* (Dublin: Gill and Macmillan, 2004), 198.
33 Seamus MacCos to Secretary, updated memo (1940), 17 March

1938 and April 1940, MSPC/A4_2, cited in Donal Ó Drisceoil, "The Military Service (1916–1923) Pensions Collection: The Brigade Activity Reports", *Atlas of the Irish Revolution*, ed. John Crowley, Donal Ó Drisceoil, and Michael Murphy (Cork: Cork University Press, 2017).

34 Dalton to Commander-in-Chief, Cork Report, 11 September 1922, MAI, IE/MA/CW/OPS/2/4.

35 Borgonovo, *The Battle for Cork*, 21.

36 Townsend, *The Republic*, 430.

37 Data compiled from UCDA, Ernie O'Malley Papers, P17a/97; Michael Harrington, *The Munster Republic: The Civil War in North Cork* (Dublin: Mercier Press 2009), IRA Brigade Activity Reports, MAI, IE/MA/MSPC/A4_5 and A4_7.

38 Borgonovo, *The Battle for Cork*, 126.

39 Ernie O'Malley, *The Singing Flame: A Memoir of the Civil War, 1922–24* (1936; reprinted, Cork: Mercier Press 2012), 282–83.

40 Cork Chamber of Commerce Annual Report, 1922, MP 507, University College Cork, cited in Borgonovo, *The Battle for Cork*, 126–27.

41 Tom Garvin, *1922: The Birth of Irish Democracy.* Dublin: Gill and Macmillan, 1996, 101–6. See also Hopkinson, *Green against Green*, 198–99.

42 D/E to Liam F, Engineering Inspector, 3rd S. Div., 29 December 1922, MAI, IE/MA/A/0990/10-12.

43 Monthly Confidential Report, for the Civic Guard, Cork East Riding, January 1923, MAI, IE/MAI/A/8454.

44 National Army Report, 21 January 1923, MAI, IE/MA/CW/OPS/2/D.

45 Hopkinson, *Green against Green*, 90.

46 *Ibid.*, 220, 273.

47 National Army Report on Railway Damage, 23 January 1923, UCDA, Richard Mulcahy Papers, P7/B/124.

48 Peter Hart, *The I.R.A. and Its Enemies: Violence and Community in Cork, 1916–1923* (Oxford: Clarendon Press, 1999), 51.

49 FM 3-24.2.

50 FM 3-07.

51 Michael Collins, notebook entry, 20 August 1922, Collins Army Barracks Museum, Cork.

52 Sean Boyne, *Emmet Dalton: British Soldier, Irish General, Film Pioneer* (Dublin: Merrion Press, 2015), 180.

53 Cabinet Meeting of the Provisional Government, minutes, 29 August 1922, NAI, D/TSCH 1/1/1.

54 Provisional Government Decision, 26 July 1922, NAI, G1/1.

55 W.T. Cosgrave, memorandum, July 1922, Fitzgerald Papers, UCDA, P4/254.

56 Michael Hopkinson, *Green against Green* (Dublin: Gill and Macmillan, 1988), 173.

57 Donal Corcoran, *Freedom to Achieve Freedom: The Irish Free State 1922–1932* (Dublin: Gill and Macmillan, 2013), 47.

58 Boyne, *Emmet Dalton*, 266, 246.

59 Railway Protection File, MAI, IE/MA/DOD/A/6943.

60 Dalton to Commander-in-Chief, 19 September 1922, MAI, IE/MA/CW/OPS/01/02/06.

61 Richard Mulcahy, Chief of General Staff, letter, 2 August 1922, UCDA, Richard Mulcahy Papers, P7/B/119.

62 Cabinet Meeting of the Provisional Government, minutes, 3 March 1922, NAI, D/TSCH 1/1/1.
63 Chairman of Great Southern & Western Railway Co., Kingsbridge, letter to Provisional [National] Government, 22 July 1922, UCDA, Richard Mulcahy Papers, P7/B/23.
64 Ministry of Economic Affairs to the Minister of Defence and Commander in Chief, letter, 25 July 1922, UCDA, Richard Mulcahy Papers, P7/B/23.
65 Chairman to the Manager Great Southern & Western Railway Co., Kingsbridge, letter, 22 July 1922.
66 General Order No. 12, from Chief of the General Staff, 2 August 1922, UCDA, Richard Mulcahy Papers, P7/B/24.
67 Cabinet Meeting of the Provisional Government, minutes, 10 September 1922, NAI D/TSCH 1/1/1.
68 Commander-in-Chief to Major General Dalton, Cork, 20 September 1922, UCDA, Richard Mulcahy Papers, P7/B/66.
69 Boyne, *Emmet Dalton*, 266. Army Organisation Report, September 1923, NAI, D/T S3361. The commanding general was Charles Russell.
70 Hopkinson, *Green against Green*, 199.
71 Russell to Chief of General staff, 25 October, 3 November 1922, UCDA, Richard Mulcahy Papers, P7/B/110.
72 O Muirithile to Commander in Chief, 23 January 1923, UCDA, Richard Mulcahy Papers P7/B/67.
73 National Army Weekly Report on Strength and Posts, 1 April 1923, NAI, D/T S3361.
74 National Army Report on the Military Situation, 15 April 1923, NAI, D/T S3361.
75 National Army Report on Operations carried out in the West Cork, and South Kerry areas, 29 April–5 May 1923, NAI, D/T S3361.
76 Hopkinson, *Green against Green*, 199.
77 Duggan, *A History of the Irish Army*, 107.
78 *An tOglach*, 5 May 1923, 22.
79 *An tOglach*, 6 October 1923, 1, 3–6, 8.
80 Railway Position Report No. 115, 30 August 1922.
81 Protection (File): Carrig Viaduct, MAI, IE/MA/DOD/A/06078.
82 Minutes of the Cork County Council Meeting, dated 13th September, 1923, Edward J. Marnane, The Cork County Council: The First Hundred Years, Cork County Library, CCCA
83 Cork County Council Meeting, minutes, 28 February 1924, *Ibid.*
84 National Army Report on the Military Situation, 21 April 1923, NAI, D/T S3361.
85 National Army Report on the Military Situation, 31 March 1923, NAI, D/T S3361.
86 Free State Operational Report to the Department of Military Statistics, 23 March 1923, MAI, IE/MA/CO/203.
87 Free State Daily Report (Cork Command), 23 March 1923, MAI, IE/MA/Co/202.
88 Free State Weekly Report (Cork Command), 15 March 1923, MAI, IE/MA/Co/183.
89 National Army Report on the Military Situation, 7 April 1923, NAI, D/T S3361.
90 National Army Report on the Military Situation, 5 May 1923, NAI, D/T S3361.

91. National Army Intelligence Report (Cork Command) 2 March 1924 MAI, IE/MA/S/12360.

Chapter 11

1. US Army, *Field Manual 3-07: Stability Operations*, 2008.
2. Jacqueline L. Hazelton, *Bullets Not Ballots: Success in Counterinsurgency Warfare* (Ithaca, NY: Cornell University Press, 2021), 8. See also Stephen T. Hosmer and Sibylle O. Crane, Hosmer and Crane, *Counterinsurgency: A Symposium, April 16–20, 1962* (Santa Monica, CA: RAND Corporation, 1963), iv.
3. FM 3-07; US Army, *FM 3-24: Counterinsurgency*, 2006.
4. See J.M. Regan, "The Politics of Utopia: Party Organisation, Executive Autonomy and the New Administration", in *Ireland: The Politics of Independence, 1922–49*, ed. Mike and John M. Regan (London: Palgrave Macmillan, 2000), 44.
5. Regan, "The Politics of Utopia", 33.
6. Cumann na nGaedheal Minute Book, 10 October 1924, University College Dublin Archives (UCDA), Desmond FitzGerald Papers, P39/1/1.
7. Tom Mahon, *The Ballycotton Job: An Incredible True Story of IRA Pirates* (Cork: Mercier Press, 2022), 136.
8. Michael Hopkinson, *Green against Green: The Irish Civil War* (Dublin: Gill and Macmillan, 2004), 89.
9. Cosgrave, Statement of Policy at the Provisional Parliament, 9 September 1923, cited in Eoin Neeson, *The Civil War in Ireland* (Cork: Mercier Press, 1966), 176.
10. Robert F. Thompson, *Defeating Communist Insurgency: Experiences from Malaya and Vietnam* (London: Chatto and Windus, 1972), 50–60, advocated the same principle in a very different context: "The government must serve all the population and must always function in accordance with the law."
11. Nadia Schadlow, *War and the Art of Governance: Consolidating Combat Success into Political Victory* (Washington, DC: Georgetown University Press, 2017), 273–77, 273–77.
12. Regan, "The Politics of Utopia", 32.
13. Ralph A. Riccio, *Irish Coastal Landings 1922* (Petersfield, UK: Mushroom Model Publications, 2012), 8; and Michael Harrington, *The Munster Republic: The Civil War in North Cork* (Cork: Mercier Press, 2009).
14. Mulcahy, notes on an interview with Cosgrave, 25 June 1923, UCDA, Richard Mulcahy Papers, P7/B/195.
15. Lord Midleton to King George V, cited in Hopkinson, *Green against Green*, 90.
16. Charles Townsend, *The Republic: The Fight for Irish Independence, 1918–1923* (London: Penguin, 2014), 420.
17. Michael Hopkinson, "The Civil War: The Opening Phase", in *Atlas of the Irish Revolution*, ed. John Crowley, Donal Ó Drisceoil, and Michael Murphy (Cork: Cork University Press, 2017), 685.
18. Lynch to Deasy, 1 September 1922, UCDA, Ernie O'Malley Papers, P17a/17.
19. Fintan O'Toole, "A Portrait of Peader O'Donnell as an Old Soldier", *Magill* (February 1982): 25–31,

cited in Ferriter, *Between Two Hells*, 34.
20 FM 3-24.
21 Cork Corporation Law and Finance Committee Meeting, minutes, 25 August 1922 and 27 September 1922, Cork City and County Archives (CCCA), CP/C/CM/LF/A.
22 Bill Kissane, *The Politics of the Irish Civil War* (Oxford: Oxford University Press, 2005), 152.
23 Regan, "The Politics of Utopia", 32.
24 Midleton, memorandum, 28 July 1922, National Archives, Public Records Office (PRO), cited in Ferriter, *Between Two Hells*, 37.
25 Gavin Maxwell Foster, *The Irish Civil War and Society: Politics, Class, and Conflict* (London: Palgrave Macmillan, 2015), 173.
26 Padraig O Caoimh, *Richard Mulcahy: From the Politics of War to the Politics of Peace, 1913–1924* (Newbridge: Irish Academic Press, 2019), 154.
27 Cited in Townsend, *The Republic*, 425.
28 Kissane, *The Politics of the Irish Civil War*, 152.
29 Townsend, *The Republic*, 423.
30 Dáil Éireann, Debates, cols. 896 and 909, 17 January 1923.
31 Belton to Middleton, 3 October 1922, PRO, Midleton Papers, 30/67/51, cited in Hopkinson, *Green against Green*, 180.
32 De Róiste Diaries, 17 November 1922, CCCA, U271/A/47.
33 National Army Report, 21 January 1923, UCDA, Richard Mulcahy Papers, P7/B/124.
34 Regan, "The Politics of Utopia", 38. A green zone is a secure centralised environment in a conflict area that is protected in order to facilitate centralised governance and command and control.
35 Executive Council, minutes, 11 January 1923, National Archives of Ireland NAI, D/TSCH 1/2/1, C.1/28.
36 Donal Corcoran, *Freedom to Achieve Freedom: The Irish Free State 1922–1932* (Dublin: Gill and Macmillan, 2013), 57.
37 Peter Coffey to W.T. Cosgrave, 25 October 1922, NAI, Department of Finance, D/Fin 519.
38 W.T. Cosgrave to Peter Coffey, 27 October 1922, NAI, Department of Finance, D/Fin 519.
39 Martin Maguire, "The Civil Service, The State and the Irish Revolution, 1886–1938", PhD dissertation (Trinity College Dublin, 2005), 215.
40 P. Hyland to W.T. Cosgrave, 5 December 1922, NAI, Department of Finance, D/Fin 519.
41 Ronan Fanning, *The Irish Department of Finance*, 56–88, cited in Maguire, *The Civil Service and the Revolution in Ireland, 1912–38*, 'Shaking the Blood-stained Hand of Mr Collins (Manchester: Manchester University Press, 2010). 215.
42 Ronan Fanning, "Britain's Legacy; Government and Administration", in *Ireland and Britain since 1922: Irish Studies*, ed. P.J. Drudy (Cambridge: 1986), 51.
43 Sean Dooney, *The Irish Civil Service* (Dublin: Mount Salus Press, 1976), 1.
44 Regan, "The Politics of Utopia", 33.
45 Cumnann na nGaedheal Standing Committee, minutes, 10 October 1924, UCDA, Desmond FitzGerald Papers, P39/1/1.

46 Foster, *The Irish Civil War and Society*, 181.
47 Regan, "The Politics of Utopia", 33.
48 Maguire, "The Civil Service", 241.
49 *Final Report of the Commission of Inquiry into the Civil Service, 1932–35* (Dublin: Stationery Office, n.d.), para. 8.
50 Borgonovo, *The Battle for Cork*, 56.
51 De Róiste Diaries, 3 August 1922, CCCA, U271/A/45.
52 John P. Duggan, *A History of the Irish Army* (Dublin: Gill and MacMillan, 1991), 97.
53 Borgonovo, *The Battle for Cork*, 125.
54 Sean Boyne, *Emmet Dalton: British Soldier, Irish General, Film Pioneer* (Dublin: Merrion Press, 2015), 205.
55 Notes for the Daily List of Suggestions, GHQ Dublin, 26 September 1922, UCDA, Richard Mulcahy Papers P7/B/119.
56 Boyne, *Emmet Dalton*, 205.
57 Commander General Staff to Major General Dalton, Cork, 14 August 1922, UCDA, Richard Mulcahy Papers, P7/B/70.
58 Notes for the Daily List of Suggestions, GHQ Dublin, 26 September 1922.
59 De Róiste Diaries, 4 September 1922, CCCA, U271/A/46.
60 Brian Girvin, *From Union to Union: Nationalism, Democracy and Religion in Ireland–Act of Union to EU* (Dublin: Gill and Macmillan, 1962), 63.
61 Tom Garvin, *1922: The Birth of Irish Democracy*, cited in Kissane, *The Politics of the Irish Civil War*, 96.
62 Kissane, *The Politics of the Irish Civil War*, 64.
63 Neeson, *The Civil War in Ireland*, 144.
64 Kissane, *The Politics of the Irish Civil War*, 152.

Chapter 12

1 Gavin Maxwell Foster, *The Irish Civil War and Society: Politics, Class, and Conflict* (London: Palgrave Macmillan, 2015), 172.
2 Mike Cronin and John M. Regan, eds., *Ireland: The Politics of Independence, 1922–49* (London: Palgrave Macmillan, 2000), 144–45.
3 P.J. Cain and A.G. Hopkins, *British Imperialism: Crisis and Deconstruction 1914–1990* (London: Longman, 1993), 81.
4 Michael Hopkinson, *Green against Green: The Irish Civil War* (Dublin: Gill and Macmillan), 2004), 273.
5 Donal Corcoran, *Freedom to Achieve Freedom: The Irish Free State 1922–1932* (Dublin: Gill and Macmillan, 2013), 47
6 J.J. Lee, *Ireland 1912–85: Politics and Society* (Cambridge: Cambridge University Press, 1989) 217.
7 Cronin and Regan, eds., *Ireland*, 149.
8 John P. Duggan, *A History of the Irish Army* (Dublin: Gill and Macmillan, 1991), 74.
9 *Ibid.*, 87.
10 John Borgonovo, *The Battle for Cork: July–August 1922* (Cork: Mercier Press, 2011), 56.
11 Cabinet Meeting of the Provisional Government, minutes, 7 July 1922, NAI, D/TSCH 1/1/1.
12 Cronin and Regan, eds., *Ireland*, 144–45.
13 Charles Townsend, *The Republic, The Fight for Irish Independence,*

      1918–1923 (London: Penguin, 2014), 426.
14 Borgonovo, *The Battle for Cork*, 56.
15 Townsend, *The Republic*, 421.
16 Eoin Neeson, *The Civil War in Ireland* (Cork: Mercier Press, 1966), 133.
17 Eli Berman, Joseph H. Felter, and Jacob N. Shapiro, with Vestal McIntyre, *Small Wars, Big Data: The Information Revolution in Modern Conflict* (Princeton, NJ: Princeton University Press, 2018), 16–17.
18 Jacqueline L. Hazelton, *Bullets Not Ballots: Success in Counterinsurgency Warfare* (Ithaca, NY: Cornell University Press, 2021), 11.
19 Borgonovo, *The Battle for Cork*, 35.
20 *Irish Independent*, 2 August 1922; *Irish Times*, 3 August 1922.
21 De Róiste Diaries, 4 July 1922, CCCA, U271/A/45.
22 Dr W. Coogan to Brigade Adjutant, 2 IRA Division, letter, 4 March 1922, University College Dublin Archives (UCDA), Con Moloney Papers, P9/154.
23 De Róiste Diaries, 6 July 1922, CCCA, U271/A/45. See also his entry for the previous day.
24 Hopkinson, *Green against Green*, 131.
25 Cork Corporation Law and Finance Committee Meeting, minutes, 25 August 1922 and 27 September 1922, CCCA, CP/C/CM/LF/A.
26 *Ibid*.
27 Borgonovo, *The Battle for Cork*, 29.
28 *Cork Examiner*, 3 June 1922.
29 Conference on Ireland at Colonial Office, London, 26 May 1922, Parliamentary Archives, Westminster (PAW), UK, Lloyd George Papers, LG/184/3/12.
30 Townsend, *The Republic*, 439.
31 Neeson, *The Civil War in Ireland*, 145.
32 Borgonovo, *The Battle for Cork*, 29.
33 Neeson, *The Civil War in Ireland*, 145.
34 *Ibid*.
35 *Irish Times*, 23 August 1922.
36 De Róiste Diaries, 5 July 1922, Cork City and County Archives (CCCA), U271/A/45.
37 Dalton to Commander-in-Chief, 12 August 1922, UCDA, Richard Mulcahy Papers, P/7/B/20.
38 Sean Boyne, *Emmet Dalton: British Soldier, Irish General, Film Pioneer* (Dublin: Merrion Press, 2015), 205.
39 National Army Report on the Military Situation, 15 April 1923, NAI, D/T S3361.
40 Provisional Government Decision, 7 August 1922, NAI, D/T, S1590.
41 US Army, *Field Manual 3-24.2: Tactics in Counterinsurgency*, 2009.
42 Micheál Martin, *Freedom to Choose: Cork Party Politics in Ireland 1918–1932* (Cork: The Collins Press, 2009), 77.
43 De Róiste Diaries, 4 August 1922, CCCA, U271/A/45.
44 Neeson, *The Civil War in Ireland*, 155.
45 Boyne, *Emmet Dalton*, 217.
46 *Ibid*.
47 Michael Collins, notebook entry, 21 August 1922, Collins Army Barracks Museum, Cork.
48 Meda Ryan, *The Day Michael Collins Was Shot*, 55–57, cited in Borgonovo, *The Battle for Cork*, 131.
49 Emmet Dalton, interview with Padraigh O Raghallaigh, RTÉ radio, February–March 1977, cited in Boyne, *Emmet Dalton*, 218.
50 Boyne, *Emmet Dalton*, 207.

51 *Ibid.*
52 Hopkinson, *Green against Green*, 131.
53 Liam Lynch to Ernie O'Malley, 4 October 1922, in *"No Surrender Here!" The Civil War Papers of Ernie O'Malley, 1922–1924*, ed. Cormac O'Malley and Anne Dolan (Dublin: Lilliput Press, 2007), 255.
54 Martin, *Freedom to Choose*, 77.
55 Lynch to O'Malley, 1 October 1922, UCDA, Richard Mulcahy Papers, P7 A/81.
56 De Róiste Diaries, 9 November 1922, CCCA, U271/A/47.
57 US Army, *Field Manual 3-07: Stability Operations*, 2008.
58 K. O'Higgins, typescript copy of an article or letter to a US newspaper 1922–23, UCDA, Richard Mulcahy Papers, P35 C/160.
59 Hopkinson, *Green against Green*, 89. Ferriter, *Between Two Hells*, 31, agrees with this figure.
60 Cabinet Meeting of the Provisional Government, minutes, 3 March 1922, NAI, D/TSCH G1/1.
61 Cainbet Meeting of the Provisional Government, minutes, 8 March 1922, NAI, D/TSCH G1/1.
62 Cork Corporation Meeting, minutes, 25 February, 4, 10, 24 March, 7 April 1922, CCCA, CP/CO/M14, cited in Borgonovo, *The Battle for Cork*, 32.
63 *Ibid.*
64 Neeson, *The Civil War in Ireland*, 144.
65 De Róiste Diaries, 4 August 1922 and 13 July 1922, CCCA, U271/A/45.
66 *Irish Times*, 26 July 1922. See also *Irish Independent*, 27 July 1922; *Cork Examiner*, 27 July 1922.
67 Borgonovo, *The Battle for Cork*, 34.
68 *Ibid.*, 52.
69 *Cork Examiner*, 15 August 1922.
70 O'Connell Report, UCDA, Richard Mulcahy Papers.
71 Declaration by Cork Unemployed Central Committee to the Citizens of Cork, 12 August 1922, cited in Neeson, *The Civil War in Ireland*, 154–55.
72 *Cork Examiner*, 9 September 1922.
73 *Irish Times*, 6 October 1922.
74 National Army Report on the Military Situation, 7 April 1923, NAI, D/T S3361.
75 National Army Report on the Military Situation, 15 April 1923, NAI, D/T S3361.
76 National Army Report on the Military Situation, 21 April 1923, NAI, D/T S3361.
77 National Army Report on the Military Situation, 5 May 1923, NAI, D/T S3361.
78 *Irish Times*, 26 July 1922; *Irish Independent*, 27 July 1922; *Cork Examiner*, 27 July 1922.
79 National Army Report on the Military Situation, 19 May 1923, NAI, D/T S3361.
80 "Problems of Peace", Free State, 25 June 1923, cited in Foster, *The Irish Civil War and Society*, 174.
81 National Army Fortnightly Review No. 1 (Cork Command), 16 November 1923, NAI, D/T S12360.
82 *Ibid.*
83 National Army Intelligence Report (Cork Command), 2 March 1924, MAI, IE/MA/S/12360.
84 Corcoran, *Freedom to Achieve Freedom*, 53.
85 J.M. Regan, "The Politics of Utopia: Party Organisation, Executive Autonomy and the New

Administration", in *Ireland: The Politics of Independence, 1922–49*, ed. Mike and John M. Regan (London: Palgrave Macmillan, 2000), 35.
86 Ibid., 47.
87 Hopkinson, *Green against Green*, 264.
88 Eunan O'Halpin, *Defending Ireland: The Irish State and Its Enemies since 1922* (Oxford: Oxford University Press, 1999), 17.

Conclusion

1 National Army Report for Week Ending 26 May 1923, University College Dublin Archives (UCDA), Richard Mulchay Papers, P7/B/139.
2 Donal Corcoran, *Freedom to Achieve Freedom: The Irish Free State 1922–1932* (Dublin: Gill and Macmillan, 2013), 95.
3 Diarmaid Ferriter, *Between Two Hells: The Irish Civil War* (London: Profile Books, 1921), 118.
4 Draft Copy of Roll of Deceased Personnel – Irish Civil War, provided to the author by Military Archives Ireland (MAI), 24 January 2022.
5 Tom Garvin, *1922: The Birth of Irish Democracy* (Dublin: Gill and Macmillan, 1996), 164.
6 Hazelton, *Bullets Not Ballots*, 2.
7 US Government Interagency Counterinsurgency Initiative, *U.S. Government Counterinsurgency Guide* (Washington, DC: US Government Printing Office, 2009), 4.
8 Colin Gray, *Another Bloody Century: Future Warfare* (London: Phoenix Press, 2005), 222; Frank Ledwidge, *Losing Small Wars: British Military Failures in the 9/11 Wars* (London and New Haven, CT: Yale University Press, 2017), 186.
9 Berman, Felter, and Shapiro, *Small Wars, Big Data*, 321.
10 American theorists Stephen Hosmer and Sybille Crane characterise the good governance theory as a list of requirements to defeat an insurgency. They suggest that the first items on this list are to "identify and redress the political, economic, military, and other issues fuelling the insurgency" and in so doing undermine the cause of the insurgents and win over the neutral majority of the population (*Counterinsurgency: A Symposium, April 16–20, 1962* [Santa Monica, CA: RAND Corporation, 1963], iv). American academic Nadia Schadlow agrees but argues for a combination of kinetic and non-kinetic actions, asserting that the tasks of good governance are not separate from conventional war (*War and the Art of Governance: Consolidating Combat Success into Political Victory* [Washington, DC: Georgetown University Press, 2017], 273–77).
11 Berman, Felter, and Shapiro, *Small Wars, Big Data*, 305–8.
12 *Final Report of the Commission of Inquiry into the Civil Service, 1932–35* (Dublin: Stationery Office, n.d.), para. 8.
13 O'Higgins Memorandum, 11 January 1923, UCDA, Richard Mulcahy Papers, P7b/96.
14 Brian Girvin, *From Union to Union: Nationalism, Democracy and Religion in Ireland—Act of Union to EU* (Dublin: Gill and Macmillan, 1962), 63.

15. John P. Duggan, *A History of the Irish Army* (Dublin: Gill and MacMillan, 1991), 88.
16. Charles Townsend, *The Republic, The Fight for Irish Independence, 1918–1923* (London: Penguin, 2014), 428–29.
17. *Irish Independent*, 21 July 1922.
18. Ralph A. Riccio, *Irish Coastal Landings 1922* (Petersfield, UK: Mushroom Model Publications, 2012), 34.
19. Dalton to Commander-in-Chief, letter, 11 September 1922, MAI, IE/MA/CW/OPS/2/4.
20. Sean Boyne, *Emmet Dalton: British Soldier, Irish General, Film Pioneer* (Dublin: Merrion Press, 2015), 246.
21. Jacqueline L. Hazelton, *Bullets Not Ballots: Success in Counterinsurgency Warfare* (Ithaca, NY: Cornell University Press, 2021), 5.
22. Boyne, *Emmet Dalton*, 246.
23. Frank Ledwidge, *Losing Small Wars: British Military Failures in the 9/11 Wars* (London and New Haven, CT: Yale University Press, 2017), 186.
24. Porch, *Counterinsurgency*, 320.
25. Galula, *Counterinsurgency Warfare*, 28, 13.
26. Ledwidge, *Losing Small Wars*, 175.
27. Galula, *Counterinsurgency Warfare*, 53; Gentile, *Wrong Turn*, xvii.
28. Robert Thompson, *Defeating Communist Insurgency: The Lessons of Malaya and Vietnam* (New York: Praeger, 1966), 111–13.
29. Michael Crawshaw, "The Evolution of British COIN", attachment to MOD JDP 3-40 (undated UK Government publication), para. 1.
30. Gentile, *Wrong Turn*, 16.
31. David Galula, *Counterinsurgency Warfare: Theory and Practice* (Westport, CT: Praeger Security International, 1964), 53.
32. Michael Hopkinson, *Green against Green: The Irish Civil War* (Dublin: Gill and Macmillan, 2004), 182.
33. General Survey for the Period Ending 17 October 1923, MAI, IE/MA/CW/OPS/3/B.
34. Ibid.
35. John Nagl, Foreword to Galula, *Counterinsurgency Warfare*, ix.
36. Berman, Felter, and Shapiro, *Small Wars, Big Data*, 27.
37. Ibid., 273.
38. Joseph H. Felter, "Sources of Military Effectiveness in Counterinsurgency; Evidence from the Philippines", in *The Sword's Other Edge; Trade-offs in the Pursuit of Military Effectiveness*, ed. Daniel Reiter (New York, Cambridge University Press, 2017).
39. Michael Few, "Interview with Dr. John Arquilla: How Can French Encounters with Irregular Warfare in the 19th Century Inform COIN in Our Time?" *Small Wars Journal* (30 November 2010), http://smallwarsjournal.com/blog/journal/docs-temp/608-arquilla.pdf.
40. Samuel P. Huntington, *Political Order in Changing Societies* (New Haven, CT: Yale University Press, 1968), 23.
41. Paul Staniland, *Networks of Rebellion: Explaining Insurgent Cohesion and Collapse* (Ithaca, NY: Cornell University Press, 2014), 6.
42. Porch, *Counterinsurgency*, 161.
43. Dave Grossman, *On Killing: The Psychological Cost of Learning to Kill in*

War and Society (Boston: Little, Brown and Company), 89–90.

44   Peter Hart, *The I.R.A. and Its Enemies: Violence and Community in Cork, 1916–1923* (Oxford: Clarendon Press, 1999), 209, 264.

45   Eli Berman, Joseph H. Felter, and Jacob N. Shapiro, with Vestal McIntyre, *Small Wars, Big Data: The Information Revolution in Modern Conflict* (Princeton, NJ: Princeton University Press, 2018), 273.

46   Ibid.

47   Calton Younger, *Ireland's Civil War* (New York: Taplinger Publishers, 1968), 476.

48   Mulcahy to Collins, memorandum, UCDA, Richard Mulcahy Papers, P7/C/35.

49   John Borgonovo, *The Battle for Cork: July–August 1922* (Cork: Mercier Press, 2011), 31.

50   Hopkinson, *Green against Green*, 239.

51   National Army Report on Operations Carried out in the West Cork, and South Kerry Areas, 29 April–5 May 1923, NAI, D/T S3361.

52   Boyne, *Emmet Dalton*, 181–82.

53   National Army Report on Strength and Posts, 1 April 1923, NAI, D/T S3361.

54   Sean Lehane to Ernie O'Malley, 15 October 1922, in *"No Surrender Here!" The Civil War Papers of Ernie O'Malley, 1922–1924*, ed. Cormac O'Malley and Anne Dolan (Dublin: Lilliput Press, 2007), 282.

55   Free State Army Intelligence Report (Cork Command), 2 March 1924, MAI, IE/MA/S/12360.

56   Cover memorandum RE: SIC scheme from Min for Home Affairs, 5 April 1923, NAI, DT S582cited in Gavin M. Foster, *The Irish Civil War and Society: Politics, Class, and Conflict* (London: Palgrave Macmillan, 2015), 133.

57   Eunan O'Halpin, *Defending Ireland: The Irish State and Its Enemies since 1922* (Oxford: Oxford University Press, 1999), 33.

58   Peter Hart, *The I.R.A. and Its Enemies: Violence and Community in Cork, 1916–1923* (Oxford: Clarendon Press, 1999), 209, 264.

59   William Kautt, *Arming the Irish Revolution: Gunrunning and Arms Smuggling, 1911–1922* (Dublin: Irish Academic Press, 2010), 151–52.

60   1st Southern Division Meeting, 26 February 1923, UCDA, Richard Mulcahy Papers, P7/B/89.

61   Nagl, *Knife Fights*, 116.

62   Ibid., 116.

63   Army Code 71451, *Design for Operations: The British Military Doctrine (1989)*, vii.

64   John Nagl, *Learning to Eat Soup with a Knife: Counterinsurgency Lessons from Malaya and Vietnam* (Chicago: University of Chicago Press, 2005).

65   A. Walter Dorn and Michael Vare, "The Rise and Demise of the 'Three Block War'", *Canadian Military Journal* 10, no. 1 (2009): 38–45.

66   David Benest, "Aden to Northern Ireland", cited in Frank Ledwidge *Losing Small Wars, British Military Failure in the 9/11 Wars* (London: Yale University Press), 180.

67   Galula, *Counterinsurgency Warfare*, 73.

68   John A. Nagl, *Knife Fights: A Memoir of Modern War in Theory and Practice*

69. Nagl, *Learning to Eat Soup with a Knife*.
70. Mulcahy to Mac Mahon, 12 December 1922, UCDA, Richard Mulcahy Papers, P7/B/153.
71. Duggan, *A History of the Irish Army*, 109.
72. Cabinet Meeting of the Provisional Government, minutes, 10 September 1922, NAI, D/TSCH/1/1/1.
73. Costello at Army Inquiry, UCDA, Richard Mulcahy Papers, P7/C/25.
74. O'Halpin, *Defending Ireland*, 16.
75. Townsend, *The Republic*, 421–22.
76. Mulcahy to Mac Eoin, 14 August 1922, UCDA, Seán MacEoin Papers, P151/161/5.
77. US Army, *Field Manual 3-24: Counterinsurgency*, 2006.
78. Trinquier, *Modern Warfare*, 45.
79. Nagl, *Knife Fights*, 117.
80. Galula, *Counterinsurgency Warfare*, 85.
81. Ibid., 57.
82. Hazelton, *Bullets Not Ballots*, 11; Nagl, *Knife Fights*, 130.
83. As a 22-year-old platoon commander living in the villages of South Lebanon in the 1990s, I had regular meetings with the local mayors and mukhtars about the ongoing security and welfare of the inhabitants.
84. Nagl, *Learning to Eat Soup with a Knife*, 28.
85. Trinquier, *Modern Warfare*, 17.
86. Galula, *Counterinsurgency Warfare*, 4.
87. Nagl, Foreword to Galula, *Counterinsurgency Warfare*, ix.
88. Roger Trinquier, *Modern Warfare: A French View of Counterinsurgency* (1964; reprint, Westport CT: Praeger Security International, 2006), 45.
89. Galula, *Counterinsurgency Warfare*, 57.
90. Berman, Felter, and Shapiro, *Small Wars, Big Data*, 17.
91. Nagl, *Knife Fights*, 130.
92. Galula *Counterinsurgency Warfare Theory and Practice*, 85.
93. National Army General Surveys of the Situation for Weeks Ending 31 March 1923, 7 April 1923, 15 April 1923, 21 April 1923, 28 April 1923, NAI, D/T S3361.
94. Brian McCarthy, Untitled MA thesis (University College Dublin, 1977), 1–7.
95. *Irish Independent*, 13 June 1977.
96. Corcoran, *Freedom to Achieve Freedom*, 113.
97. Berman, Felter, and Shapiro, *Small Wars, Big Data*, 273.
98. National Army Report on Operations Carried out in the West Cork and South Kerry Areas, 29 April–5 May 1923, NAI, D/T S3361.
99. Berman, Felter, and Shapiro, *Small Wars, Big Data*, 321.
100. John Nagl, *Learning to Eat Soup with a Knife: Counterinsurgency Lessons from Malaya and Vietnam* (Chicago: University of Chicago Press, 2005), 28.
101. Ibid., 309.
102. Schadlow, *War and the Art of Governance*, 273–77.
103. Berman, Felter, and Shapiro, *Small Wars, Big Data*, 321.

104 John A. Nagl, Foreword to David Galula, *Counterinsurgency Warfare*, ix.
105 Crawshaw, "The Evolution of British COIN", para. 1.